AF553983

MODERN HOSPITALITY AND TOURISM MANAGEMENT

MODERN HOSPITALITY AND TOURISM MANAGEMENT

Atul Shrivastava

CENTRUM PRESS
NEW DELHI-110002 (INDIA)

CENTRUM PRESS

H.O.: 4360/4, Ansari Road, Daryaganj,
New Delhi-110002 (India)
Tel: 23278000, 23261597, 23255577, 23286875

B.O.: No. 1015, Ist Main Road, BSK IIIrd Stage,
IIIrd Phase, IIIrd Block, Bangalore-560085 (INDIA)
Tel: 080-41723429

Email: centrumpress@gmail.com
Visit us at: www.centrumpress.com

Modern Hospitality and Tourism Management

First Edition, 2010

ISBN 978-93-80540-98-6

PRINTED IN INDIA

Printed at Balaji Offset, Delhi.

Contents

Preface

According to the World Travel and Tourism Council (1997), the economics of the 21st century will be dominated by three industries: telecommunications, information technology and tourism. The travel and tourism industries have grown by 500% in the last 25 years and it is estimated that by the year 2007 tourists will spend US$884 billion in foreign countries on tourism related activities. Travel and tourism represents a broad range of related industries. The growth of these industries has opened up many new job opportunities for graduates.

It is interesting to realise that in 1997 travel and tourism provides 10.5% of the total world employment, with up to 25% of all employment, in some areas, such as the Caribbean. It has been estimated that, by 2007, more than 100 million people worldwide will be employed in this sector. Because of this, tourism is now seen to be of importance to most countries of the world.

During this time, the nature of tourism has developed in scope and direction, away from traditional activities, such as the sunshine sand and sea holidays to a wide range of new activities such as cultural tourism, adventure tourism, sports and leisure activities and ecotourism.

As per the Travel and Tourism Competitiveness Report 2009 by the World Economic Forum, India is ranked 11th in the Asia Pacific region and 62nd overall, moving up three places on the list of the world's attractive destinations. It is ranked the 14th best tourist destination for its natural resources and 24th for its cultural resources, with many World Heritage sites, both natural and cultural, rich fauna, and strong creative industries in the country. India also bagged 37th rank for its air transport network. The India travel and tourism industry ranked 5th in the long-term (10-year) growth and is expected to be the second largest employer in the world by 2019.

This book touches all crucial aspects of management of modern tourism and hospitality industry. The book will delight and enlighten one and all concerned be they-students, researchers, planners of this field.

—Atul Shrivastava

1

Hotel Management Principles and Guidelines

Accounting Principles

The lodging industry was reportedly one of the first industries to develop "definitive standards to provide specific guidance to accountants and operators. The standards evolved because uniformity of layout and presentation were, and are, still not stressed under U.S.

Generally Accepted Accounting Principles (GAAP)." Those standards were and are contained in the Uniform System of Accounts for the Lodging Industry (USALI), which is published by the American Hotel and Motel Association.

While the accounting profession may not have seen fit to develop GAAP standards specifically applicable to the lodging industry, the USALI has been widely adopted within the industry. Although there is no requirement that a lodging operator use the USALI, the degree of compliance with this time-tested, turnkey system is substantial. The primary reason for widespread adoption of the USALI has been comparability. Lodging operators tend to use financial statement data generated by competitors as a benchmark against which to measure their own operations. If comparability is lacking, then there are no benchmarks.

Additionally, while the system was developed for use within the United States, many hotel operators around the world have adopted the USALI. Financial statements prepared for external users, are based on GAAP. In addition to other items commonly found in most financial statements, lodging industry financials are likely to report on such items as China, Glassware, Silver, Linen, and Uniforms (CGSLU), and the House Bank.

The USALI is a highly departmentalized system of accounting, and includes Departmental Statements of Income. There are two main department classifications in a hotel: operating and overhead. The operating (revenue-producing) departments include rooms, food and beverage, telecommunications, and similar departments. The overhead departments include administrative and general, data processing, human resources, transportation, marketing, guest entertainment, energy costs, and property operation and maintenance.

The USALI itself provides for up to 30 departmental statements, which include, in addition to those already mentioned: telecommunications, garage and parking, golf shop, golf pro shop, guest laundry, health centre, swimming pool, tennis, tennis pro shop, other operated departments, rentals and other income, human resources, information services, security, franchise fees, management fees, rent, property taxes and insurance, interest expense, depreciation and amortization, income taxes, house laundry, salaries and wages and payroll taxes and employee benefits.

The principal differences between a hotel's transactions and internal control and those of other businesses are found in the revenue cycle. Room revenue is the most important source of income to a hotel. The front desk is the centre of the hotel's operation and the place where the guest ledger, which summarizes and accumulates all charges to guests using the hotel facilities, is maintained.

Some of the functions performed by front desk personnel are registering guests, recording room revenue, recording food and beverage and other guest charges, checking out guests, and settling guests' bills. There are numerous articles and books that further explain the hotel business. For more information, refer to *Montgomery's Auditing* by O'Reilly, Vincent M., et al., Twelfth Edition, New York: Wiley, 1998.

Montgomery's Auditing recommends the following substantive tests for room revenue for financial statement purposes:

- Review reconciliations of rooms occupied per the front desk to the housekeeper's daily inspection report or the exception report
- Compare the room rate charged on the guest folio with that on the guest registration and room rack for a selected number of folios
- Trace room charges to guest folios and compare with established rates
- Trace cash receipts to the cashier's report and the cash receipts journal Montgomery's Auditing recommends the following for revenue deductions (allowances):
- Determine that adjustments (credits) made to guests' accounts in connection with overcharges, disputed charges or rate changes were properly approved
- Review supporting documentation for propriety
- Trace credit postings to individual guest folios.

From a tax audit standpoint, the available descriptions of hotel operations would seem to suggest considerable opportunity for manipulation of both revenue and expenses. Room rates vary considerably depending on a variety of factors-e.g., group rates versus individual rates, etc. The occupancy rate would appear to be another area of potential concern.

While these concerns may not be overly great in the case of publicly traded companies who have to undergo an audit in the post Sarbanes-Oxley atmosphere, there may be of considerable concern with non-publicly traded companies.

Additionally, one of the newest areas that is gaining significance in the industry is the barter transaction. A barter transaction occurs when a property agrees to provide accommodation and/or other services in exchange for external services, for example advertising.

While USALI recognizes barter transactions as executory contracts that do not need to be recorded in the financial statements until service is provided or received, it suggests that to provide more complete information for decision-making, the internal records reflect the transaction by recording an asset and a liability at the time the barter transaction is negotiated.

The value assigned to this transaction should be a conservative average of the market rate for similar accommodations or services at the property, per the USALI. When services are provided by the property, revenues are recorded and charged to the barter liability. On the other side, the expense is offset against the barter asset account when the service is received. For external reporting purposes, USAL suggests that the asset and liability accounts be netted and reflected as a current asset or liability. This will result in revenues and expenses associated with the barter transaction being reported in different periods·

Ratio analysis, in general, comprises the same types of ratios used in almost any industry. However, there are a few industry specialized ratios peculiar to hotels and/or restaurants of which one should be aware.

- Average Room Rate = Rooms Revenue divided by Paid Rooms Occupied.
- Average Food Check = Total Food Revenue divided by Number of Covers. Covers refer to guests served in the food operation during the period.

A key recent addition is RevPar, which stands for Revenue per Available Room. It is calculated as either: Rooms Revenue divided by Rooms Available for Sale, or as Rooms Revenue divided by Rooms Available. The USALI expresses a preference for the second computation because "the purpose of the ratio is to determine whether the inventory of rooms is being managed optimally. Therefore, the denominator should also include rooms out of order and temporary house use rooms."

The USALI also discusses a sample chart of accounts, which uses a twelve-digit numbering system, consisting of four clusters of three digits each. The first three digits are the property number. The second three digits are the revenue departments or cost centres. The third three digits are the major accounts on the balance sheet or income statement and the final three digits are sub-accounts useful for analysis and control. Obviously, this may vary considerably from taxpayer to taxpayer.

The descriptions contained in this guide only scratch the surface of standard practices within the hotel industry which are either unique to the hotel industry, or are uncommon in most other industries. A partial listing of available publications is provided elsewhere within this guide should additional information be required.

Information Systems

The following are examples of some of the information system products that are available to hotel operators:

Lodging Touch Property Management System

The system is divided into various modules which can interact with the front office, group sales, guest history, accounts receivable, travel agencies, and yield management. Hoteliers can search and retrieve guest information by various fields, including name, address, confirmation numbers, and other fields. In addition, the system allows users to search for accounts using any criteria.

Paragon AS/400 Front Office

Planning for a guest's stay includes managing accommodations, aggressive pricing, marketing, forecasting, and implementing reporting controls. The Paragon system claims a flexible system that provides information in order to achieve optimal standards. The system provides information and feedback to measure financial impact and quality.

Paragon can manage the complete hotel system. Paragon can be integrated with Paragon Back Office, Central Reservations, and complementary products. Some benefits claimed by the Paragon include improved customer service, efficient internal operations, and control over financial data integrity.

Other key features include:

- Easy reservation input
- Optimal return on rooms by providing flexible rate configuration and maximum room occupancy
- Access availability by room type, total hotel and group.
- Provide confirmation letters and pre-printed registration cards.
- Capture additional guest information through hotel configurable fields.
- Maintain wait lists
- Provide flexible package configurations.

CLS Software Property Management System

This system can support properties of all sizes, from 50 to 1,000 rooms. They also claim a comprehensive integrated modular system that links together all aspects of the hotel function. The system comes in domestic and international versions.

Other key features include:

- Ease of data entry
- Over 200 interface solutions
- Technical Support-24-hours a day, 7-days a week, 365-days a year
- Over 25 years of experience.

Hotel Information Systems' epitome® Project Management System for UNIX

Hotel Information Systems offers a wide variety of other hotel management systems, namely, epitome® Project Management System for UNIX. This system can be utilized with the hotel's current IT system.

Industry Operating Procedures

Some hotels are heavily involved in franchising activities. Franchisees will pay a fixed percent of receipts to a franchiser for advertising and royalties. Some hotel franchisers will lease the structure to the franchisee for a monthly rate and/or a percentage of sales.

The internal controls of these chain hotels are extensive; conversely, individual independent hotels do not always enjoy the same degree of controls over operations.

Ownership takes diverse forms, ranging from publicly-held companies to individuals. Included within this span are churches and other not-for-profit organizations, municipalities, partnerships and REITs. Of the various ownership arrangements, REITs seem to provide some of the more interesting, and perhaps more involved sets of rules.

Many firms desire to convert to the REIT status because the taxable income that is distributed to the shareholders is not taxed. Therefore, REITs avoid double taxation.

Effective January 1, 2001, REITs were allowed to wholly own taxable subsidiaries. These taxable subsidiaries were, in turn, allowed to lease hotels from the related REIT and/or its affiliates, provided certain conditions were met, and provided the subsidiary did not manage or operate any hotels or health care facilities.

These comments are some highlights of the REIT status. A full analysis the law applying to REITs is clearly beyond the scope of this document.

Also beyond the scope of this document are numerous potential employment tax issues, unrelated business income issues in the case of non-profits, and any other areas which generally fall outside the purview of LMSB. Nevertheless, it should be kept in mind that the hotel industry entails a great variety of business arrangements which include not merely hotel owners, but also hotel operators, designers, builders and so on.

Government Regulatory Requirements

Federal Requirements

The Federal Trade Commission (FTC) publishes the rulebook for promotional allowance marketing, titled Guides for Advertising Allowances and Other Merchandising Payments and Services, these guides are usually referred to as "The Guides," "the FTC Guides" or the "Fred Meyer Guides."

Text of the Americans with Disabilities Act, Public Law 336 of the 101st Congress, enacted July 26, 1990.

The ADA prohibits discrimination and ensures equal opportunity for persons with disabilities in employment, State and local government services, public accommodations, commercial facilities, and transportation. It also mandates the establishment of TDD/telephone relay services.

State Requirements

Each state has their own specific requirements and regulations regarding the manufacture, sale, resale, and consumption of alcoholic beverages.

Local Requirements

Many localities have controls over the purchase, sale, resale and consumption of alcoholic beverages.

Significant Law and Important Issues

Emerging or Other Significant Issues

Issue	*Brief Summary of Issue*
Depreciable Life of a Hotel's Small wares Asset Account and Treatment of Replacements	When a hotel opens a location, they will purchase thousands of dollars worth of small wares (towels, sheets, blankets, glassware, china, silverware, linen, etc.). A potential issue had been identified relating to the recovery period of these assets and how to treat the replacement costs of these items.
Losses Incurred When a Hotel is Closed	Is a taxpayer entitled to deduct the difference between the adjusted basis of the property and its appraised value when a location is closed but not disposed of? Some taxpayers are taking the position that when the building is owned, they are entitled to a loss in the form of bonus depreciation equal to the difference between the adjusted basis and the appraised value of the building, when a decision is made to close an unprofitable location. The current IRS position is that a loss on the Section 1250 property is not allowed until an actual disposition (sale or abandonment) has occurred. The mere closing of the property is not an actual disposition.
Deferral of Gift Card Sales	Are taxpayers properly following the rules for deferral under Treas. Reg. § 1.451-5? Is a CAM required? Was an information schedule attached to the tax return? Is income from unredeemed gift cards brought into income after 2 years? Was a separate company set up to manage the

program? Can the taxpayer track the outstanding liability?

Guest Loyalty/Reward Programs

1. What is the proper character of a reward point? Is a reward point a "rebate or refund" as provided in Treas. Reg. § 1.461-4(g)(3) or a "trading stamp or premium coupon" as provided in Treas. Reg. § 1.451-4(a)? The characterization will affect the timing of expense recognition. Whereas a trading stamp or premium coupon may reduce gross income at the time of the corresponding sale, a rebate or refund will not reduce gross income until payment is made to the person to which the liability is owed. Furthermore, when is the liability fixed: at the time a customer is issued or redeems a reward certificate? 2. What is the cost of a reward point? How was the estimated average cost of redeeming each point computed? Did the retailer include only the costs to acquire the merchandise, cash, or other property required to redeem the points, or did the taxpayer include other costs such as advertising catalogs, transporting and storing merchandise, operating redemption centres, etc.?3. What methodology was used to estimate future redemptions? Does the methodology result in a reasonably accurate estimate of the points outstanding at the end of the taxable year that will ultimately be presented for redemption? Although an expense may be deductible before it is due and payable, the liability must be firmly established. Is the liability fixed prior to the customer's

accumulation of the minimum number of points needed to earn a reward certificate? Does the methodology take into consideration any expiration of previously earned points?. Does the recurring item exception provided under Treas. Reg. § 1.461-5 apply if the reward certificate is determined to constitute a rebate?

Cost Segregation Studies

Many hotels are the subject of cost segregation studies. An Audit Technique Guide (ATG) for the preparation and examination of cost segregation studies was initially issued in April 2004 and was most recently updated in January 2006. The primary goal is to provide examiners with an understanding of why cost segregation studies are performed by taxpayers, how such studies are prepared, and what to look for in the review and examination of these studies. This guide will also assist taxpayers and practitioners in understanding some of the items the Service will consider to support property allocations based on these studies. Included in the ATG is industry specific guidance for land-based casinos, restaurants, and retail establishments which were previously issued as Industry Director Directives. It should be noted that this ATG is not an official Service pronouncement and may not be cited as authority.

Contributions of Hotel Beds

Some of the problems encountered during examinations are as follows: Contribution made to an organization that is not a qualifying organization.· Fair market value (this is the area where most disputes between the taxpayer and the Service occur).

WOTC/WTW Claims

Rev. Rul. 2003-112 provided guidance on whether an individual meets the family membership requirements permitting certification for the WOTC and WTW credits. Some states may have applied a narrower definition in issuing certificates. Many taxpayers are currently filing claims using the revenue ruling as justification. These claims SHOULD NOT be allowed without proper substantiation. The current Service position is that additional credit should only be allowed when the taxpayer has documented certification from the state agencies.

Tax Abatements

At issue is the proper tax treatment on State & Local Economic Development Subsidies. This might include inducements & Enticements to persuade companies to relocate or maintain their investment in that particular area. Some taxpayers are taking the position that they are entitled to a deduction for a tax abatement. Further, they account for the abatement as income under IRC § 118 and then reduce basis in long life assets or land under IRC § 362. This accounting treatment is an emerging issue in all industries.

FICA Tax Tip Credit

·Should a taxpayer be allowed a credit under section 45B on Service Charges allocated to servers? · Should a taxpayer be allowed a credit under section 45B on both directly tipped and indirectly tipped employees? · Should a taxpayer be allowed a credit under section 45B for the difference paid for minimum wages for the first 90 days for employees under age 21? These are some of the issues that hotels with restaurants will face. When a service fee is charged by the restaurant, typically on large parties, banquets, or catering, these amounts are not eligible for the FICA tax tip credit under IRC § 45B.

Franchising Fees

Some hotels are requiring nonrefundable franchisee fees upfront, perhaps several years before the franchisees actually get their hotels. When examining franchisers, you should inquire as to their policy for reporting these advance fees. Some are properly including them in income and some are not.

Upfront Payments

In some situations vendors will enter into long term agreements with hotels. These contracts typically call for a large up-front payment from the vendor to the hotel. In return the recipient agrees to purchase product for a given time period or the recipient agrees to purchase a stated amount of product in the future with no time period mentioned. The contracts will usually stipulate that the vendor will either be the exclusive supplier of the product or that the vendor is the primary vendor and will receive preferential placement of the product for an extended period of time. Typically in hotels you may see this from the soft drink provider.

Lobbying Deductions	The principal issue is whether costs incurred to influence legislation that impacts a taxpayer's business or industry are deductible as ordinary and necessary business expenses under IRC § 162(a). The general audit approach is to determine if the activity is covered by IRC § 162(e). If yes, no deduction is permitted. If no, the activity is deductible to the extent it meets the requirements of IRC § 162(a). Generally, IRC § 162 (e) (1) provides for no deduction of amounts paid or incurred in connection with any of the following four activities: 1. "Influencing legislation" (i.e., direct lobbying of the legislature); 2. Participating in a political campaign of a candidate for public office; 3. Attempting to influence the public regarding elections, legislative matters, or referendums (i.e. grassroots lobbying); or; 4. Communicating with "covered executive branch officials." Treas. Reg. § 1.162-29 defines "influencing legislation" as any attempt to influence legislation through a lobbying communication and all ancillary activities engaged in for the purpose of making or supporting a lobbying communication. One area that is often overlooked is dues paid to trade associations. The following website allows you to search by company name and see who is registered to lobby on the company's behalf and the amount of lobbying-related income from the company/client.

Industry Resources

Websites

Name of Site	*Summary and Available Information*
Int'l Assn of Amusement Parks and Attractions	Provides a variety of information about this industry segment.
Travel Industry Assn of America	Gives an overview of this related industry.
Cornell, School of Hotel Admin.	Links to hospitality education links around the country.
Hotel Resource	"The Resource for Hospitality Professionals sponsored by The Buyer's Guide"
Int'l Tax Treatment of REITS	Self explanatory
FASB Summaries	FASB Summaries
AICPA Home Page	Information from the AICPA
Rutgers Resources	Information from business library
CPA Journal Home Page	Self-explanatory
Wall Street Journal Home Page	Self-explanatory
Internal Auditing Web Page	Self-explanatory
Stock History	Self-explanatory
Company Profiles	Self-explanatory
Tax and Accounting Sites	Links to CPA Sites
Search SEC documents	Self-explanatory
SEC home page	Self-explanatory
Library of Congress	Self-explanatory
Thomas Legislative Research	Self-explanatory
TCU Professor-Tax Links	Provides links to various tax sites
News Articles	Self-explanatory
News Articles	Self-explanatory
Tax Gateway	Provides links to various sites
Wall Street Research Net	Information on publicly traded hotels
Corporate Information	Information on companies

The Failure of Hotels

According to Cuisine Scene Hospitality Solutions more than 200 restaurants, cafes or catering companies close down every week in Australia. Those that are now open probably won't be around in five years. Only 5% of restaurants open today will be operating in 10 years. More and more competitors are opening every day, wage costs increase, cost of goods continue to go up and staff turnover is always a problem. The overall average net profit in the hospitality industry is only 1.5%.

Cuisine Scene identifies 10 reasons for hospitality businesses failing to achieve their full potential.

Lack of Consistency

Most restaurants, cafes and catering companies forget the importance of constantly striving for consistency in every aspect of their establishment. Consistency of product, service and concept will provide a competitive edge. Clear and thorough systems will ensure a solid base from which all your staff can achieve a consistently high level of product and service, whether you're there or not.

Selecting and Retaining the Right Staff

Your front line and key personnel are crucial to your business success. Attracting and keeping the right staff is a difficult and time-consuming operation. It demands a documented and thorough chain of employment focusing on relevant issues from an attractive job advertisement through effective interviews, orientation, and development path. The problem of staff recruitment is present in almost all restaurants, cafes, and hotels that fail to reach their full potential. Ensuring you get the best staff means your competitor can't.

Incorrect Menu Structure

Effective menus increase sales without changing food and beverage costs. There are psychological factors that guide your guest's decision when choosing their meals. A thorough knowledge of these factors helps you achieve a menu that really performs.

Ineffective or Nonexistent Marketing

Most restaurants, cafes and hotels that fail to reach their full potential often lose thousands of dollars on marketing that is unmeasurable, ineffective or too expensive. Brand recognition and product placement are vital to a successful hospitality business. Competition is fierce and if you don't know your target market well, how will know how to get them in the door?.

Little Understanding of Key Figures

Many businesses have little or no understanding of the key elements involved in establishing key performance indicators as critical business controls. The break even point is one of the most important success indicators you need. What are your fixed and variable costs?. Other indicators include contribution margins, yields, gross profits, wage costs, server sales analysis, stock values, and many other important key figures allow you to know at anytime, how well your business, and its staff, are performing. Set up reliable benchmarks and access to key performance indicators that allow you to measure your business performance without having to be there.

Work on the Business, not in it

Streamline your restaurant, cafe or catering business so it runs itself when your not there. Allow yourself to step back and critically assess the indicators that help you determine where your business is heading. Trust your systems and key personnel to manage things when your not there, but ensure they know you are always watching from a distance. Stepping out of the business will allow you to think outside the box and give you the freedom to play a major part in the strategic planning of your business and not get caught up with time consuming day to day operations. Cuisine Scene can assist you to rethink how you look at your business.

Poorly Presented Concept or Branding

A well thought out concept gives an impression of professionalism and confidence. Acceptable lighting, sound, and decor are critical to the success of your restaurant, cafe or catering business. It is the crucial element that completes the entire experience for your guests. Consider speed of service, menu variety, menu value, first impressions, kids facilities and complaint handling. What does it take to give your establishment the competitive edge it deserves? Good food? Good Service? Effective marketing? Yes to all of these but a strong concept will tie them all together and leave your competition wondering where they went wrong? And your guests wondering what they will discover on their next visit!

Any restaurant, cafe, or hotel that wants to stay in the spotlight needs to be dynamic. There needs to be an emotional connection on some level with your target market. Be prepared to refine (not change) your brand as industry trends and clientele dictate. Your brand should be evident throughout all your marketing, advertising and premises. Stop and look from the customer's perspective every week. Ask yourself about the standard and speed of service. What do you see? What do you hear? What do you feel about the experience?

Lack of Integrated Business Systems

Not only is it imperative to have these integrated business systems and procedures in place but is it critical that you know how to use them. Everything needs to be clear, detailed and on paper. Job descriptions, checklists, sales analysis sheets, labour control reports, workplace safety security guidelines, phone script sheets and functions bookings procedures should all be set down. All staff must have access to the information at any time and be accountable for completing or using it. The systems must be regularly updated and creating them should involve relevant staff as much as possible.

Ineffective Control of Your POS System

Most point of sale (POS) systems in restaurants, cafes and hotel businesses today are outdated, obsolete and not providing the speed of information necessary to closely monitor day to day operations. Update it and make the most of it. A great POS System will pay for itself and boost sales at the same time, not to mention the added value when an effective staff incentive program is tied into it. Hospitality staff motivational software is one of the best ways to analyse and compare your server sales/product mix. It will even improve your menu profitability across the board. Effective and easy to use POS systems integrated with your back office reports and systems will also ensure you have your critical KPIs at your fingertips. Add-ons such as stock control, reservations, and labour programs will increase the effectiveness of your system. Cuisine Scene can show you how a cost effective POS system can manage your tables during a shift and organise your reservations.

No Structured Business Plan

96% of all businesses do not have a structured business plan involving detailed systems, marketing plans, forecasts and budgets. It is essential to know where you are headed and how you're going to get there. Without a structured business plan it is easy to wonder why you don't have control over your business.

Guidelines of Employment in the Hotel Sector

The growth of the hotel industry is linked closely to this sector. Across the nation, hotels and motels are a welcome haven for weary travellers. For vacationing families and persons whose jobs take them out of town, a comfortable room, good food, and a helpful hotel staff can make being away from home an enjoyable experience. They may be overnight guests at a highway hotel, spend several days at a towering five star hotel, or relax for a week at a large resort complex with tennis courts, a golf course and a variety of other recreational facilities. Rise in corporate activity in India has increased the importance of the business traveller and the hotel industry is now focusing on business with this segment.

Manpower requirements for hotels is on the rise. Star hotels require specialized trained staff for their various departments: food and beverage, housekeeping, accounting, marketing, recreation and other services, computer applications, financial management, engineering, maintenance, security, fire fighting and public relations. These jobs have become increasingly challenging and in recent times. With sophisticated technology gaining prominence automation will play a major role in the service sector but the compulsions of personalised attention in this service industry will continue.

Human resource employed by the hotel industry up to 2001 has match the extension of room space, almost an additional 1,25,000 rooms. Each room in a five star hotel needs 3 persons in jobs with direct responsibilities while many more persons indirectly assist the core group. The core professionals entering the industry have been over 200,000 in this century.

Types of Hotels

Employment opportunity in hotels varies within the industry and is largely dependent on the size of the hotel, the clientele it caters to and the purpose it is made for. Generally the largest work force of hotel executives and other staff are found in five star hotels. The smaller star hotels employ staff according to the guest capacity. There are hotels in cosmopolitan towns which have a larger inflow and hence need a well trained, efficient staff to cope up with the guests booked with them. In smaller towns work may be comparatively less. Hotels catering to business travellers, located at crucial places in the city, are staffed for precise and efficient functioning.

Tourism has been promoted earnestly in the last decade which has provided a boom to the hotel industry. Most tourist destinations such as hills, beaches, game sanctuaries, famous religious shrines have hotels to cater to the needs of the tourists. The beaches of Goa for instance have b-each resort hotels while hill stations like Mussourie, Darjeeling, Ooty have convenient hill resort hotels. At international airports we find hotels which cater to transit passengers and foreign travellers. These airport hotels have an ambiance of grandeur which is designed to present the stately grace of this country. Foreign tourists in fact are lured by the exquisite hospitality at the famous palace hotels. Taking the tourist to an era of royalty resplendent with all its fineries, these hotels have attracted foreigners from all parts of the world. Some famous palace hotels are at Jaipur, Mysore, Udaipur, Jodhpur.

Travel by road has introduced highway hotels for Indian and foreign travellers. Located on highways, connecting major cities, these hotels provide facilities for lodging and boarding, medical facilities for emergencies, communication facilities, etc.

New concepts in hotels are also being introduced. Heritage hotels at important pilgrim locations, temple towns, wildlife sanctuaries and heritage locations are being developed with the specific aim of providing the best hospitality to the tourist. Growth plans of the tourism industry include setting up of integrated sports resorts. These complexes will be equipped to provide the best sports facilities and will have hotels to cater to the sportsperson's needs. Trainers, coaches, players from all over the world will then meet and share experiences at these sports complex hotels.

Hotels with a rural ambience are being designed at famous towns like Chidambaram, Puttaparthi, Rameshwaram,

Mahabaliburam, Pondicherry, Sarnath, Bodhgaya. These hotel resorts are aimed to provide cultural experiences, including vedas, yoga, meditation, classical arts and folk arts, for the foreign tourists. This would give authentic Indian cultural experience to the international tourists for the first time in our country.

Hotels on wheels began with the train 'Palace on wheels'. Designed to provide the luxury of a star hotel, this is an air conditioned train. Tamil Nadu Government proposes to build and operate a similar train to operate through the temple towns of Tamil Nadu. Other States may also follow suit.

Business centres and hotels have also recently gained popularity among business firms, the finance sector or any organized sector which must meet in conferences, meetings and seminars. Catering for such groups is a challenge for any hotelier. Conferences are held in such centres where the necessary atmosphere and facilities are almost inbuilt.

This description covers the kinds of hotels we have today in our country and the hotels we expect to have in the near future.

Nature of Work

Jobs in a Hotel

The Hotel Industry has, as said earlier, a great variety in terms of size, clientele it aims to serve, and its location. However, for the efficient functioning of any hotel-large or small, work is divided among key departments. Most large hotels have an organizational hierarchy in its various departments and the functionaries are allocated responsibilities according to levels of professional development.

Management jobs-In all hotels, hotel managers and assistant managers work to ensure that guests' visits are pleasant. Hotel managers are responsible for the efficient and profitable operation of their establishments. In a small hotel, with limited staff, a single manager may direct all aspects of operations. However, large hotels may employ hundreds of workers, and the manager may be aided by a number of assistant managers assigned among departments responsible for various aspects of operations. The general manager has overall responsibility for the operation of the hotel. Within guidelines established by the owners of the hotel or executives of the hotel chain, the general manager sets room rates, allocates funds to departments, approves expenditures, and establishes norms of service to guests, the standard of housekeeping, food quality, decoration and banquet operations. Assistant managers ensure that the day-to-day operations of their departments meet the general manager's standards.

Resident managers live in hotels and are on call 24 hours a day to resolve problems or emergencies, although they normally work for scheduled hour in a day, but, as the senior most assistant managers, they oversee the day-to-day operations of the hotel. Under the supervision and guidance of the top management work the various department heads.

Departmental Operations

Catering management-The catering department has at the management level the Food and Beverage Manager and the Banquet Manager. The Food and Beverage Manager plans organizes and controls the work of the catering department. For efficient and profitable operation of restaurants and institutional food service facilities, managers and assistant managers select and appropriately price interesting menu items, ensure efficient use of food and other supplies, achieve consistent quality in food preparation and service, recruit and train appropriate number of workers, supervise their work, and attend to the various administrative aspects of the business.

In most restaurants and institutional catering services, the manager is assisted by one or more assistant managers, depending on the size and business hours of the establishment. In large establishments, as well as in many others that offer fine dining, the management team consists of a general manager, one or more assistant managers, and an executive chef. The Executive Chef is in charge of the operation of the kitchen, while the assistant managers supervise service in the dining room and other areas of the operation.

Restaurant and Food Service Managers meet with sales representatives of restaurant suppliers to place orders to replenish stocks of tableware, linens, paper, cleaning supplies, cooking utensils, furniture and fixtures. They also arrange for equipment maintenance and repairs. They maintain records of hours and wages of employees, payrolls, and taxes, etc. Since evenings and weekends are popular dining periods, night and weekend work is demanding. However, many managers of institutional catering service work more conventional hours because factory and office canteens are often open only on weekdays for breakfast and lunch.

Banquet Managers often work under pressure simultaneously coordinating a wide range of activities. When problems occur, it is the responsibility of the manager to resolve them with least disruption to customers. The job can be hectic during peak dining hours, and dealing with irate customers or uncooperative employees can be particularly stressful.

Catering operations-The Catering department includes the culinary department, the steward department and the food service department.

Culinary department is at the very heart of this industry. Cuisines of different countries and types are prepared and served in the restaurants housed in the Hotel. The hotel employs Executive Chefs to head each of these specialized kitchens under whose direction chef de parties turn out exquisite preparations and meals.

The Steward is at the head of the restaurant arrangements. He sees that everything is in order for the food service department. The servicing of food is a skill which requires expert training. Under the Maitre d' Hotel are the trained hotel personnel who serve and attend to the guests in the hotel with drinks and food.

Food and beverage service workers deal with customers in all kinds of dining establishments from small informal diners to large restaurants. Waiters and waitresses take customers orders and serve food and beverages. How this is done depends on the type of establishment.

Coffee shops require fast, efficient service, whereas in finer restaurants the service is more formal and personnel. Bartenders fill the drink orders given to them by waiters. Bartenders must be able to mix drinks accurately and quickly and also operate the cash register. They are responsible for ordering and maintaining an inventory of liquor and other supplies. Hosts and hostesses welcome guests, escort guests to their table. Counter attendants take orders and serve food at counters. Fast food workers take orders and accept payment from customers standing at counters of fast food restaurants. They may cook and package foods. The job is very hectic during parties and conventions.

***Front office department*-**The first people to welcome guests in a hotel are the personnel in the front office.

Front Office Managers coordinate reservations and room assignments and train and direct the hotel's front desk staff that deals with the public. They ensure that guests are handled courteously and efficiently, complaints and problems are resolved, and requests for special services are carried out.

The Front Office Manager oversees the work of receptionists, information clerk, reservation clerk and other services personnel like bell captain, bell boy and doorman. At the reception the guest 'checks in' and is assisted to go with his baggage to the room with bellboys in attendance. The bell captain supervises the work of bell boys. The information clerk keeps telephonic messages for guests and passes them through the bell captain to guests on their arrival at the hotel.

***Housekeeping department*-**A hotel is like a big 'home'. It requires the same kind of upkeep and maintenance as a home but on a very large scale. Hotels hence have a house keeping department to look after cleanliness in rooms, lounges, lobby, restaurant, dining halls and parks etc. The interiors too are maintained and decorated with flowers, potted plants and paintings. The department has at its head the Executive Housekeeper.

Executive Housekeepers are responsible for ensuring that guest rooms, meeting and banquet rooms and public areas are clean, orderly and well maintained. They train, schedule and supervise the work of housekeepers, inspect rooms and order cleaning supplies. They work with a team of housekeepers, maids, cleaners, seamstresses. Aesthetic upkeep and maintenance of equipment is often a round the clock job. Shift duties are assigned to most of this staff.

There are floor supervisors in charge of rooms on a floor. They supervise the work of room maids and linen maids and train them according to the requirements of the hotel. Every day the room maids/boys make the beds and clean the rooms. They change the bed linen and arrange toilet towels. Chamber boys and maids clean the toilets. Linen maids collect bed sheet, towels, tablecloths and napkins and send them for laundry. They keep the stock in order. Log books have to maintained by the housekeeper.

Accounting department-As any industry, the hotel industry deals with personnel, materials, sales, equipment, maintenance etc. There is constant turnover of money. This work of managing money matters is done by the accounting department. The Chief Accountant, a chartered accountant, has a team of accountants, auditors, cashiers and accounting clerks working in the department. Chief Accountant works directly under the executive Assistant Manager.

Marketing department-Marketing of services is a major task in most upcoming hotels. People are generally not aware of services they can avail for business purposes, seminars, conventions, parties, celebrations or while on a holiday. They, nevertheless, would like to compare services of different hotels and then select the most appropriate. Sales and marketing division works to identify the needs of prospective customers and sell the services which have been developed.

Engineering department-Engineering department procures, installs and maintains all equipment used in hotels.

Personnel department-Personnel department is engaged in the process of recruiting and training fresh personnel as well as providing in service training. It looks into the personnel needs and requirements of its employees (Also refer to section on Personnel Management).

Forecasting department-Forecasting department plays a key role in the enhancement of profitability of this hospitality business. From projecting growth in terms of business to arranging financial investments is the task of this department. Generally experienced finance people head this department of financial analysts and market researchers.

Work Environment

Employees in most of the hotel operational areas enjoy pleasant, clean and comfortable working conditions. Most large hotel have well equipped kitchen with modern amenities, good ventilation and comfortable work space. The office staff work with automated electronic office systems which provides the best job conditions.

Hotels work on a 24 hours, seven day week schedule and so employees have to keep to shifts normally three in a day. Holiday and Sunday shifts may also be rotated among staff. The work environment is pleasant but workers are on their feet much of the day. Housekeepers and their assistant staff perform physically strenuous duties.Since the major responsibility of hotel staff is to ensure that guests are comfortable it is often very trying to ensure that the individual needs of hundreds of guests are met. The job demands a consistent personal appeal which may be hard to maintain at all times.

Pleasing difficult customers can be challenging. The employees can, nevertheless, take pride in providing pleasurable stay in the hotel. The ambiance in a hotel is one of precision, quick feedback and consequent appraisals. Senior managers work fixed hours and as resident managers stay at the hotel premises.

Personal Characteristics

This dynamic and variegated sector offers a whole range of jobs for young men and women with an outgoing and pleasant personality, a flair for creativity and capacity for hard work. Above all this sector is for people who like people. Along with flair and flamboyance, it is essential to have a sense of discipline, commitment and dedication in order to succeed in this line. Hoteliering may seem glamorous but at the same time it is very tough and taxing. Hoteliering is not a career but a life style. A person is either attitudinal or aptitudinally suited or not suited at all. A gregarious, socially oriented person can find this work pleasurable, while it may be tedious to person with introverted disposition. The challenge of the career lies not only in remuneration it fetches but also in the responsibility, career progression, team spirit and the pride of working for an organisation enjoying great esteem.

Employment Avenues

Options for Hotel Management Graduates

- Restaurant Management
- Club Management

- Cruise Ship Hotel Management
- Hospital Administration and Catering
- Institutional and Industrial Catering
- Airline Catering and Cabin Services
- Manufacturers and Suppliers of Hotel and Restaurant Equipment & Services
- Hotel and Catering Institutes
- Hotel and Tourism Associations
- Catering Departments in Banks and Insurance Houses
- With Government owned Catering Departments, e.g., Railway, Armed Forces, Ministerial Conventions, etc.
- Insurance servicing
- Front office in service sector
- Call centres.

Options for Graduates from other Disciplines in the Hotel Industry

The Hotel Industry also inducts graduates from other disciplines directly to its in-house training programmes.

Graduates in -Home Science, Tourism, Arts/Science/Commerce can enter as Hotel Executive Trainee, Chef Trainee, Kitchen Stewarding Executive, Trainee, Housekeeping Management Trainee, Trainee Captain, Trainee Floor Supervisor, Trainee Front Office Assistant, Trainee Guest Relations, Executive, Assistants in Accounts, Personnel, Restaurant Cashier, Audit, Purchase Stores, Security, Restaurant Hostess Degree holders in Engineering (Electrical/Mechanical) can enter as Trainee Engineer.

Options for Post Graduates in the Hotel Industry

For post graduate degree/diploma holders in Hotel Management & Tourism, MBA's (Marketing, Finance, Materials, Personnel), Chartered/Cost Accountants, M.Tech's, M.Sc (Horticulture), M.Sc (Home Science), Hotel Administration, post graduate diploma holders in Advanced food production, employment in middle and senior managerial positions is offered in Operations, Finance, Personnel, Purchase, Marketing, Engineering, Horticulture, Catering departments of hotels.

Further Promotions are on Merit

Hierarchical Levels

Level 1: Trainee or apprentice stage for persons new to the industry or starting in a department in which they have no previous experience.

Level 2: People at this level are either skilled workers or tradesmen. They may be recent Hotel Management Graduates or have worked in similar positions for one to three years.

Level 3: At the semiprofessional level are people with considerable experience. They may carry out supervisory functions as well as their respective job functions.

Level 4: Department heads are usually responsible for a designated "department" or section of the overall operation. On the job and college experience are typical qualifications required.

Level 5: Work at the management level involves more planning, organizing and controlling of others' work than actually dealing with guests or handling food and beverages. Extensive training and experience is necessary.

Level 6: This is the top management or executive level: the persons/positions here handle the overall management of the property and its human resources, with special concern for long-term planning of financial, marketing and staff development matters. A business or hotel school degree and extensive experience at the management level are basic qualifications required.

Guidelines for Foreign Investment

Foreign Direct Investment (FDI) plays a crucial role in the accelerated economic growth of the country. Over the years, FDI inflow in India is increasing. Government is encouraging Foreign Direct Investment (FDI) in all the vital sectors of the economy.

FDI in India is permitted as under the following forms of investments:

- Through financial collaborations.
- Through joint ventures and technical collaborations.
- Through capital markets via Euro issues.
- Through private placements or preferential allotments.

FDI is not permitted in the following industrial sectors:

- Arms and ammunition.
- Atomic Energy.
- Railway Transport.
- Coal and lignite.
- Mining of iron, manganese, chrome, gypsum, sulphur, gold, diamonds, copper, zinc.

Approval of Foreign Direct Investment in India

Foreign direct investments in India are approved through two routes:

Automatic Approval by RBI

The Reserve Bank of India accords automatic approval within a period of two weeks (provided certain parameters are met) to all proposals involving:

- foreign equity up to 50% in 3 categories relating to mining activities
- foreign equity up to 51% in 48 specified industries.
- foreign equity up to 74% in 9 categories.

FDI on automatic route is not allowed in the following cases:

- Proposals that require an industrial licence and cases where foreign investment is more than 24% in the equity capital of units manufacturing items reserved for the small scale industries.
- Proposals in which the foreign collaborator has a previous venture/tie-up in India.
- Proposals relating to acquisition of shares in an existing Indian company in favour of a Foreign/Non-Resident Indian (NRI)/Overseas Corporate Body (OCB) investor; and
- Proposals falling outside notified sectoral policy/caps or under sectors in which FDI is not permitted and/or whenever any investor chooses to make an application to the Foreign Investment Promotion Board and not to avail of the automatic route.

FIPB Route

FIPB stands for Foreign Investment Promotion Board which approves all other cases where the parameters of automatic approval are not met. Normal processing time is 4 to 6 weeks. FIPB has Secretary, Department of Economic Affairs as its chairman. The other members of the boards are Secretary, Department of Industrial Policy & Promotion, Commerce Secretary and Foreign Secretary. The government has set up Foreign Investment Implementation Authority (FIIA) to facilitate quick translation of FDI approvals into implementation by providing a pro-active one stop after care service to foreign investors, help them obtain necessary approvals and by sorting their operational problems.

Hotel and Tourism is one of the most booming sectors in Indian economy. It has contributed heavily in the Gross Domestic Product of India. 100 percent FDI is permitted in the Hotel and Tourism in India under various approvals. Under Automatic route, FDI is allowed only up to 51 percent in this industry. As per FDI guidelines for hotel and tourism industry in India, following are the sectors, in hotels, which have been receiving the maximum amount of FDI Inflows for the past few years:

- Restaurants
- Beach resorts
- Tourist complexes which facilitates accommodation and catering to the tourists.

As per FDI guidelines for hotel and tourism industry in India, following are the sectors in tourism which have been receiving the maximum amount of FDI Inflows for the past few years:

- Travel agencies
- Tour operating agencies and Tourist transport operating agencies
- Units which facilitates cultural, adventure and wild life experience to tourists
- Units providing surface, air and water transport facilities to tourists
- Sectors which offers leisure, entertainment, amusement, sports, and health related facilities to the tourists
- Convention/Seminar units and organizations.

FDI in Hotels and Tourism Industries in India:

- 100 percent FDI is permitted in the hotel and tourism industry in India under various approvals
- Hotels offer restaurants, beach resorts, and other tourist complexes which provide accommodation or catering and food facilities to tourists
- Tourism Sector includes tour operating agencies and tourist transport operating agencies, units which offer cultural, adventurous and wild life experiences to tourists, and various other entertainment programs which include, water sport activities, leisure games, amusement parks as well as the health care units
- Automatic approval for foreign technology in the hotel and tourism sector will be availed if 3 percent of the total expense of the project occupies infrastructural developments
- Up to 3 percent of the net turn over is payable as marketing fee under automatic route
- 10 percent of the gross operating profit is payable as management fee under automatic route 100% FDI is permissible in the sector on the automatic route.

The term hotels include restaurants, beach resorts, and other tourist complexes providing accommodation and/or catering and food facilities to tourists. Tourism related industry include travel agencies, tour operating agencies and tourist transport operating agencies, units providing facilities for cultural, adventure and wild life experience to tourists, surface, air and water transport facilities to tourists, leisure, entertainment, amusement, sports, and health units for tourists and Convention/Seminar units and organizations. For foreign technology agreements, automatic approval is granted if

i. up to 3% of the capital cost of the project is proposed to be paid for technical and consultancy services including fees for architects, design, supervision, etc.

ii. up to 3% of net turnover is payable for franchising and marketing/publicity support fee, and up to 10% of gross operating profit is payable for management fee, including incentive fee.

2

Staffing for Housekeeping Operations

Staffing is the third sequential function of management. Up until now the executive housekeeper has been concerned with planning and organizing the housekeeping department for the impending opening and operations.

Now the executive housekeeper must think about hiring employees within sufficient time to ensure that three of the activities of staffing—selection (including interviewing), orientation, and training—may be completed before opening. Staffing will be a major task of the last two weeks before opening.

The development of the Area Responsibility Plan and the House Breakout Plan before opening led to preparation of the Department Staffing Guide, which will be a major tool in determining the need for employees in various categories. The housekeeping manager and laundry manager should now be on board and assisting in the development of various job descriptions. The hotel human resources department would also have been preparing for the hiring event. They would have advertised a mass hiring for all categories of personnel to begin on a certain date about two weeks before opening. Even though this chapter reflects a continuation of the executive housekeeper's planning for opening operations, the techniques described apply to any ongoing operation, except that the magnitude of selection, orientation, and training activities will not be as intense. Also, the fourth activity—development of existing employees—is normally missing in opening operations but is highly visible in ongoing operations.

Job Specifications

Job specifications should be written as job descriptions are prepared. Job specifications are simple statements of what the various incumbents to positions will be expected to do. An example of a job specification for a section housekeeper is as follows:

Job Specification—Example

Section Housekeeper (hotels) [often Guestroom Attendant—GRA] The incumbent will work as a member of a housekeeping team, cleaning and servicing for occupancy of approximately 18 hotel guestrooms each day.

Work will generally include the tasks of bed making, vacuuming, dusting, and bathroom cleaning. Incumbent will also be expected to maintain equipment provided for work and load housekeeper's cart before the end of each day's operation. Section housekeepers must be willing to work their share of weekends and be dependable in coming to work each day scheduled.

Employee Requisition

Once job specifications have been developed for every position, employee requisitions are prepared for first hirings (and for any follow-up needs for the human resources department). Note the designation as to whether the requisition is for a new or a replacement position and the number of employees required for a specific requisition number.

The human resources department will advertise, take applications, and screen to fill each requisition by number until all positions are filled. For example, the first requisition for GRAs may be for 20 Staffing Housekeeping Positions GRAs. The human resources department will continue to advertise for, take applications, and screen employees for the housekeeping department and will provide candidates for interview by department managers until 20 GRAs are hired. Should any be hired and require replacing, a new employee requisition will be required.

Staffing Housekeeping Positions

There are several activities involved in staffing a housekeeping operation. Executive housekeepers must select and interview employees, participate in an orientation program, train newly hired employees, and develop employees for future growth. Each of these activities will now be discussed.

Sources of Employees

Each area of the has its own demographic situations that affect the availability of suitable employees for involvement in housekeeping or environmental service operations. For example, in one area, an exceptionally high response rate from people seeking food service work may occur and a low response rate from people seeking housekeeping positions may occur. In another area, the reverse may be true, and people interested in housekeeping work may far outnumber those interested in food service.

Surveys among hotels or hospitals in your area will indicate the best source for various classifications of employees. Advertising campaigns that will reach these employees are the best method of locating suitable people.

Major classified ads associated with mass hirings will specify the need for food service personnel, front desk clerks, food servers, housekeeping personnel, and maintenance people. Such ads may yield surprising results. If the volume of response for housekeeping personnel is insufficient to provide a suitable hiring base, the following sources may be investigated:

1. Local employment agencies
2. Flyers posted on community bulletin boards
3. Local church organizations
4. Neighborhood canvass for friends of recently hired employees
5. Direct radio appeals to local homemakers
6. Organizations for underprivileged ethnic minorities, and mentally disabled people (It should be noted that many mentally disabled persons are completely capable of performing simple housekeeping tasks and are dependable and responsible people seeking an opportunity to perform in a productive capacity.)

If these sources do not produce the volume of applicants necessary to develop a staff, it may become necessary to search for employees in distant areas and to provide regular transportation for them to and from work.

Staffing for Housekeeping Operations

If aliens are hired, the department manager must take great care to ensure that they are legal residents of this country and that their green cards are valid. More than one hotel department manager has had an entire staff swept away by the Department of Immigration after hiring people who were illegal aliens. Such unfortunate action has required the immediate assistance of all available employees (including management) to fill in.

Processing Applicants

Whether you are involved in a mass hiring or in the recruiting of a single employee, a systematic and courteous procedure for processing applicants is essential.

For example, in the opening of the Los Angeles Airport Marriott, 11,000 applicants were processed to fill approximately 850 positions in a period of about two weeks. The magnitude of such an operation required a near assembly-line technique, but a personable and positive experience for the applicants still had to be maintained.

The efficient handling of lines of employees, courteous attendance, personal concern for employee desires, and reference to suitable departments for those unfamiliar with what the hotel or hospital has to offer all become earmarks for how the company will treat its employees.

The key to proper handling of applicants is the use of a control system whereby employees are conducted through the steps of application, prescreening, and if qualified, reference to a department for interview.

Note the opportunity for employees to express their desires for a specific type of employment. Even though an employee may desire involvement in one classification of work, he or she may be hired for employment in a different department. Also, employees might not be aware of the possibilities available in a particular department at the time of application or may be unable to locate in desired departments at the time of mass hirings.

Employees who perform well should therefore be given the opportunity to transfer to other departments when the opportunities arise. According to laws regulated by federal and state Fair Employment Practices Agencies (FEPA), no person may be denied the opportunity to submit application for employment for a position of his or her choosing. Not only is the law strict on this point, but companies in any way benefiting from interstate commerce (such as hotels and hospitals) may not discriminate in the hiring of people based on race, color, national origin, or religious preference. Although specific hours and days of the week may be specified, it is a generally accepted fact that hotels and hospitals must maintain personnel operations that provide the opportunity for people to submit applications without prejudice.

Prescreening Applicants

The prescreening interview is a staff function normally provided to all hotel or hospital departments by the *human resources* section of the organization. Prescreening is a preliminary interview process in which unqualified applicants—those applicants who do not meet the criteria for a job as specified in the job specification–special qualifications—are selected (or screened) out. For example, an applicant for a secretarial job that requires the incumbent to take shorthand and be able to type 60 words a minute may be screened out if the applicant is not able to pass a relevant typing and shorthand test. The results of prescreening are usually coded for internal use and are indicated on the Applicant Processing Record If a candidate is screened out by the personnel section, he or she should be told the reason immediately and thanked for applying for employment.

Applicants who are not screened out should either be referred to a specific department for interview or, if all immediate positions are filled, have their applications.

Staffing Housekeeping Positions

Placed in a department pending file for future reference. All applicants should be told that hiring decisions will be made by individual department managers based on the best qualifications from among those interviewed.

A suggested agenda for a prescreening interview is as follows:

1. The initial contact should be cordial and helpful. Many employees are lost at this stage because of inefficient systems established for handling applicants.
2. During the prescreening interview, try to determine what the employee is seeking, whether such a position is

available, or, if not, when such a position might become available.

3. Review the work history as stated on the application to determine whether the applicant meets the obvious physical and mental qualifications, as well as important human qualifications such as emotional stability, personality, honesty, integrity, and reliability.
4. Do not waste time if the applicant is obviously not qualified or if no immediate position is available.

When potential vacancies or a backlog of applicants exists, inform the candidate. Be efficient in stating this to the applicant. Always make sure that the applicant gives you a phone number in order that he or she may be called at some future date. Because most applicants seeking employment are actively seeking immediate work, applications more than 30 days old are usually worthless.

If at all possible, an immediate interview by the department manager should be held after screening. If this is not possible, a definite appointment should be made for the candidate's interview as soon as possible.

The Interview

An interview should be conducted by a manager of the department to which the applicant has been referred. In ongoing operations, it is often wise to also allow the supervisor for whom the new employee will work to visit with the candidate in order that the supervisor may gain a feel for how it would be to work together. The supervisor's view should be considered, since a harmonious relationship at the working level is important. Although the acceptance of an employee remains a prerogative of management, it would be unwise to accept an employee into a position when the supervisor has reservations about the applicant.

Certain personal characteristics should be explored when interviewing an employee. Some of these characteristics are native skills, stability, reliability, experience, attitude toward employment, personality, physical traits, stamina, age, sex, education, previous training, initiative, alertness, appearance, and personal cleanliness. Although employers may not discriminate against race, sex, age, religion, and nationality, overall considerations may involve the capability to lift heavy objects, enter men's or women's restrooms, and so on. In a housekeeping (or environmental services) department, people should be employed who find enjoyment in housework at home. Remember that character and personality cannot be completely judged from a person's appearance.

Also, it should be expected that a person's appearance will never be better than when that person is applying for a job.

Letters of recommendation and references should be carefully considered. Seldom will a letter of recommendation be adverse, whereas a telephone call might be most revealing.

If it were necessary to select the most important step in the selection process, interviewing would be it. Interviewing is *the* step that separates those who will be employed from those who will not. Poor interviewing techniques can make the process more difficult and may produce a result that can be both frustrating and damaging for both parties. In addition, inadequate interviewing will result in gaining incorrect information, being confused about what has been said, suppression of information, and, in some circumstances, complete withdrawal from the process by the candidate.

The following is a well-accepted list of the steps for a successful interview process.

1. *Be prepared.* Have a checklist of significant questions ready to ask the candidate. Such questions may be prepared from the body of the job description.
2. *Find a proper place to conduct the interview. The* applicant should be made to feel comfortable. The interview should be conducted in a quiet, relaxing atmosphere where there is privacy that will bringabout a confidential conversation.
3. *Practice.* People who conduct interviews should practice interviewing skills periodically. Several managers may get together and discuss interviewing techniques that are to be used.
4. *Be tactful and courteous.* Put the applicant at ease, but also control the discussion and lead to important questions.
5. *Be knowledgeable.* Be thoroughly familiar with the position for which the applicant is interviewing in order that all of the applicant's questions may be answered. Also, have

a significant background knowledge in order that general information about the company may be given.

6. *Listen.* Encourage the applicant to talk. This may be done by asking questions that are not likely to be answered by a yes or no. If people are comfortable and are asked questions about themselves, they will usually speak freely and give information that specific questions will not always bring out. Applicants will usually talk if there is a feeling that they are not being misunderstood.
7. *Observe.* Much can be learned about an applicant just by observing reactions to questions, attitudes about work, and, specifically, attitudes about providing service to others. Observation is a vital step in the interviewing process.

Interview Pitfills

Perhaps of equal importance to the interviewing technique are the following pitfalls, which should be avoided while interviewing.

1. Having a feeling that the employee will be just right based on a few outstanding characteristics rather than on the sum of all characteristics noted.
2. Being influenced by neatness, grooming, expensive clothes, and an extroverted personality—none of which has much to do with housekeeping competency.
3. Overgeneralizing, whereby interviewers assume too much from a single remark (for instance, an applicant's assurance that he or she "really wants to work").
4. Hiring the "boomer," that is, the person who always wants to work in a new property; unfortunately, this type of person changes jobs whenever a new property opens.
5. Projecting your own background and social status into the job requirement. Which school the applicant attended or whether the applicant has the "proper look" is beside the point. It is job performance that is going to count.
6. Confusing strengths with weaknesses, and vice versa. What is construed by one person to be overaggressiveness might be interpreted by another as confidence, ambition, and potential for leadership, the last two traits being in chronic short supply in most housekeeping departments. These

are the very characteristics that make it possible for management to promote from within and develop new supervisors and managers.

7. Being impressed by a smooth talker—or the reverse: assuming that silence reflects strength and wisdom. The interviewer should concentrate on what the applicant is saying rather than on how it is being said, then decide whether his or her personality will fit into the organization.
8. Being tempted by overqualified applicants. People with experience and education that far exceed the job requirements may be unable for some reason to get jobs commensurate with their backgrounds. Even if such applicants are not concealing skeletons in the closet, they still tend to become frustrated and dissatisfied with jobs far below their level of abilities.

The application of the techniques and avoidance of the pitfalls will be valuable tools in the selection of competent personnel for the housekeeping and environmental service departments.

For many years, the approach of many managers was to write a job description and then fill it by attempting to find the perfect person. This approach may overlook many qualified people, such as disadvantaged people or slow learners. Job descriptions may be analyzed in two ways when filling positions: (1) what is actually required to do the work, and (2) what is desirable. Is the ability to read or write really necessary for the job? Is the ability to learn quickly really necessary? A person who does not read or write or who is a slow learner can be trained and can make an excellent employee. True, it may take additional time, but the reward will be a loyal employee as well as less turnover. It has been proven many times that those who are disadvantaged or slightly retarded, once trained, will perform consistently well for longer periods. There are agencies who seek out companies that will try to hire such people.

Results of the Interview

If the results of an interview are negative and rejection is indicated, the candidate should be informed as soon as possible. A pleasant statement, such as "Others interviewed appear to be more qualified," is usually sufficient.

This information can be handled in a straightforward and courteous manner and in such a way that the candidate will appreciate the time that has been taken during the interview.

When the results of the interview are positive, a statement indicating a favourable impression is most encouraging.

However, no commitment should be made until a *reference check* has been conducted.

Reference Checks

In many cases, reference checks are made only to verify that what has been said in the application and interview is in fact true. Many times applicants are reluctant to explain in detail why previous employment situations have come to an end. It is more important to hear the actual truth about a prior termination from the applicant than it is to hear that they simply have been terminated.

Reference checks, in order of desirability, are as follows:

1. Personal (face-to-face) meetings with previous employers are the least available but provide the most accurate information when they can be arranged.
2. Telephone discussions are the next best and most often used approach. For all positions, an in-depth conversation by telephone between the potential new manager and the prior manager is most desirable; otherwise a simple verification of data is sufficient to ensure honesty.
3. The least desirable reference is the written recommendation, because managers are extremely reluctant to state a frank and honest opinion that may later be used against them in court.

Applicants who are rated successful at an interview should be told that a check of their references will be conducted, and, pending favourable responses, they will be contacted by the personnel department within two days. Applicants who are currently employed normally ask that their current employer not be contacted for a reference check. This request should be honoured at all times. Applicants who are currently working usually want to give proper notice to their current employers. If the applicant chooses not to give notice, chances are no notice will be given at the time he or she leaves your hotel.

In some cases, the applicant gives notice and, upon doing so, is "cut loose" immediately. If such is the case, the applicant should be told to contact the department manager immediately in order that the employee may be put to work as soon as possible.

Interview Skills Versus Turnover

There is no perfect interviewer, interviewee, or resultant hiring or rejection decision in regard to an applicant. We can only hope to improve our interviewing skills in order that the greatest degree of success in employee retention can be obtained. The executive housekeeper should expect that 25 percent of initial hires into a housekeeping department will not be employed for more than three months. (This is primarily because the housekeeping skills are easily learned and the position is paid at or near minimum wage.) Some new housekeeping departments have as much as a 75 percent turnover rate in the first three months of operation.

Orientation

A carefully planned, concerned, and informational orientation program is significant to the first impressions that a new employee will have about the hospital or hotel in general and the housekeeping department in particular. Too often, a new employee is told where the work area and restroom are, given a cursory explanation of the job, then put to work. It is not uncommon to find managers putting employees to work who have not even been processed into the organization, an unfortunate situation that is usually discovered on payday when there is no paycheck for the new employee. Such blatant disregard for the concerns of the employee can only lead to a poor perception of the company. A planned orientation program will eliminate this type of activity and will bring the employee into the company with personal concern and with a greater possibility for a successful relationship.

A good orientation program is usually made up of four phases: employee acquisition, receipt of an employee's handbook, tour of the facility, and an orientation meeting.

Employee Acquisition

Once a person is accepted for employment, the applicant is told to report for work at a given time and place, and that place should be the personnel department. Preemployment procedures can take as much as one-half day, and department managers eager to start new employees to work should allow time for a proper employee acquisition into the organization. Employment Checklist similar to those used by most personnel offices to ensure that nothing is overlooked in assimilating a new person into the organization.

At this time it should be ensured that the application is complete and any additional information pertaining to employment history that may be necessary to obtain the necessary work permits and credentials is on hand. Usually the security department records the entry of a new employee into the staff and provides instructions regarding use of employee entrances, removing parcels from the premises, and employee parking areas. Application for work permits, and drug testing, will be scheduled where applicable. All documents required by the hotel's health and welfare insurer should be completed, and instructions should be given about immediately reporting accidents, no matter how slight, to supervisors. The federal government requires that every employer submit a W-4 (withholding statement) for each employee on the payroll.

The employee must complete this document and give it to the company. Mandatory deductions from pay should be explained (federal and state income tax and Social Security FICA), as should other deductions that may be required or desired. The PAF is serially numbered, is created from data stored on magnetic discs, and is maintained in the employee's personnel file. When a change has to be made, such as job title, marital status, or rate of pay, the PAF is retrieved from the employee's record, changes are made *under* the item to be changed, and the corrected PAF is used to change the data in the computer storage. Once new information is stored, a new PAF is created and placed in the employee's record to await the next need for processing. A long-time employee might have many PAFs stored in the personnel file.

When either regular or special performance appraisals are given, the last (most current) PAF will be used to record the appraisal. A standard form used to record such appraisals, as well as written warnings and matters involving terminations. These forms are usually found on the reverse side of the PAF. Since performance appraisals may signify a raise in pay, the appropriate pay increase information would be indicated on the front side of the PAF. All recordings on PAFs, whether on one side or both, require the submission of data, storage of information, and creation of a new PAF to be stored in the employee's record.

The PAF and performance appraisal system should be thoroughly explained to the new employee, along with assignment of a payroll number. The employer should also explain how and when the staff is paid and when the first paycheck may be expected.

The Employee Handbook

The new employee should be provided with a copy of the hotel or hospital employee's handbook and should be told to read it thoroughly. Since the new housekeeping employee is not working just for the housekeeping department but is to become integrated as a member of the entire staff, reading this handbook is extremely important to ensure that proper instructions in the rules and regulations of the hotel are presented. The handbook should be developed in such a way as to inspire the new employee to become a fully participating member of the organization.

Familiarization Tour of the Facilities

Upon completion of the acquisition phase, a facility tour should be conducted for one or all new employees. For new facilities, access to the property should be gained within about one week before opening, and many new employees can be taken on a tour simultaneously. It is possible for employees to work in the hotel housekeeping department for years and never to have visited the showroom, dining rooms, ballrooms, or even the executive office areas. A tour of the complete facility melds employees into the total organization, and a complete informative tour should *never* be neglected. For ongoing operations, after acquisition, the new employee may be turned over to a department supervisor, who becomes the tour director. An appreciation of the total involvement of each employee is strengthened when a facilities tour is complete and thorough. If necessary, the property tour might be postponed until after the orientation meeting; however, the orientation activity of staffing is not complete until a property tour is conducted.

Orientation Meeting

The orientation meeting should not be conducted until the employee has had an opportunity to become at least partially familiar with the surroundings. After approximately two weeks, the employee will have many questions about experiences, the new job, training, and the rules and regulations listed in the Property and Department Handbooks.

Employee orientation meetings that are scheduled too soon fail to answer many questions that will develop within the first two weeks of employment.

The meeting should be held in a comfortable setting, with refreshments provided. It is usually conducted by the director of human resources and is attended by as many of the facility managers as possible.

Most certainly, the general manager or hospital administration members of the executive committee, the security director, and the new employees' department heads should attend. Each of these managers should have an opportunity to welcome the new employees and give them a chance to associate names with faces. All managers and new employees should wear name tags. In orientation meetings, a brief history of the company and company goals should be presented.

A planned orientation meeting should not be concluded without someone stressing the importance of each position. Every position must have a purpose behind it and is therefore important to the overall functioning of the facility. An excellent statement of this philosophy was once offered by a general manager who said, "The person mopping a floor in the kitchen at 3:00 A.M. is just as valuable to this operation as I am—we just do different things."

The orientation meeting should be scheduled to allow for many questions. And there should be someone in attendance who can answer *all of them*.

Although the new employee will be gaining confidence and security in the position as training ends and work is actually performed, informal orientation may continue for quite some time. The formal orientation, however, ends with the orientation meeting (although the facility tour may be conducted after the meeting). Finally, it should be remembered that good orientation procedures lead to worker satisfaction and help quiet the anxieties and fears that a new employee may have. When a good orientation is neglected, the seeds of dissatisfaction are planted.

Training

General

The efficiency and economy with which any department will operate will depend on the ability of each member of the organization to do his or her job. Such ability will depend in part on past experiences, but more commonly it can be credited to the type and quality of training offered. Employees, regardless of past experiences, always need some degree of training before starting a new job. Small institutions may try to avoid training by hiring people who are already trained in the general functions with which they will be involved. However, most institutions recognize the need for training that is specifically oriented toward the new experience, and will have a documented training program.

Some employers of housekeeping personnel find it easier to train completely unskilled and untrained personnel. In such cases, bad or undesirable practices do not have to be trained out of an employee. Previous experience and education should, however, be analyzed and considered in the training of each new employee in order that efficiencies in training can be recognized. If an understanding of department standards and policies can be demonstrated by a new employee, that portion of training may be shortened or modified. However, skill and ability must be demonstrated before training can be altered. Finally, training is the best method to communicate the company's way of doing things, without which the new employee may do work contrary to company policy.

First Training

First training of a new employee actually starts with a continuation of *department* orientation. When a new employee is turned over to the housekeeping or environmental services department, orientation usually continues by familiarizing the employee with *department rules and regulations.* Many housekeeping departments have their own department employee handbooks.

A Systematic Approach to Training

Training may be defined as those activities that are designed to help an employee begin performing tasks for which he or she is hired or to help the employee improve performance in a job already assigned. The purpose of training is to enable an employee to begin an assigned job or to improve upon techniques already in use. In hotel or hospital housekeeping operations, there are three basic areas in which training activity should take place: skills, attitudes, and knowledge.

Skills Training

A sample list of skills in which a basic housekeeping employee must be trained follows:

1. *Bed making:* Specific techniques; company policy
2. *Vacuuming:* Techniques; use and care of equipment
3. *Dusting:* Techniques; use of products
4. *Window and mirror cleaning:* Techniques and products
5. *Setup awareness:* Room setups; what a properly serviced room should look like
6. *Bathroom cleaning:* Tub and toilet sanitation; appearance; methods of cleaning and results desired
7. *Daily routine:* An orderly procedure for the conduct of the day's work; daily communications
8. *Caring for and using equipment:* Housekeeper cart; loading
9. *Industrial safety:* Product use; guest safety; fire and other emergencies.

The best reference for the skills that require training is the job description for which the person is being trained.

Attitude Guidance

Employees need guidance in their attitudes about the work that must be done. They need to be guided in their thinking about rooms that may present a unique problem in cleaning. Attitudes among section housekeepers need to be such that, occasionally, when rooms require extra effort to be brought back to standard, it is viewed as being a part of rendering service to the guest who paid to enjoy the room.

Carol Mondesir, director of housekeeping, Sheraton Centre, Toronto, states that:

A hotel is meant to be enjoyed and, occasionally, the rooms are left quite messed up. However, as long as they're not vandalized, it's part of the territory. The whole idea of being in the hospitality business is to make the guest's stay as pleasant as possible. The rooms are there to be enjoyed. Positive relationships with various agencies and people also need to be developed.

The following is a list of areas in which attitude guidance is important:

1. The guest/patient
2. The department manager and immediate supervisor
3. A guestroom that is in a state of great disarray
4. The hotel and company
5. The uniform
6. Appearance
7. Personal hygiene.

Meeting Standards

The most important task of the trainer is to prepare new employees to meet standards. With this aim in mind, sequence of performance in cleaning a guestroom is most important in order that efficiency in accomplishing day-to-day tasks may be developed.

In addition, the *best method* of accomplishing a task should be presented to the new trainee. Once the task has been learned, the next thing is to meet standards, which may not necessarily mean doing the job the way the person has been trained.

Knowledge Training

Areas of knowledge in which the employee needs to be trained are as follows:

1. Thorough knowledge of the hotel layout; employee must be able to give directions and to tell the guest about the hotel, restaurants, and other facilities
2. Knowledge of employee rights and benefits
3. Understanding of grievance procedure
4. Knowing top managers by sight and by name.

Ongoing Training

There is a need to conduct ongoing training for all employees, regardless of how long they have been members of the department. There are two instances when additional training is needed: (1) the purchase of new equipment, and (2) change in or unusual employee behavior while on the job.

When new equipment is purchased, employees need to know how the new equipment differs from present equipment, what new skills or knowledge are required to operate the equipment, who will need this knowledge, and when. New equipment may also require new attitudes about work habits.

Employee behavior while on the job that is seen as an indicator for additional training may be divided into two categories: events that the manager witnesses and events that the manager is told about by the employees.

Events that the manager witnesses that indicate a need for training are frequent employee absence, considerable spoilage of products, carelessness, a high rate of accidents, and resisting direction by supervisors.

Events that the manager might be told about that indicate a need for training are that something doesn't work right (product isn't any good), something is dangerous to work with, something is making work harder.

Although training is vital for any organization to function at top efficiency, it is expensive. The money and man-hours expended must therefore be worth the investment.

There must be a balance between the dollars spent training employees and the benefits of productivity and high-efficiency performance. A simple method of determining the need for training is to measure performance of workers: Find out what is going on at present on the job, and match this performance with what should be happening. The difference, if any, describes how much training is needed.

In conducting performance analysis, the following question should be asked: Could the employee do the job or task if his or her life depended on the result? If the employee *could not* do the job even if his or her life depended on the outcome, there is a deficiency of knowledge (DK). If the employee could have done the job if his or her life depended on the outcome, but did not, there is a deficiency of execution (DE). Some of the causes of deficiencies of execution include task interference, lack of feedback (employee doesn't know when the job is being performed correctly or incorrectly), and the balance of consequences (some employees like doing certain tasks better than others).

If either deficiency of knowledge or deficiency of execution exists, training must be conducted. The approach or the method of training may differ, however. Deficiencies of knowledge can be corrected by training the employee to do the job, then observing and correcting as necessary until the task is proficiently performed. Deficiency of execution is usually corrected by searching for the underlying cause of lack of performance, not by teaching the actual task.

Training Methods

There are numerous methods or ways to conduct training. Each method has its own advantages and disadvantages, which must be weighed in the light of benefits to be gained. Some methods are more expensive than others but are also more effective in terms of time required for comprehension and proficiency that must be developed. Several useful methods of training housekeeping personnel are listed and discussed.

On-the-job Training

Using on-the-job training (OJT), a technique in which "learning by doing" is the advantage, the instructor demonstrates the procedure and then watches the students perform it. With this technique, one instructor can handle several students. In housekeeping operations, the instructor is usually a GRA who is doing the instructing in the rooms that have been assigned for cleaning that day. The OJT method is not operationally productive until the student is proficient enough in the training tasks to absorb part of the operational load.

Simulation Training

With simulation training, a model room (unrented) is set up and used to train several employees. Whereas OJT requires progress toward daily production of ready rooms, simulation requires that the model room not be rented. In addition, the trainer is not productive in cleaning ready rooms.

The advantages of simulation training are that it allows the training process to be stopped, discussed, and repeated if necessary. Simulation is an excellent method, provided the trainer's time is paid for out of training funds, and clean room production is not necessary during the workday.

Coach-pupil Method

The coach-pupil method is similar to OJT except that each instructor has only one student (a one-to-one relationship). This method is desired, provided that there are enough qualified instructors to have several training units in progress at the same time.

Lectures

The lecture method reaches the largest number of students per instructor. Practically all training programs use this type of instruction for certain segments. Unfortunately, the lecture method can be the dullest training technique, and therefore requires instructors who are gifted in presentation capabilities. In addition, space for lectures may be difficult to obtain and may require special facilities.

Conferences

The conference method of instruction is often referred to as workshop training. This technique involves a group of students who formulate ideas, do problem solving, and report on projects. The conference or workshop technique is excellent for supervisory training.

Demonstrations

When new products or equipment are being introduced, demonstrations are excellent. Many demonstrations may be conducted by vendors and purveyors as a part of the sale of equipment and products. Difficulties may arise when language barriers exist. It is also important that no more information be presented than can be absorbed in a reasonable period of time; otherwise misunderstandings may arise.

Training Aids

Many hotels use training aids in a conference room, or post messages on an employee bulletin board. Aside from the usual training aids such as chalkboards, bulletin boards, charts, graphs, and diagrams, photographs can supply clear and accurate references for how rooms should be set up, maids' carts loaded, and routines accomplished.

Most housekeeping operations have films on guest contact and courtesy that may also be used in training. Motion pictures speak directly to many people who may not understand proper procedures from reading about them. Many training techniques may be combined to develop a well-rounded training plan.

Development

It is possible to have two students sitting side by side in a classroom, with one being trained and the other being developed. Recall that the definition of training is preparing a person to do a job for which he or she is hired or to improve upon performance of a current job.

Development is preparing a person for advancement or to assume greater responsibility. The techniques are the same, but the end result is quite different. Whereas training begins after orientation of an employee who is hired to do a specific job, upon introduction of new equipment, or upon observation and communication with employees indicating a need for training, development begins with the identification of a specific employee who has shown potential for advancement. Training for promotion or to improve potential is in fact development and must always include a much neglected type of training— supervisory training.

Many forms of developmental training may be given on the property; other forms might include sending candidates to schools and seminars. Developmental training is associated primarily with supervisors and managerial development and may encompass many types of experiences.

Note the various developmental tasks that the trainee must perform over a period of 12 months.

Development of individuals within the organization looks to future potential and promotion of employees. Specifically, those employees who demonstrate leadership potential should be developed through supervisory training for advancement to positions of greater responsibility.

Unfortunately, many outstanding workers have their performance rewarded by promotion but are given no development training. The excellent section housekeeper who is advanced to the position of senior housekeeper without the benefit of supervisory training is quickly seen to be unhappy and frustrated and may possibly become a loss to the department. It is therefore most essential that individual potential be developed in an orderly and systematic manner, or else this potential may never be recognized.

While undergoing managerial development as specified, student and management alike should not lose sight of the primary aim of the program, which is the learning and potential development of the trainee, not departmental production. Even though there will be times that the trainee may be given specific responsibilities to oversee operations, clean guestrooms, or service public areas, advantage should not be taken of the trainee or the situation to the detriment of the development function. Development of new growth in the trainee becomes difficult when the training instructor or coordinator is not only developing a new manager but is also being held responsible for the production of some aspect of housekeeping operations.

Records and Reports

Whether you are conducting a training or a development program, suitable records of training progress should be maintained both by the training supervisor and the student. Periodic evaluations of the student's progress should be conducted, and successful completion of the program should be recognized. Public recognition of achievement will inspire the newly trained or developed employee to achieve standards of performance and to strive for advancement.

Once an employee is trained or developed and his or her satisfactory performance has been recognized and recorded, the person should perform satisfactorily to standards. Future performance may be based on beginning performance after training. If an employee's performance begins to fall short of standards and expectations, there has to be a reason other than lack of skills.

The reason for unsatisfactory performance must then be sought out and addressed. This type of follow-up is not possible unless suitable records of training and development are maintained and used for comparison.

Evaluation and Performance Appraisal

Although evaluation and performance appraisal for employees will occur as work progresses, it is not uncommon to find the design of systems for appraisal as part of organization and staffing functions. This is true because first appraisal and evaluation occurs during training, which is an activity of staffing. Once trainees begin to have their performance appraised, the methods used will continue throughout employment. As a part of training, new employees should be told how, when, and by whom their performances will be evaluated, and should be advised that questions regarding their performance will be regularly answered.

Probationary Period

Initial employment should be probationary in nature, allowing the new employee to improve efficiency to where the designated number of rooms cleaned per day can be achieved in a probationary period (about three months). Should a large number of employees be unable to achieve the standard within that time, the standard should be investigated. Should only one or two employees be unable to meet the standard of rooms cleaned per day, an evaluation of the employee in training should either reveal the reason why or indicate the employee as unsuitable for further retention. An employee who, after suitable training, cannot meet a reasonable performance standard should not be allowed to continue employment. Similarly, an employee who has met required performance standards in the specified probationary period should be continued into regular employment status and thus achieve a reasonable degree of security in employment.

Evaluation

Evaluation of personnel is an attempt to measure selected traits, characteristics, and productivity. Unfortunately, evaluations are generally objective in nature, and raters are seldom trained in the art of subjective evaluation. Initiative, self-control, and leadership ability do not lend themselves to measurement; therefore such characteristics are estimated. How well they are estimated depends to a great extent on the person doing the estimating. Two raters using the same form and rating the same person will probably arrive at different conclusions. Certain policies on the use of evaluations should be established so that they are understood by both the person doing the evaluating and the person being evaluated. These policies must be established and disseminated by management. In order to establish such policies, the following questions, among others, must be answered and communicated to all those involved in the evaluation: What will evaluations be used for? Will evaluations influence promotions, become a part of the em ployee's record, be used as periodic checks, or be used for counseling and guidance? What qualities are going to be evaluated? Who is going to be evaluated? Who will do the evaluating? Reliable evaluations require careful planning and take considerable time, skill, and work. An evaluation must be understood by the employee.

Evaluation should be used at the end of a probationary period, and the employee must understand at the beginning of the period that he or she will be observed and evaluated. Each item, as well as what impact the evaluation will have on future employment, should be explained to the employee. People undergoing periodic evaluations, such as at the end of one year's employment, should also know why evaluations are being conducted and what may result from the evaluation. In both situations, the evaluation should be used for counseling and guidance so that performance may be improved.

Prospects for Development via International Business

International Business Development evolves through the normal processes of trade, foreign direct investment (FDI), capital flows, migration, and the advancement of technology in undeveloped nations. In order to achieve sustainable global business development, business professionals often must finds ways of adapting to the cultures and societies within which they operate and conduct business.

As the globalization of economies, societies, and cultures continues, and nations become more integrated through networks of exchange, international business development and global strategic management continues to evolve. Global firms that employ business development professionals in multiple locations who share the exact same body of knowledge, ethics, practices, and standards benefit from a shared body of knowledge and ethics. These companies are well positioned for growth, as are the societies in which they operate.

The international business development and global strategic management industry is a specialized field of commerce that penetrates existing markets, and often creates new ones, by introducing new products and services to businesses, individuals, non-profit organizations, and government agencies. Topics that are common to international business development include ethics, philosophy, economics, politics, marketing, management, and technology. International business development professionals require knowledge of the legalities of strategic relationships, licensing, partnering, intellectual property, emerging technologies, fair practices, cultural differences, international marketing, information management, knowledge management, finance, and advertising, all of which affect business development within a culture and its economy.

The early debate on the role of foreign direct investment (FDI) in developing countries has been neatly characterized as "colourful and fluid" (Balasubramanyam, 1985). One reason for the colourfulness of this debate was its emergence within the politically-charged birth of development economics *per se* and related attempts to co-opt it into disparate wider political-economic postures. This points forward to my, hopefully calmer, concern here with the parallel need to *evaluate* transnational corporations (TNCs) as participants in the processes of globalization. Another factor in leaving the early debates open and fluid was the lack of a commonly agreed methodology for analysing, in a convincing manner, an observable mode of international transaction (FDI) with an obvious potential for a wide-ranging diversity of often intangible or unmeasurable implications. This meant that much early analysis of the developmental effects of FDI fractured around detailed investigations of specific aspects of a wide range of separate areas of concern (e.g. extent and appropriateness of technology transfer; job generation and employment conditions; the allegation of decapitalization; balance-of-payments and trade effects; bargaining mechanisms; spillovers; industry structure).

If early theorizing of the TNC helped to explain the indecisiveness of attempts to evaluate the implications of FDI, then the subsequent analysis of these firms, now most usefully positioned at the interface of business strategy and economics, provides methodologies that are highly attuned to elucidation of issues of globalization and development. Central to this analysis, and to the lines of argument developed here, is a preference for *organizing* an understanding of *diversity*, rather than simplifying it or assuming it away. Two vectors of diversity define the structure of our subsequent analysis.

Operation of Pricing Decisions and Strategies

Pricing is a fundamental aspect of financial modeling, and is one of the four Ps of the marketing mix. The other three aspects are product, promotion, and place. It is also a key variable in microeconomic price allocation theory.

Price is the only revenue generating element amongst the four Ps, the rest being cost centres. Pricing is the manual or automatic process of applying prices to purchase and sales orders, based on factors such as: a fixed amount, quantity break, promotion or sales campaign, specific vendor quote, price prevailing on entry, shipment or invoice date, combination of multiple orders or lines, and many others. Automated systems require more setup and maintenance but may prevent pricing errors. The needs of the consumer can be converted into demand only if the consumer has the willingness and capacity to buy the product. Thus pricing is very important in marketing.

Questions Involved in Pricing

Pricing involves asking questions like:

- *How much to charge for a product or service?* This question is that a typical starting point for discussions about pricing, however, a better question for a vendor to ask is-How much do customers *value* the products, services, and other intangibles that the vendor provides.
- What are the pricing objectives?
- Do we use profit maximization pricing?
- How to set the price?: (cost-plus pricing, demand based or value-based pricing, rate of return pricing, or competitor indexing)
- Should there be a single price or multiple pricing?
- Should prices change in various geographical areas, referred to as zone pricing?
- Should there be quantity discounts?
- What prices are competitors charging?
- Do you use a price skimming strategy or a penetration pricing strategy?
- What image do you want the price to convey?
- Do you use psychological pricing?

- How important are customer price sensitivity (e.g. "sticker shock") and elasticity issues?
- Can real-time pricing be used?
- Is price discrimination or yield management appropriate?
- Are there legal restrictions on retail price maintenance, price collusion, or price discrimination?
- Do price points already exist for the product category?
- How flexible can we be in pricing? : The more competitive the industry, the less flexibility we have.
  - o The price floor is determined by production factors like costs (often only variable costs are taken into account), economies of scale, marginal cost, and degree of operating leverage
  - o The price ceiling is determined by demand factors like price elasticity and price points
- Are there transfer pricing considerations?
- What is the chance of getting involved in a price war?
- How visible should the price be?-Should the price be neutral? (ie.: not an important differentiating factor), should it be highly visible? (to help promote a low priced economy product, or to reinforce the prestige image of a quality product), or should it be hidden? (so as to allow marketers to generate interest in the product unhindered by price considerations).
- Are there joint product pricing considerations?
- What are the non-price costs of purchasing the product? (e.g..: travel time to the store, wait time in the store, disagreeable elements associated with the product purchase-dentist-> pain, fishmarket-> smells)
- What sort of payments should be accepted? Pricing

What a Price should Do

A well chosen price should do three things:

- achieve the financial goals of the company (e.g., profitability)
- fit the realities of the marketplace (Will customers buy at that price?)

- support a product's positioning and be consistent with the other variables in the marketing mix
  - o price is influenced by the type of distribution channel used, the type of promotions used, and the quality of the product
    - * price will usually need to be relatively high if manufacturing is expensive, distribution is exclusive, and the product is supported by extensive advertising and promotional campaigns
    - * a low price can be a viable substitute for product quality, effective promotions, or an energetic selling effort by distributors

From the marketer's point of view, an efficient price is a price that is very close to the maximum that customers are prepared to pay. In economic terms, it is a price that shifts most of the consumer surplus to the producer. A good pricing strategy would be the one which could balance between the price floor (the price below which the organization ends up in losses) and the price ceiling (the price beyond which the organization experiences a no demand situation).

Definitions

Pricing is the process of determining what a company will receive in exchange for its products. Pricing factors are manufacturing cost, market place, competition, market condition, Quality of product.

The effective price is the price the company receives after accounting for discounts, promotions, and other incentives.

Price lining is the use of a limited number of prices for all your product offerings. This is a tradition started in the old five and dime stores in which everything cost either 5 or 10 cents. Its underlying rationale is that these amounts are seen as suitable price points for a whole range of products by prospective customers. It has the advantage of ease of administering, but the disadvantage of inflexibility, particularly in times of inflation or unstable prices.

A loss leader is a product that has a price set below the operating margin. This results in a loss to the enterprise on that particular item, but this is done in the hope that it will draw customers into the store and that some of those customers will buy other, higher margin items.

Promotional pricing refers to an instance where pricing is the key element of the marketing mix.

The price/quality relationship refers to the perception by most consumers that a relatively high price is a sign of good quality. The belief in this relationship is most important with complex products that are hard to test, and experiential products that cannot be tested until used (such as most services). The greater the uncertainty surrounding a product, the more consumers depend on the price/quality hypothesis and the more of a premium they are prepared to pay. The classic example of this is the pricing of the snack cake Twinkies, which were perceived as low quality when the price was lowered. Note, however, that excessive reliance on the price/quantity relationship by consumers may lead to the raising of prices on all products and services, even those of low quality, which in turn causes the price/quality relationship to no longer apply.

Premium pricing (also called prestige pricing) is the strategy of consistently pricing at, or near, the high end of the possible price range to help attract status-conscious consumers. A few examples of companies which partake in premium pricing in the marketplace include Rolex and Bentley. People will buy a premium priced product because:

1. They believe the high price is an indication of good quality;
2. They believe it to be a sign of self worth-"They are worth it"-It authenticates their success and status-It is a signal to others that they are a member of an exclusive group;
3. They require flawless performance in this application-The cost of product malfunction is too high to buy anything but the best-example : heart pacemaker.

The term Goldilocks pricing is commonly used to describe the practice of providing a "gold-plated" version of a product at a premium price in order to make the next-lower priced option look more reasonably priced; for example, encouraging customers to see business-class airline seats as good value for money by offering an even higher priced first-class option. Similarly, third-class railway carriages in Victorian England are said to have been built without windows, not so much to punish third-class customers (for which there was no economic incentive), as to motivate those who could afford second-class seats to pay for them instead of taking the cheaper option. This is also known as a potential result of price discrimination.

The name derives from the Goldilocks story, in which Goldilocks chose neither the hottest nor the coldest porridge, but instead the one that was "just right". More technically, this form of pricing exploits the general cognitive bias of aversion to extremes. This practice is known academically as "framing". By providing three options (i.e. small, medium, and large; first, business, and coach classes) you can manipulate the consumer into choosing the middle choice and thus, the middle choice should yield the most profit to the seller, since it is the most chosen option.

Demand-based pricing is any pricing method that uses consumer demand-based on perceived value-as the central element. These include : price skimming, price discrimination and yield management, price points, psychological pricing, bundle pricing, penetration pricing, price lining, value-based pricing, geo and premium pricing. Pricing factors are manufacturing cost, market place, competition, market condition, quality of product.

Multidimensional pricing is the pricing of a product or service using multiple numbers. In this practice, price no longer consists of a single monetary amount (e.g., sticker price of a car), but rather consists of various dimensions (e.g., monthly payments, number of payments, and a downpayment). Research has shown that this practice can significantly influence consumers' ability to understand and process price information.

The 9 Laws of Price Sensitivity

In their book, "The Strategy and Tactics of Pricing", Thomas Nagle and Reed Holden outline 9 laws or factors that influence a buyer's price sensitivity with respect to a given purchase:

Reference Price Effect

Buyer's price sensitivity for a given product increases the higher the product's price relative to perceived alternatives. Perceived alternatives can vary by buyer segment, by occasion, and other factors.

Difficult Comparison Effect

Buyers are less sensitive to the price of a known/more reputable product when they have difficulty comparing it to potential alternatives.

Switching Costs Effect

The higher the product-specific investment a buyer must make to switch suppliers, the less price sensitive that buyer is when choosing between alternatives.

Price-Quality Effect

Buyers are less sensitive to price the more that higher prices signal higher quality. Products for which this effect is particularly relevant include: image products, exclusive products, and products with minimal cues for quality.

Expenditure Effect

Buyers are more price sensitive when the expense accounts for a large percentage of buyers' available income or budget.

End-Benefit Effect

The effect refers to the relationship a given purchase has to a larger overall benefit, and is divided into two parts:

Derived demand: The more sensitive buyers are to the price of the end benefit, the more sensitive they will be to the prices of those products that contribute to that benefit.

Price proportion cost: The price proportion cost refers to the percent of the total cost of the end benefit accounted for by a given component that helps to produce the end benefit (e.g., think CPU and PCs). The smaller the given components share of the total cost of the end benefit, the less sensitive buyers will be to the component's price.

Shared-cost Effect

The smaller the portion of the purchase price buyers must pay for themselves, the less price sensitive they will be.

Fairness Effect

Buyers are more sensitive to the price of a product when the price is outside the range they perceive as "fair" or "reasonable" given the purchase context.

The Framing Effect

Buyers are more price sensitive when they perceive the price as a loss rather than a forgone gain, and they have greater price sensitivity when the price is paid separately rather than as part of a bundle.

Approaches

Pricing as the most effective profit lever. Pricing can be approached at three levels. The industry, market, and transaction level.

Pricing at the industry level focuses on the overall economics of the industry, including supplier price changes and customer demand changes.

Pricing at the market level focuses on the competitive position of the price in comparison to the value differential of the product to that of comparative competing products.

Pricing at the transaction level focuses on managing the implementation of discounts away from the reference, or list price, which occur both on and off the invoice or receipt.

Tactics

Micromarketing is the practice of tailoring products, brands (microbrands), and promotions to meet the needs and wants of microsegments within a market. It is a type of market customization that deals with pricing of customer/product combinations at the store or individual level.

Pricing Mistakes

Many companies make common pricing mistakes. Bernstein's article "Supplier Pricing Mistakes" outlines several which include:

- Weak controls on discounting
- Inadequate systems for tracking competitor selling prices and market share
- Cost-Up pricing
- Price increases poorly executed
- Worldwide price inconsistensies
- Paying sales reps on dollar volume vs. addition of profitability measures.

3

Hotel Accounting

Accounting department-As any industry, the hotel industry deals with personnel, materials, sales, equipment, maintenance etc. There is constant turnover of money. This work of managing money matters is done by the accounting department. The Chief Accountant, a chartered accountant, has a team of accountants, auditors, cashiers and accounting clerks working in the department. Chief Accountant works directly under the executive Assistant Manager.

Accounting serves a purpose beyond presenting the historical financial position of a hotel. Timely accounting information, properly presented, is information that management can use to improve future performance and compare income and expenses to past performance and future goals.

The Uniform System of Accounts, endorsed by the American Hotel and Lodging Association, is used to present financial information. Additionally, statistics that are useful in analyzing the financial statements are included. Full supplementary schedules and any backup documentation is available to the owner at any time. We will assist client asset managers in the preparation of their internal reports.

Accounting data is processed using an offsite Application Service Provide (ASP) over the internet. This enables our hotels to input daily revenue and statistical data while accounts payable is processed regularly. The end result is that managers, owners and corporate staff can review financial data on line at any time over the internet using a web browser. Using our ASP accounting is accomplished using the most advantageous arrangement for the hotel. We can either perform all of the accounting, from disbursements to statement processing, at our corporate office or decentralize any portion of the process to the hotel level. At HVS Hotel Management, tight internal and cash controls, combined with strong manager responsibility, are key to maximizing profitability.

Generally Accepted Accounting Principles

Generally Accepted Accounting Principles (GAAP) is the americanized term used to refer to the standard framework of guidelines for financial accounting used in any given jurisdiction which are generally known as Accounting Standards. GAAP includes the standards, conventions, and rules accountants follow in recording and summarizing transactions, and in the preparation of financial statements.

Overview

Financial accounting is information that must be assembled and reported objectively. Third-parties who must rely on such information have a right to be assured that the data are free from bias and inconsistency, whether deliberate or not. For this reason, financial accounting relies on certain standards or guides that are called "Generally Accepted Accounting Principles" (GAAP). Principles derive from tradition, such as the concept of matching. In any report of financial statements (audit, compilation, review, etc.), the preparer/auditor must indicate to the reader whether or not the information contained within the statements complies with GAAP.

- Principle of regularity: Regularity can be defined as conformity to enforced rules and laws.
- Principle of consistency: This principle states that when a business has once fixed a method for the accounting treatment of an item, it will enter all similar items that follow in exactly the same way.
- Principle of sincerity: According to this principle, the accounting unit should reflect in good faith the reality of the company's financial status.
- Principle of the permanence of methods: This principle aims at allowing the coherence and comparison of the financial information published by the company.

- Principle of non-compensation: One should show the full details of the financial information and not seek to compensate a debt with an asset, a revenue with an expense, etc.
- Principle of prudence: This principle aims at showing the reality "as is" : one should not try to make things look prettier than they are. Typically, a revenue should be recorded only when it is *certain* and a provision should be entered for an expense which is *probable.*
- Principle of continuity: When stating financial information, one should assume that the business will not be interrupted. This principle mitigates the principle of prudence: assets do not have to be accounted at their disposable value, but it is accepted that they are at their historical value.
- Principle of periodicity: Each accounting entry should be allocated to a given period, and split accordingly if it covers several periods. If a client pre-pays a subscription (or lease, etc.), the given revenue should be split to the entire time-span and not counted for entirely on the date of the transaction.
- Principle of Full Disclosure/Materiality: All information and values pertaining to the financial position of a business must be disclosed in the records.
- Principle of Utmost Good Faith: All the information regarding to the firm should be disclosed to the insurer before the insurance policy is taken.

Accounting Cycle and Financial Statements

Financial statements are official records that document the financial activities of a business. They provide a view into the financial condition as well as the profitability of the business. Financial statements are prepared as part of the accounting cycle.

There are four basic types of financial statements:

Balance Sheet Financial Statement

The Balance Sheet gives a snapshot overview of a company's financial condition at a given point in time. (This differs from the other financial statements in that it is the only one that reflects a single point in time; the other statements report on activities over a period of time. In fact, with a 'beginning' balance sheet and the other statements, you have enough information to build an 'ending' balance sheet for any period of time.)

Remember, it is called a 'balance' sheet because the amount of assets should equal (or 'balance') the sum of the liabilities and owner's equity.

Income Statement

The Income Statement reports on a business' profit and loss from operations over a given period of time. It can also be referred to as a Profit and Loss Statement or P&L Statement. Depending on financial requirements, businesses will prepare either a Single-Step Income Statement or a Multi-Step Income Statement.

Statement of Retained Earnings

The Retained Earnings Statement shows the changes in the owner's equity in a business over a given period of time by highlighting the equity positions at the beginning and end of the reporting period.

Statement of Cash Flow

The Cash Flow Statement reports on a business' cash flow from operations, financing, and investment activities over a given period. It shows how money has flowed into and out of the company, and generally demonstrates the short-term viability of the company's cash position.

The statement of cash flow also explains how the cash position can change independently of profit — $1 million in sales on credit can make the income statement profitable, but without the cash the company might be in dire financial straits.

The Accounting Cycle is a series of steps which are repeated every reporting period. The process starts with making accounting entries for each transaction and goes through closing the books. Use this tutorial for an overview of the accounting cycle, covering activities required both during and at the end of the accounting period.

Accounting Cycle-Introduction

The Accounting Cycle is a series of steps which are repeated every reporting period. The process starts with making accounting entries for each transaction and goes through closing the books.

Accounting Cycle-Steps During the Accounting Period

These accounting cycle steps occur during the accounting period, as each transaction occurs:

1. Identify the transaction through an original source document (such as an invoice, receipt, cancelled check, time card, deposit slip, purchase order) which provides:
   - o date
   - o amount
   - o description (account or business purpose)
   - o name and address of other party (if practical)
2. Analyze the transaction – determine which accounts are affected, how (increase or decrease), and how much
3. Make Journal entries – record the transaction in the journal as both a debit and a credit
   - o journals are kept in chronological order
   - o journals may include sales journal, purchases journal, cash receipts journal, cash payments journal, and the general journal
4. Post to ledger – transfer the journal entries to ledger accounts
   - o ledger is kept by account
   - o ledger accounts may be T-account form or include balances
   - o (Learn more about the Chart of Accounts.)

Accounting Cycle: Steps at the End of the Accounting Period

These accounting cycle steps occur at the end of the accounting period:

1. Trial Balance – this is a calculation to verify the sum of the debits equals the sum of the credits. If they don't balance, you have to fix the unbalanced trial balance before you go on to the rest of the accounting cycle. (If they do balance you could still have a problem, but at least it balances!)
2. Adjusting entries – prepare and post accrued and deferred items to journals and ledger T-accounts
3. Adjusted trial balance – make sure the debits still equal the credits after making the period end adjustments

4. Financial Statements – prepare income statement, balance sheet, statement of retained earnings, and statement of cash flows (this can occur at other points in time with appropriate adjustments)
5. Closing entries – prepare and post closing entries to transfer the balances from temporary accounts (such as the revenue and expenses from the income statement to owner's equity on the balance sheet).
6. After-Closing trial balance – final trial balance after the closing entries to make sure debits still equal credits.

Accounting Concept of Income

The concept of 'income' is different to the economists and accountants. Economists concept of income is that of 'real income' meaning thereby the increase-in real terms of the ownership funds between two points of time.

In accounting the term income is known as 'net profit'. It was stated earlier:

Sales-Merchandising cost = Gross profit and Gross profit-Expenses of doing business = Net profit

In other words, Revenue-Expenses = Net profit.

These terms are explained below:

Revenue

It is the monetary value of the products sold or services rendered to the customers during the period. It results from sales services and source like interest, dividend and commission etc. For example, sales affected by the business and charge made for services rendered by the business constitutes revenue. However, all cash receipt may nott be revenue.

Thus, money borrowed leads to cash receipt but it does not constitute revenue. Similarly additional capital brought in increases proprietor's funds but it is not revenue.

Expenses/Cost of (Doing Business)

Expenditure incurred by the business to earn revenue is termed as expense or cost of doing business. Examples of expenses are raw materials consumed, salaries, rent, depreciation, advertisement etc.

Cash v/s Accrual Basis of Accounting

Small business, individual professionals and non-trading concerns usually adopt cash basis of accounting. Under this system, incomes are considered to have been earned only when received ill cash and expenses are considered to have been incurred only actually paid. Hence, under this system the profit or loss of an accounting period is the difference between incomes received and the expenses paid. Though the cash basis of accounting is simple (no adjustment is required) but il loses its comparability.

Under accrual basis all incomes are credited to the period in which earned irrespective of the fact whether received or not. Similarly, all expenses are debited to the period in which incurred irrespective of the fact whether paid or not. It is a scientific basis of accounting, though a bit difficult.

Matching Concept. Requires that expenses should be matched to the revenues of the appropriate accounting period. So we must determine what are the revenues earned during a particular accounting period and the expenses incurred to earn these revenues. It is the matching concept which justifies accrual basis of accounting.

Accruals and Deferrals

Accounting is expected to measure or ascertain the net income of the business during the accounting period. Normally, it is the calendar year (1st January to 31st December) but in other cases it may be Financial year (Ist April to 31st March) or any other period according to the convention of the business community of the area. The combined impact of matching concept and the accounting period concept on accounting has resulted in accruals and deferrals.

Accrued or Outstanding Expenses

It is the term which denotes that expenditure has been incurred during the accounting period but the same has not been paid in cash e.g. Salary, Rent, Wage etc. becoming due but not paid.

Deferred or Pre-paid Expenses

It is the term which denotes that payment in cash has been made "in advance but the full benefit of this payment has not been reaped by the current accounting period, e.g., Insurance paid in advance.

Accrued or Outstanding Income

It is the term which denotes that the income has been earned but the cash has not been received against the same. Income has accrued due but not received e.g. Interest on investments etc.

Differed or Received in-advance Income

It is the term which denotes income which has been received (in cash) in advance but it has not been earned so far e.g. rent received in advance. All the accruals and deferrals arc not be adjusted at the end of the accounting period (end-period adjustments) in order to find out the income of the business during the period under review. The procedure of ascertaining (i) business income and (ii) financial position is being described, in detail below:

In fact, these arc two most important of many objectives of book-keeping. In order to know the profits earned by him he prepares a trading and loss account and in order to know the financial position of his business on the last day of the financial period he prepares a balance sheet.

Such accounts are called 'Final Accounts'. Preparation of final accounts is the concluding step of accounting cycle. In fact, final accounts include a number of accounts (i) Manufacturing/ Production account, (ii) Trading account, (iii) Profit and loss account and (iv) Balance sheet.

Practically balance sheet is a statement but for accounting purposes here it is treated as a part vital accounts.

The preparation of above all or any of the above accounts depends upon the nature of the business being carried on by the business concerned. In case of a manufacturing business manufacturing account, trading account, profit and loss account and balance sheet form the parts of final accounts whereas in case of trading business all other accounts are prepared with the exception of manufacturing account. Each of these accounts provide a specific vital information to businessman to help to control and organize the business activities in a batter way.

Internal Control for Food and Beverage Sales

As in nearly all hotel departments, F&B outlets of a hotel might operate under the following systems:

Manual Systems

In small organizations where the manager or the owner is available in nearly all hotel operations, manual systems are preferred. For, there is no need for an investment in computers, though a lot of human errors, as far as control is concerned, might be observed. The forms that must be used in a manual system are:

Captain Order

This form is a written format of the guest order. This is an internal control document prepared in three copies by the waiter/ waitress. A copy is sent to kitchen for food production, a copy to service bar for the drinks to be prepared and the last copy to the cashier for opening a guest check.

On the captain order, no monetary information takes place. Rather, the order of the guest, the table no., the waiter ID, and number of guest(s) are only filled.

Captain orders help as to control the relation between the waiter, kitchen, service bar and cashier.

Guest Check (F&B check, "Adisyon")

By recording F&B item prices on the captain order, the cashier prepares the guest check. Had any cancellations or additions from the initial captain order occurred, the cashier should make the necessary changes.

As far as payment is concerned, the guest might opt for:

a) Charging to his/her room. In this case, the waiter shall insert the room number and take the guest signature on the guest check,

b) Cash, Credit Card, Bank Check or personal check. In this case, the waiter shall get the due amount from the guest; bring the collection to the cashier, who shall prepare the necessary legal document for sales along with the various internal control vouchers needed. In manual systems, cash register machine is used for this purpose. To illustrate, the cashier rings up the sale on the cash register and gives the guest the cash register bill.

At the end of his/her shift, the cashier should take the "Z" report from the cash register, attach it to various guest checks opened, the captain orders, and the total cash received in that very shift. Later, it is the responsibility of the Hotel Manager or Accounting Managers to verify the total shown on the cash register tape against the total cash receipts and the total developed from the serially numbered guest checks. While doing so, the unit prices recorded on the guest checks have to be also verified from the price list.

Semi-Automated Systems

In larger organizations, maintaining internal control by observation and one to one verifications is not applicable. In cases where business owners want to benefit from computerized systems but cannot afford financially to set up a fully automated system, it is better to get use of an individual Posting Machine for the various F&B outlets' operations.

In such systems, there is no need for the verification of unit prices on the guest checks as the computer automatically posts the prices.

The other advantage is, as the guest check printed from the posting machine is facing the legal requirements, there is no need to use cash register machine or to create another legal document. At the end of each shift, the cashier shall count the cash receipts and compare them with the total generated from guest checks. The accounting department does the verification.

In semi-computerized accounting systems there is no interface with the other hotel departmental systems. This is one of the biggest disadvantages of this very system since it involves extra control work for other departments and functions. For example, the Night Auditor must control and post all the data again to the Front Office system. This is time consuming and subject to numerous posting errors. In practice, this might generate significant late charge amounts, and hence might affect seriously the financial position of the hotel.

Fully Automated Systems

In big organizations, manual or semi-automated systems cannot be applicable because of the huge amount of the number of transactions, their control, and the large amount of money associated to them.

In fully automated systems, in order to maintain an adequate internal control and information flow, the individual computers must be electronically connected to each other. The major advantages of the system are:

1. On-line information is available
2. No need for re-entering data
3. Minimum internal control requirement.

Debit and Credit

Debit and credit are formal bookkeeping and accounting terms. They are the most fundamental concepts in accounting, representing the two sides of each individual transaction recorded in any accounting system. A debit transaction indicates an asset or an expense transaction, a credit indicates a transaction that will cause a liability or a gain. A debit transaction can also be used to reduce a credit balance or increase a debit balance. A credit transaction can be used to decrease a debit balance or increase a credit balance.

Debits and credits are a system of notation used in bookkeeping to determine how and where to record any financial transaction. In bookkeeping, instead of using addition '+' and subtraction '-' symbols, a transaction uses the symbol DR (Debit) or CR (Credit). In double-entry bookkeeping debit is used for asset and expense transactions and credit is used for liability, gain and equity transactions.

For bank transactions, money in is treated as a debit transaction and money out is treated as a credit transaction. Traditionally, transactions are recorded in two columns of numbers: debits in the left hand column, credits in the right hand column. Keeping the debits and credits in separate columns allows each to be recorded and totalled independently. Where the total of the debit value amounts is lower than the total of the credit value amounts a balancing debit value is posted to that nominal ledger account. That nominal ledger account is now "balanced". An account can have either a credit value balance or a debit value balance but not both.

Origin of the Terms Debit and Credit

The term debit comes from Middle French *debet* from Latin *debitum* "that which is owed" (the neuter past participle of *debere* "to owe"). Debit is abbreviated to Di (for debtor). The term credit comes from the Latin *creditum* meaning "that which is entrusted or loaned" from the past participle of *credere* "to trust or entrust". Credit is abbreviated to Ck (for creditor).

Operational Principles

·Debit generally represents any depletion in the resources held by the entity while credit represents increment of the resources held by the entity. Hence, debits to an account are negative/depletions in the accounting entity's resources while credits are positive/increments in the same.

Real Accounts

- In real accounts any increment in assets held by the entity is reflected by increasing the relevant asset account and depletion by crediting the asset account.
- If any asset account is debited then it is on account of increment in the value or acquisition of that liability or owner's equity which decreases the resources held by the entity.

As the total resources held by the entity cannot indigenously increment themselves the depletion has to be matched with a fall in resources within the entity.

Personal Accounts

- In Personal Accounts debiting the personal account of any external entity increases the value of the liabilities receivable from that entity thus augmenting the resources of the accounting entity.
- Similarly crediting the personal account of any external entity reduces the value of monies receivable from that entity thus reducing the resources of the accounting entity.

Nominal Accounts

- In Nominal Accounts the Expense accounts whenever debited are done as the Expense incurred represents the Goods and/or Services acquired for ssumption by the entity and hence are temporary increments in the resources of the consumers.
- In Nominal Accounts the Income accounts are credited as the Income earned represents the Epistolary representation of an entity

Examples

1. when you pay rent with cash: you increase rent (expense) by debiting, and decrease cash (asset) by credit.
2. when you receive cash for a sale: you increase cash (asset) by debiting, and increase sales (revenue) by credit.
3. when you buy equipment (asset) with cash: You increase equipment (asset) by debiting, and decrease cash (asset) by credit.
4. when you borrow with a cash loan: You increase cash (asset) by debiting, and increase loan (liability) by credit.

Depreciation and Double-entry Book Keeping System

Depreciation

Depreciation is a term used in accounting, economics and finance to spread the cost of an asset over the span of several years.

In common speech, depreciation is the reduction in the value of an asset due to usage, passage of time, wear and tear, technological outdating or obsolescence, depletion, inadequacy, rot, rust, decay or other such factors.

In accounting, however, depreciation is a term used to describe any method of attributing the historical or purchase cost of an asset across its useful life, roughly corresponding to normal wear and tear. It is of most use when dealing with assets of a short, fixed service life, and which is an example of applying the matching principle per generally accepted accounting principles. Depreciation in accounting is often mistakenly seen as a basis for recognizing impairment of an asset, but unexpected changes in value, where seen as significant enough to account for, are handled through write-downs or similar techniques which adjust the book value of the asset to reflect its current value.

The use of depreciation affects the financial statements and in some countries the taxes of companies and individuals. The recording of depreciation will cause an expense to be recognized, thereby lowering stated profits on the income statement, while the net value of the asset (the portion of the historical cost of the asset that remains to provide future value to the company) will decline on the balance sheet. Depreciation reported for accounting and tax purposes may differ substantially.

Depreciation and its related concept, amortization (generally, the depreciation of intangible assets), are non-cash expenses. Neither depreciation nor amortization will directly affect the cash flow of a company, as both are accounting representations of expenses attributable to a given period. In accounting statements, depreciation may neither figure in the cash flow statement, nor be "added back" to net income (along with other items) to derive the operating cash flow. Depreciation recognized for tax purposes will, however, affect the cash flow of the company, as tax depreciation will reduce taxable profits; there is generally no requirement that treatment of depreciation for tax and accounting purposes be identical. Where depreciation is shown on accounting statements, the figure usually does not match the depreciation for tax purposes.

Because of its non-standardized derivation, depreciation is a key component of EBITDA, a metric used to gauge the worth of a company independent of tax-jurisdiction effects and capitalization structure.

Salvage value is the estimated value of an asset at the end of its useful life. In accounting, the salvage value of an asset is its remaining value after depreciation. This is also known as residual value or scrap value. It is the net cash inflow that occurs when the asset is liquefied at the end of its life. Salvage value can be negative if the residual asset requires special treatment to terminate—for example, used nuclear materials or CRT's containing lead. In economics, depreciation is the decrease in the economic value of the capital stock of a firm, nation or other entity, either through physical depreciation, obsolescence or changes in the demand for the services of the capital in question. If capital stock is C_0 at the beginning of a period, investment is *I* and depreciation *D*, the capital stock at the end of the period, C_1, is $C_0 + I\text{-}D$.

Accounting

A company needs to report depreciation accurately in its financial statements in order to achieve two main objectives:

1. matching its expenses with the income generated by means of those expenses, and
2. ensuring that the asset values in the balance sheet are not overstated.

Depreciation is an attempt to write-off the cost of Non Current Asset over its useful life. The word write-off means to turn it into an expense. For example, an entity may depreciate its equipment by 15% per year. This rate should be reasonable in aggregate (such as when a manufacturing company is looking at all of its machinery), and consistently employed. However, there is no expectation that each individual item declines in value by the same amount, primarily because the recognition of depreciation is based upon the allocation of historical costs and not current market prices.

Accounting standards bodies have detailed rules on which methods of depreciation are acceptable, and auditors should express a view if they believe the assumptions underlying the estimates do not give a true and fair view.

Recording Depreciation

For historical cost purposes, assets are recorded on the balance sheet at their original cost; this is called the historical cost. Historical cost minus all depreciation expenses recognized on the asset since purchase is called the book value. Depreciation is not taken out of these assets directly. It is instead recorded in a contra asset account: an asset account with a normal credit balance, typically called "accumulated depreciation". Balancing an asset account with its corresponding accumulated depreciation account will result in the net book value. The net book value will never fall below the salvage value, meaning that once an asset is fully depreciated, no further expenses will be taken during its life. Salvage value is the estimated value of the asset at the end of its useful life. In this way, total depreciation for an asset will never exceed the estimated total cash outlay (depreciable basis) for the asset. The exception to this is in many price-regulated industries (public utilities) where salvage is estimated net of the cost of physically removing the asset from service. (Decommissioning a nuclear power plant is a nontrivial expense.) If the expected cost of removal exceeds the expected raw (or gross) salvage, then the net of the two (called net salvage) may be negative. In this case, the depreciation recorded on the regulated books may exceed the depreciable basis. Companies have no obligation to dispose of depreciated assets, of course, and many fully depreciated assets continue to generate income.

Recording a depreciation expense will involve a credit to an accumulated depreciation account. The corresponding debit will involve either an expense account or an asset account that represents a future expense, such as work in progress. Depreciation is recorded as an adjusting journal entry.

A write-down is a form of depreciation that involves a partial write off. Part of the value of the asset is removed from the balance sheet. The reason may be that the book value (accounted value) of the fixed asset has diverged from the market value and causes the company a loss. An example of this would be a revaluation of goodwill on an acquisition that went bad.

Methods of Depreciation

There are several methods for calculating depreciation, generally based on either the passage of time or the level of activity (or use) of the asset.

Straight-line Depreciation

Straight-line depreciation is the simplest and most-often-used technique, in which the company estimates the salvage value of the asset at the end of the period during which it will be used to generate revenues (useful life) and will expense a portion of original cost in equal increments over that period. The salvage value is an estimate of the value of the asset at the time it will be sold or disposed of; it may be zero or even negative. Salvage value is also known as scrap value or residual value.

Declining-Balance Method

Depreciation methods that provide for a higher depreciation charge in the first year of an asset's life and gradually decreasing charges in subsequent years are called accelerated depreciation methods. This may be a more realistic reflection of an asset's actual expected benefit from the use of the asset: many assets are most useful when they are new. One popular accelerated method is the declining-balance method. Under this method the Book Value is multiplied by a fixed rate.

*Annual Depreciation = Depreciation Rate * Book Value at Beginning of Year*

The most common rate used is double the straight-line rate. For this reason, this technique is referred to as the double-declining-balance method. To illustrate, suppose a business has an asset with $1,000 Original Cost, $100 Salvage Value, and 5 years useful life. First, calculate straight-line depreciation rate. Since the asset has 5 years useful life, the straight-line depreciation rate equals (100%/5) 20% per year. With double-declining-balance method, as the name suggests, double that rate, or 40% depreciation rate is used.

Activity Depreciation

Activity depreciation methods are not based on time, but on a level of activity. This could be miles driven for a vehicle, or a cycle count for a machine. When the asset is acquired, its life is estimated in terms of this level of activity. Assume the vehicle above is estimated to go 50,000 miles in its lifetime. The per-mile depreciation rate is calculated as: ($17,000 cost-$2,000 salvage)/50,000 miles = $0.30 per mile. Each year, the depreciation expense is then calculated by multiplying the rate by the actual activity level.

Units of Time Depreciation

Units of Time Depreciation is similar to units of production, and is used for depreciation equipment used in mine or natural resource exploration, or cases where the amount the asset is used is not linear year to year.

A simple example can be given for construction companies, where some equipment is used only for some specific purpose. Depending on the number of projects, the equipment will be used and depreciation charged accordingly.

Taxes

When a company spends money for a service or anything else that is short-lived, this expenditure is usually immediately tax deductible in some countries, and the company enjoys an immediate tax benefit.

To be eligible for depreciation, an asset must have two features:

1. it has a useful life beyond the taxable year (essentially why it was capitalized in the first place), and
2. it wears out, decays, declines in value due to natural causes, or is subject to exhaustion or obsolescence.

Therefore, when a company buys an asset that will last longer than one year, like a computer, car, or building, the company cannot immediately deduct the cost and enjoy an immediate large tax benefit. Instead, the company must *depreciate* the cost over the useful life of the asset, taking a tax deduction for a part of the cost each year. Eventually the company does get to deduct the full cost of the asset, but this happens over several years. In the US, the IRS's depreciation schedule for any given class of asset is fixed, and is related to typical durability. A computer may depreciate completely over five years; a nonresidential building, usually 39 years. The maximum allowable useful life under US income tax regulations is 40 years. Though the IRS does allow a small choice of permutations for depreciation life and acceleration, it does not allow a taxpayer to invent any arbitrary asset life. Other countries have other systems, many simply eliminate all choice altogether. In these jurisdictions accounting depreciation and tax depreciation are almost always significantly different numbers, as in many instances a form of "accelerated depreciation" can be used for tax purposes to lower (taxable) net income in a given period (or, in some instances, a fixed asset may be allowed to be expensed for tax purposes; Section 179 of the Internal Revenue Code allows for this treatment in some circumstances). Technically, these are not considered "tax reductions" but tax deferrals: lowering taxable income now by increasing expenses should increase future taxable income (and taxes) at a later date.

In the US, there are generally five variables that a taxpayer must take into account when computing the correct depreciation deduction:

1. the depreciation base (the asset's cost basis),
2. the asset's class life (estimated life expectancy of the asset),
3. the applicable recovery period (the number of years the taxpayer can claim depreciation deductions),
4. the applicable depreciation method, and
5. the applicable convention (§ 168(d)(4) of the code—generally the half-year convention).

Economics

In economics, the value of a capital asset is equal to the present value of the flow of services the asset will generate in future, appropriately adjusted for uncertainty. Economic depreciation over a given period is the reduction in the remaining value of future services. Under certain circumstances, such as an unanticipated increase in the price of the services generated by an asset, its value may increase rather than decline. Depreciation is then negative.

National Accounts

In national accounts the decline in the aggregate capital stock arising from the use of fixed assets in production is referred to as consumption of fixed capital (CFC). Hence, CFC is equal to the difference between aggregate gross fixed capital formation (gross investment) and net fixed capital formation (net investment) or between Gross National Product and Net National Product. Unlike depreciation in business accounting, CFC in national accounts is, in principle, not a method of allocating the costs of past expenditures on fixed assets over subsequent accounting periods. Rather, fixed assets at a given moment in time are valued according to the remaining benefits to be derived from their use.

Double-entry Bookkeeping System

The double-entry bookkeeping system was started in 13th century and refers to a set of rules to record financial information in a financial accounting system wherein every transaction or event impacts at least two different accounts. In modern accounting this is done using debits and credits, and serves as a kind of error-detection system: if, at any point, the sum of debits does not equal the corresponding sum of credits, then an error has occurred.

Since there are several different types of errors that can occur which result in equal sums for debits and credits, double-entry accounting is not a guarantee that no errors exist. However, it is still useful.

Significance

Double-entry bookkeeping has been considered a fundamental innovation and a cornerstone of Capitalism by such thinkers as Werner Sombart and Max Weber, Sombart writing in "Medieval and Modern Commercial Enterprise" that:

"*The very concept of capital* is derived from this way of looking at things; one can say that *capital, as a category, did not exist before double-entry bookkeeping*. Capital can be defined as that amount of wealth which is used in making profits and which enters into the accounts."

Timeline

Century	*Development Stage*
551-479 BCE	Confucius is described, by Sima Qian and other sources, as having endured a poverty-stricken and humiliating youth and been forced, upon reaching manhood, to undertake such petty jobs as accounting and caring for livestock.
Roman Empire	The origins of a primitive double-entry system may possibly be traced as far back as the Roman Empire, in ""*ex Oratione Ciceronis pro Roscio Comaedo*", and *Naturalis Historiae Plinii, lib. 2, cap. 7* where the advised system was *"That the one side of their book was used for Debitor, the other for Creditor"* (*Huic Omnia Expensa. Huic Omnia Feruntur accepta et in tota Ratione mortalium sola. Utramque Paginam facit.*).
12th	Later there are traces of the double-entry system in the accounting of the Islamic world from at least the 12th century.
13th	The earliest extant records that follow the modern double-entry form are those of Amatino Manucci, a Florentine merchant at the end of the 13th century.
14th	Some sources suggest that Giovanni di Bicci de' Medici introduced this method for the Medici bank in the 14th century.
15th	By the end of the 15th century, the merchant venturers of Venice used this system widely. Luca Pacioli, a monk and collaborator of Leonardo da Vinci, first codified the system in a mathematics textbook of 1494. Pacioli is often called the "father of accounting" because he was the first to publish a detailed description of the double-entry system, thus enabling others to study and use it.

Accounts

An accounting system records, retains and reproduces financial information relating to financial transaction flows and financial position. Financial Transaction Flows primarily encompass inflows on account of incomes and outflows on account of expenses. Elements of financial position, including property, money received, or money spent, are assigned to one of the primary groups i.e. assets, liabilities, and equity.

Within these primary groups each distinctive asset, liability, income and expense is represented by its respective "account". An account is simply a record of financial inflows and outflows in relation to the respective asset, liability, income or expense. Income and expense accounts are considered temporary accounts, since they only represent the inflows and outflows which are absorbed in the financial position elements on completion of the time period.

Books of Accounts

It does this by ensuring that each individual financial transaction is recorded in at least two different nominal ledger accounts within the financial accounting system. The two entries have equal amounts and opposite signs, so that when all entries in the accounts are summed, the total is exactly the same, in other words the accounts balance. This is a partial check that each and every transaction has been correctly recorded. The transaction is recorded as a "debit entry" (Dr.) in one account, and a "credit" (Cr.) entry in the other account. A debit entry generally means that value has been added to the account, and a credit entry means that value is being subtracted from the account. The debit entry will be recorded on the debit side (left hand side) of a nominal ledger account and the credit entry will be recorded on the credit side of a nominal ledger account. A nominal ledger has a Debit side and a Credit side. If the total of the entries on the debit side is greater than the total on the credit side of the nominal ledger account then that account is said to have a debit balance.

As there are two entries for each transaction, hence the expression Double-Entry is used. As the total of the debit entries equals the total of the credit entries, when the nominal ledger accounts are listed in columns, the left column for accounts with net Debit balances and the right column for accounts with net Credit balances, then the total of all the Debit balances will equal the total of all the Credit balances. If this does not happen then an error has been made somewhere.

An example of an entry being recorded twice for double-entry bookkeeping would be a supplier's invoice for stationery costing $100. The expense or Debit entry is Stationery Nominal Ledger a/c $100 Dr (showing that $100 has been spent on stationery) and the Credit entry is to the Supplier's Control Nominal Ledger a/c $100 Cr (showing that we now owe the supplier $100). This transaction has now been recorded twice in the financial accounting system and the total value is $100 for both Debit and Credit values.

Double entry is only used within the nominal ledgers. It is not used in the daybooks, which normally do not form part of the nominal ledger system. The information from the daybooks themselves will be taken and used within the nominal ledger and it is the nominal ledgers that will ensure the integrity of the resulting financial information created from the daybooks (provided that the information recorded in the daybooks is correct).

(The reason for this is to limit the number of entries in the nominal ledger: entries in the daybooks can be totalled before they are entered in the nominal ledger. If there are only a relatively small number of transactions it may be simpler instead to treat the daybooks as an integral part of the nominal ledger and thus of the double entry system.)

However as can be seen from the examples of daybooks shown below, it is still necessary to check, within each daybook, that the postings from the daybook balance.

The double entry system uses nominal ledger accounts. From these nominal ledger accounts a Trial balance can be created. The trial balance lists all the nominal ledger account balances. The list is split into two columns, with debit balances placed in the left hand column and credit balances placed in the right hand column. Another column will contain the name of the nominal ledger account describing what each value is for. The total of the debit column must equal the total of the credit column.

From the Trial balance the Profit and Loss Statement and the Balance Sheet can then be produced. The Profit and Loss statement will contain nominal ledger accounts that are Income or Expense type nominal ledger accounts. The Balance Sheet will contain nominal ledger accounts that are Asset or Liability accounts.

Bookkeeping process

The book keeping process primarily refers to recording the financial effects of financial transactions only into accounts. The variation between manual and any electronic accounting system simply stems from the latency between the recording of the financial transaction and its getting posted in the relevant account. This delay absent in electronic accounting systems due to instantenous posting into relevant accounts is not replicated in manual systems thus giving rise to primary books of accounts such as Sales Book, Cash Book, Bank Book, Purchase Book for recording the immediate effect of the financial transaction.

In the normal course of business, a document is produced each time a transaction occurs. Sales and purchases usually have invoices or receipts. Deposit slips are produced when lodgements (deposits) are made to a bank account. Cheques are written to pay money out of the account. Bookkeeping involves, first of all, recording the details of all of these source documents into multi-column journals (also known as a books of first entry or daybooks). For example, all credit sales are recorded in the Sales Journal, all Cash Payments are recorded in the Cash Payments Journal. Each column in a journal normally corresponds to an account. In the single entry system, each transaction is recorded only once. Most individuals who balance their cheque-book each month are using such a system, and most personal finance software follows this approach.

After a certain period, typically a month, the columns in each journal are each totaled to give a summary for the period. Using the rules of double entry, these journal summaries are then transferred to their respective accounts in the ledger, or book of accounts. For example the entries in the Sales Journal are taken and a debit entry is made in each customer's account (showing that the customer now owes us money) and a credit entry might be made in the account for "Sale of Class 2 Widgets" (showing that this activity has generated revenue for us). This process of transferring summaries or individual transactions to the ledger is called posting. Once the posting process is complete, accounts kept using the "T" format undergo balancing, which is simply a process to arrive at the balance of the account.

As a partial check that the posting process was done correctly, a working document called an unadjusted trial balance is created. In its simplest form, this is a three column list. The first column contains the names of those accounts in the ledger which have a non-zero balance. If an account has a debit balance, the balance amount is copied into column two (the debit column). If an account has a credit balance, the amount is copied into column three (the credit column). The debit column is then totalled and then the credit column is totalled. The two totals must agree-this agreement is not by chance-because under the double-entry rules, whenever there is a posting, the debits of the posting equal the credits of the posting. If the two totals do not agree, an error has been made either in the journals or during the posting process. The error must be located and rectified and the totals of debit column and credit column recalculated to check for agreement before any further processing can take place.

Once the accounts balance, the accountant makes a number of adjustments and changes the balance amounts of some of the accounts. These adjustments must still obey the double-entry rule. For example, the "Inventory" account asset account might be changed to bring them into line with the actual numbers counted during a stock take. At the same time, the expense account associated with usage of inventory is adjusted by an equal and opposite amount. Other adjustments such as posting depreciation and prepayments are also done at this time. This results in a listing called the adjusted trial balance. It is the accounts in this list and their corresponding debit or credit balances that are used to prepare the financial statements.Finally financial statements are drawn from the trial balance, which may include:

- the income statement, also known as the statement of financial results, profit and loss account, or P&L
- the balance sheet, also known as the statement of financial position
- the cash flow statement
- the statement of retained earnings, also known as the statement of total recognised gains and losses or statement of changes in equity.

Abbreviations used in Bookkeeping

- A/C-Account
- A/R-Accounts Receivable
- A/P-Accounts Payable
- B/S-Balance Sheet
- c/d-Carried down
- b/d-Brought down
- c/f-Carried forward
- b/f-Brought forward
- Dr-Debit
- Cr-Credit
- G/L-General Ledger; (or N/L-Nominal Ledger)
- P&L-Profit & Loss; (or I/S-Income Statement)
- PP&E-Property, Plant and Equipment
- TB-Trial Balance
- VAT-Value Added Tax
- CST-Central Sale Tax
- TDS-Tax Deducted at Source
- MAT-Minimum Alternate Tax
- EBIDTA-Earnings before Interest, Depreciation, Taxes and Amortisation.
- EBDTA-Earnings before Depreciation, Taxes and Amortisation.
- EBT-Earnings before Taxes.
- EAT-Earnings after Tax.
- PAT-Profit after tax
- PBT-Profit before tax
- Dep-Depreciation.

Debits and Credits

Double-entry bookkeeping is governed by the accounting equation. If revenue equals expenses, the following (basic) equation must be true: assets = liabilities + equity.

For the accounts to remain in balance, a change in one account must be matched with a change in another account. These changes are made by debits and credits to the accounts. Note that the usage of these terms in accounting is not identical to their everyday usage. Whether one uses a debit or credit to increase or decrease an account depends on the normal balance of the account. Assets, Expenses, and Drawings accounts have a normal balance of *debit*. Liability, Revenue, and Capital accounts have a normal balance of *credit*. On a general ledger, debits are recorded on the left side and credits on the right side for each account. Since the accounts must always balance, for each transaction there will be a debit made to one or several accounts and a credit made to one or several accounts. The sum of all debits made in any transaction must equal the sum of all credits made. After a series of transactions, therefore, the sum of all the accounts with a debit balance will equal the sum of all the accounts with a credit balance.

Debits and credits are then defined as follows:

- debit: A debit is recorded on the left hand side of a T account
- credit: A credit balance is recorded on the right hand side of a 'T' account
- Debit accounts = Asset and Expenses (also debit money received into bank accounts)
- Credit accounts = Gains (income) and Liabilities (also credit money paid out of bank accounts).

4

Service Quality Management in Hospitality and Tourism

Service Quality in Hospitality

Delivering good service to customers is the main goal that every service business strives to accomplish from time to time. The ability for a service provider to deliver quality service is considered an essential strategy for success and survival in today's competition. In this case, service encounter is a critical part of the service delivery process because it gives impact to customer's evaluations of service consumption experiences.

Therefore, there have been several studies and researches focusing on service encounter as it is believed that there is a causal relationship between the customer perception of service quality and the service encounter. Service encounter is one of the factors influencing customer perceptions of service quality, satisfaction and value as shown in the Hospitality industry is one of the service sector, with relatively high level of customer contact. The higher the level of customer contact the more numerous and longer service encounters between customers and service employees.

It implies that more attention must be focused on how to manage all the possible service encounters which will much influence the service quality of the hospitality organization and in the end the profit. Many hospitality organizations have invested considerably to develop service-delivery system which will ensure that customers will receive consistently high-quality service in every service encounter. This makes service encounter or 'moment of truth' in hospitality industry become much more important to be taken care of in the future.

While considerable research has been conducted in the service sector in general focusing on service encounters specific concern in managing service encounters in hospitality industry has received very little attention. The objectives of this article are to explore from a theoretical perspective how to manage service quality through managing the service encounters that takes place in hospitality industry. It also aims to set a framework of investigation for future empirical research.

Service Quality

Service quality is determined by what customers perceive. It means that customers play an important part in judging service quality. Very often companies define service quality apart from what the customers perceive of the quality so that time and money are poorly invested to poor quality programs. Grönroos (2000) identified two dimensions in service quality as it is perceived by customers; they are technical quality and functional quality. The technical quality is the outcome or the end result of a service production process. The functional quality is how a customer receives the service and how he experiences the simultaneous production and consumption process. All the tangibles will create the technical quality but the intangibles will generate the functional quality. For example in a restaurant setting, the delicious food served to the guest is the technical quality of a service; while how the guest is treated and served by the waiter is the functional quality.

Both of them give influence to the customer in perceiving the service quality. Very often the service provider who performs better in functional quality will gain competitive advantage when most of service providers provide relatively the same technical quality.

Service Quality Dimensions

In evaluating service quality, consumers consider five dimensions:

1. Reliability: ability to perform the promised service dependably and accurately

2. Responsiveness: willingness to help customers and provide prompt service
3. Assurance: employee's knowledge and courtesy and their ability to inspire trust and confidence
4. Empathy: caring, individualized attention given to customers
5. Tangibles: appearance of physical facilities, equipment, personnel, and written materials.

These dimensions are generally considered by consumers when they want to procure a service or when they want to estimate service quality. In the same way, these dimensions are very much contemplated when consumers experience the 'moment of truth'.

Service Encounter or "Moment of Truth"

The term service encounter and 'moment of truth' are used interchangeably when discussing the period of time where customers interact directly with a service. As it is stated by Lovelock (2002) that 'moment of truth' is "a point in service delivery where customers interact with service employees or self-service equipment and the outcome may affect perceptions of service quality". In the 'moment of truth', a careless mistake by an employee, a rude behavior or an unanticipated request by a guest can result in a dissatisfied guest. It is the crucial moment for service provider to influence customer perception of service quality. For example, a hotel guest may experience several service encounters when booking a room, checking into the hotel, being escorted to a room by a bellman, having meals in the hotel restaurant, requesting a wake-up call, using in-house services, and checking out. In these encounters hotel guests receive a picture of the hotel's service quality and each encounter contributes to the hotel guest's overall satisfaction and willingness to do business with the hotel organization again. As for the hotel, each encounter is an opportunity to deliver quality service to guests.

Positive service encounters will add up to a shared image of high service quality, whereas the negative ones will give the opposite effect. Hence, a combination of positive and negative encounters will make the customer *"feel unsure of the organization's service quality, doubtful of its consistency in service delivery, and vulnerable to the appeals of competitors"*. Besides, each encounter with different people and departments in an organization will also add to or detract from the potential for a continuing relationship.

Types of Service Encounters

There are three general types of service encounters in the hospitality industry: *remote encounters, phone encounters, and face-to-face encounters.* Remote encounters can occur without any direct human contact, such as: booking a room via the Internet. In this case the technical quality is the only point to control as there is no direct interaction with the service provider. While the phone encounter is the type of encounter between an end customer and the organization which occurs over the telephone, such as: booking a room or a table via telephone. In this case, tone of voice, employee knowledge, and effectiveness/efficiency in handling customer issues become important criteria for judging service quality.

As for face-to-face encounters, there is a direct contact between an employee and a customer. Both verbal and nonverbal behaviours are important determinants of service quality as well as the tangible cues such as employee attire, equipment, physical setting and other tangible symbols.

Analysis of Problems and Challenges in Managing Service Encounters

In order to avoid negative service encounters but ensure positive service encounters are in place, it is necessary to find out what sort of things may bring customer satisfaction and what other sort of things may cause customer dissatisfaction in a service encounter.

First of all, there are four common themes identified as the sources of customer satisfaction/dissatisfaction in memorable service encounters:

1. Recovery: employee response to service delivery system failures
2. Adaptability: employee response to customer needs and requests
3. Spontaneity: unprompted and unsolicited employee action
4. Coping: employee response to problem customers Failure to respond to the four themes accordingly will result in

customer dissatisfaction. Therefore, understanding general service behavior is important to anticipate as much as possible the positive service encounters instead of the negative ones.

Secondly, the intangibility characteristic of service becomes another problem because research has shown that customer expectations are higher for services that are more intangible than for services with more tangible features. It becomes a challenge for a hotel organization to add more tangibility in the service encounter that may lessen the chance of a larger gap between customer expectations and perceptions when a problem arises with that encounter. In this manner, the service provider can add more tangibility when delivering the service by showing directly the service process to the customer. For example: in a restaurant setting, the service provider can present directly the food preparation and cooking process to the guests so that they may experience the process by themselves and see how the food is prepared. By adding more tangibility to the service we provide, it is more unlikely for a customer to judge a service delivery quality. As a result, the service provider will be able to prevent customer dissatisfaction from occurring or at least minimize it so that service quality will be better accomplished.

Thirdly, another point of consideration should also be given to nonverbal communication when managing service encounters. It is commonly known that employee's display of affective characteristics such as *"friendliness, responsiveness, and enthusiasm positively influences customer's overall evaluation of service encounter and perceptions of service quality"*. Moreover, Sundaram and Webster add that both *"verbal and nonverbal elements of communication between the service provider and the customer influencecustomer's affect or subjective feelings, which in turn influence their evaluation of the service encounter"*.

There are several nonverbal cues influencing service encounters, they are:

1. Kinesics – body movements such as eye contact, nodding, hand shaking, smiling and adopting a relaxed and open posture;
2. Paralanguage – vocal pitch, vocal loudness or amplitude, pitch variation, pauses and fluency;

3. Proxemics – the distance and relative postures of the service provider and customer, and particularly the use of touch; and
4. Physical appearance.

Customer Perception of Service Provider Nonverbal Cues

No Nonverbal Cues Customer Perception

1. Smiling, light laughter and frequent eye contact Friendliness and courtesy
2. Head nodding Empathy, courtesy and trust
3. Frequent eye contact Credibility
4. Hand shaking Friendliness and courtesy
5. A slower speech rate, lower pitch, moderate pauses and less inflection Friendliness and credibility
6. A faster speech rate, higher pitch, high vocal intensity, and higher inflection Competence but less friendliness
7. Touch Friendliness and empathy
8. Physical attractiveness Friendliness, credibility, competence, empathy and courtesy
9. Colour and intensity of clothes Friendliness, competence and credibility.

When service employees know exactly what are expected from them in terms of nonverbal behavior besides the verbal communication, they will be able to enhance their effective communication skill verbally and non-verbally. As the effective communication skill increases, the service encounter or 'moment of truth' will more positive and the perceived service quality will be enhanced as the five dimensions of service quality are met accordingly.

Nevertheless, it needs some endeavour from the hospitality managers to build the service employee awareness of the importance of nonverbal behavior besides verbal communication in attaining effective communication skill that will enhance service quality.

Sundaram and Webster (2000) suggest that in order to make service employee more sensitive to nonverbal cues, the managers can utilize *role-playing* and show *videotapes* of actual service delivery which demonstrate both the positive and negative nonverbal cues. Continuous feedback will also be useful to remind service employees of the importance of nonverbal communication. Periodic surveys, in addition, are important to assess customers' perceptions of service employees' nonverbal behavior.

Providing incentives can be desirable to encourage service employees to implement the recommended changes in nonverbal behavior.

Thirdly, culture and purchase motivation become two other points to consider when attempting to manage service encounters. The involvement of people in service delivery implies that cultural diversities and norms quickly come into play when customers evaluate service encounters. This is obviously relevant especially in the hospitality industry where there is so much cultural exposure either with the international guests or among the service employees themselves.

The Asians and the Westerners are two different groups of people who have very different cultural backgrounds. Mattila (1999) states that Western customers care more about efficiency and timesaving of a service whereas Asian customers emphasizes on the quality of interpersonal relationship between employee and customer. Therefore, service styles in Asia are more people-oriented than in the West, where the efficiency of the service delivery is highly valued. Another thing that differentiates the two groups in terms of service expectation is that the Asians tend to expect the service employees who are lower in social status to provide customers with high

levels of service because their culture is characterized by relatively large power distance that reflect social hierarchies. On the other hand, the Western customers tend to expect more classless or democratic service as their culture less accepts of status differences.

Nevertheless, when these two different groups of culture are opposed to purchase motivation, the expectation will be different. For business customers regardless of cultural background, they tend to focus on the output not the style of the service delivery.

They are more interested in efficiency (including the speed of service) than in the functional quality of the interaction. Business customers driven by the need for efficiency might focus on the *"service outcome"* rather than on the *"feelings"* generated by the service encounter. Leisure customers, in contrast, tend to be more heterogeneous in their expectations according to their cultural background. Asian leisure customers tend to prefer *"high-context communication"* in which nonverbal cues are more important than explicit expressions. Asian leisure customers expect to be treated as *"deserving of high-quality service"* (Mattila, 1999). Likewise, some nonverbal cues may vary from culture to culture. Eye contact, for example, is very much expected by the Americans whereas in many Oriental cultures it is not proper to look in the eye too often someone who is superior. In fact, a bowed head represents a signal of respect to an authority figure.

Consequently, it is essential for hospitality organizations to develop employee training programs for guest-contact employees, such as: the Front desk employees in the hotel industry, to ensure that they are able to deliver the service the 'right' way. As for the organizations that expect to cater International guests, they need to give the employees a multicultural training program which includes a language training program and cross-cultural understanding to meet the possible cultural expectations of their foreign guests. This idea is in line with a research finding signifying that Front desk employees' performance is critical to guests' baseline evaluation of a hotel's service quality (Michael, Wooldridge and Jones, 2003). As for the restaurant, the waiters or waitresses should be trained well so that they will be more aware of how to be able to serve better according to what is expected by the guests and to have more control over the 'moment of truth'.

Service Blueprint

Service blueprints are pictures or maps of service processes that permit the people involved in designing, providing, managing, and using the service to better understand them and deal with them objectively. A service blueprint simultaneously depicts the service process and the roles of consumers, service providers, and supporting services.

Blueprints are designed by identifying and mapping a process from the consumer's point of view, mapping employee actions and support activities, and adding visible evidence of service at each consumer action step. Key components of service blueprints are consumer actions, "onstage" and "backstage" employee actions, and support processes. Service blueprint accentuates the customer interactions in the service operations processes and, that the line of visibility separated activities of the front stage, where customers obtained tangible evidence of the service, from the back office processing, which was out of customer view (Tseng et al., 1999). Hence, the service blueprint can facilitate problem solving and create thinking by identifying potential points of failure and highlighting opportunities to enhance customers' perceptions of the service.

Analysis of the Service Encounters

There are basically nine kinds of service encounters that happen in the service blueprint above as there are interactions between the service employee and the guest. First of all, when the guest calls the restaurant and books a table, there is a telephone interaction between the guest and the service employee who picks up the telephone. This is the first encounter or 'moment of truth' in which the guest will judge the service quality by evaluating the words spoken by the restaurant employee as well as the tone of voice or the nonverbal cues, in this case, the "paralanguage". In this 'moment of truth', it is very important that the service employee speaks the 'right' words in the 'right' way so that the guest will a first good impression about the service quality of the restaurant in his mind and he would want to go on to the next service encounter.

In this encounter, the guest will judge the service quality whether it is courteous, friendly, credible, competent and empathetic or not at all. Very often restaurants fail to attend to this very first encounter in the 'right' way. They fail to instill a good impression or even an excellent one about the service quality in the first place. This can happen since there is a different perception between the guest and the restaurant employee as the service provider on the "point of activation" when the first action in the service encounter begins (Hubbert et al., 1995).

It often happens that the service provider perceives that the first action in the service encounter starts when the guest actually arrives and enters the restaurant whereas the guest evaluates the first service encounter at the very first moment he or she contacts the restaurant and has the conversation with a restaurant employee.

This can be a critical point in the 'moment of truth' in which the service provider needs to take care.

Secondly, when the guest arrives at the restaurant and he is greeted by a greeter who then asks for the reservation. This leads to the second interaction between the guest and the service employee but this time, it is more than just verbal communication but also nonverbal communication as there is direct contact between the two. When greeting the guest, it is important for the service employee to also demonstrate the 'right' nonverbal cues besides the verbal and tangible cues since all those cues will compose the overall notion of the service quality. In this stage, the service encounter will confirm the previous telephone encounter when the guest evaluates the service quality. In this case the critical point will be the credibility and friendliness of the service employees in welcoming the guests.

Then for the next service encounters (number 3-5), the guest will experience the next interaction with the service employee when he or she is being escorted to the table and seated. In this case the body language matters most as there will be less verbal communication but more nonverbal communication.

Brenner (1998) noted on the powerful influence of body language on giving impact on others. The impact someone makes on others depends on what he or she actually says (7%), how he or she says it (38%), and by his or her body language (55%).

Besides, 93% of someone's emotion is communicated non-verbally without actual words. That is why it is of vital importance to pay attention to the body language and to make sure that the 'right' body language is shown during the service delivery. The body language can demonstrate whether the service employee is friendly, courteous and credible. As mentioned in the previous part it appears that some nonverbal cues are different from culture to culture.

That is why it is imperative that the service employee is aware of multicultural cues and able to perform eventually the 'multicultural' body language depending on the situation. The 'right' body language will generate good service encounters. In the end, good service encounters accumulated over time maintain a long-term exchange relationship between customers and organization. In the next service encounters (number 6-7), when the guest enjoys the meal, besides the tangible things like the meals served, decoration and atmosphere of the restaurant, the attentiveness and responsiveness of the service employees will be the important points the guest evaluates in judging the service encounter. The judgment of the service encounter will be positive when the guest's expectation is met or even exceeded.

In the last service encounters (number 8-9), even though it is the last 'moment of truth' but it is also a crucial moment to take care it will leave a 'good' or 'terrible' last impression about the overall restaurant service. When the service provider neglects this last crucial moment, it may happen that the last 'terrible' moment will distort the whole first 'good' impression.

Global Hotel Guest Privacy Policy

Our Commitment

As one of our valued guest (hereinafter "You"), it is always a pleasure to welcome You to one of our hotels. Our first priority is to offer You exceptional stays and experiences around the world.

Your full satisfaction and faith in Accor is essential to us.

We recognize that privacy is part of Your expectations as a guest. Therefore, we have designed and implemented this Hotel Guest Privacy Policy which describes how Accor uses Your Personal Information on the basis of Accor's "7 Privacy Principles" (hereinafter "Accor 7 Privacy Principles") which constitute core principles for Accor and which therefore apply throughout the Accor Group (Accor and its subsidiaries) worldwide.

Consent to this Hotel Guest Privacy Policy

You should read this Hotel Guest Privacy Policy carefully before providing us with any of Your "Personal Information" (hereinafter referred to as "PI"), i.e. any information collected and recorded in any format that identifies You personally, whether directly (e.g. name) or indirectly (e.g. phone number).

This Hotel Guest Privacy Policy is part of Accor's terms and conditions governing our hotel services. By accepting said terms and conditions, You expressly consent to this Hotel Guest Privacy Policy. Accor may use Your PI for marketing purposes. If required by applicable law, You will be requested to give Your prior express consent to receive such marketing materials.

Accor 7 Privacy Principles

The following constitute Accor 7 Privacy Principles, which apply throughout the Accor Group worldwide.

a. Transparency: when collecting and processing Your PI, we will provide You with relevant information and notice, for what purposes and who are the recipients.
b. Legitimacy: we will collect and process Your PI only for the purposes which are mentioned to You in this Hotel Guest Privacy Policy.
c. Relevance & Accuracy: we will only collect PI which is necessary for the purposes of the data processing as set out in this Hotel Guest Privacy Policy. We will take all reasonable measures to ensure You that the PI that we have stored is accurate and up to date.
d. Storage: we will keep Your PI for the period necessary for the purposes of the data processing as set out in this Hotel Guest Privacy Policy and in accordance with local law requirements.
e. Access & Rectification: we offer You ways to access, modify, correct or delete Your PI.
f. Confidentiality & Security: we will implement reasonable technical and organisational measures to protect Your PI against accidental or unlawful alteration or loss, or from unauthorized use, disclosure or access.
g. Sharing & International Transfer: we may share Your PI within the Accor Group or with third parties (such as commercial partners and service providers) for the purposes described in this Hotel Guest Privacy Policy. We will take appropriate measures to secure such sharing and transfer. If You have any questions about these Accor 7 Privacy Principles, please contact Accor Data Privacy Contact as described in section 13 of this Hotel Guest Privacy Policy.

Scope

This Hotel Guest Privacy Policy is applicable to:

a. Any data processing implemented by Accor owned and managed hotels, i.e. hotels which are part of the Accor

Group, including managed hotels, e.g. hotels operating under the following brands Sofitel, Pullman, Novotel, Grand Mercure, Mercure, MGallery, Suitehotel, Ibis, all seasons, Etap Hotel, Hotel F1, Formule 1, Studio 6, Motel6. This list is regularly updated.

b. Any Accor booking web sites, i.e. existing Accor websites, e.g. accorhotels.com. and also brand website (www.sofitel.com, www.mercure.com,...).

c. Any Accor loyalty program websites (e.g. www.a-club.com).

Although this Hotel Guest Privacy Policy does not apply to franchised hotels, Accor will use reasonable efforts to promote and request that the Accor 7 Privacy Principles be implemented by the said franchisees and that the said franchisees comply with all applicable laws in processing Your PI.

What Personal Information?

- Contact information, e.g. name, telephone numbers, e-mail addresses, postal addresses, etc.;
- Other personal details: date of birth; nationality,
- Children Information: name, birth date and age;
- Credit card details (only in transactional related system)
- Membership card numbers of any Accor loyalty program or any membership number of frequent flyer or any of Accor's partners You are registered with;
- Your dates of arrival and departure/visit from our hotels;
- our preferences and interests, e.g. smoking or non-smoking room, preferred location of Your room (low floor, high floor, etc.), type of bed, preferred newspaper, sports and cultural interests;

Any questions/comments You may have during or after Your stay in one of our hotels.

We do not knowingly collect PI from children under the age of 18, except name, date of birth and nationality as provided directly by an adult on their behalf or with adult's permission. Please make sure that Your children do not provide us with any PI without Your permission, e.g. online. If You believe Your child has submitted PI to us, please contact us so that we can delete such

PI. Generally, we do not knowingly collect sensitive information such as racial or ethnic origin, political opinions, religious or philosophical beliefs, trade union membership, health or sex life details.

In addition, depending on the applicable law, other data than those listed above may also be considered as sensitive data: credit card number, leisure habits, personal activities and hobbies, cultural habits, smoker/non-smoker status, etc. However, we may need to collect such data which may be considered as sensitive, to satisfy Your request or provide You with specific services such as specific diet or any disability access facilities. In such case, if required by applicable law, we will ask You to expressly consent that we collect and process such sensitive information.

When is My Personal Information Collected?

PI may be collected in certain circumstances including without limitation as follows:

a. Hospitality activities such as:
   - Booking of an hotel room;
   - Check in and check out;
   - Consumption during a stay in an hotel as tracked through room charges;
   - Claims, requests and/or disputes.

b. Participation in marketing programs:
   - Registering with Accor's loyalty programs;
   - Contribution to guests surveys and/or comments (e.g. "Guest Satisfaction Survey", "Contact us"; "Guests comments"; "Satisfait ou invite");
   - Contests;
   - Subscription to newsletters, to receive e-mail offers or promotions.

c. Provision of information by third party service providers:

d. Internet activities:
   - Connection to any Accor websites (IP address, session cookies);
   - Fill in of an online collection form (e.g. online bookings, questionnaire, etc.).

What are the Purposes?

We use Your PI for the following purposes:

a. To manage Your reservation and booking:
   - To book and reserve Accor hotel rooms and requested accommodation;
   - To establish and maintain business records and comply with accounting requirements;
   - For back office processing; including managing a list of undesirable guests, further to a non-payment, or to improper behaviour, etc.

b. To manage Your stay at the hotel:
   - To track consumption (telephone, bar, Internet, pay TV...);
   - To access rooms.

c. To improve our hospitality services, including:
   - To process Your PI in Accor's Clients Relationship Management (CRM) program;
   - To better understand Your needs and requests;
   - To tailor our products and services to better suit Your desires.

d. To send You newsletters, promotions and marketing material about tourism, hospitality or services, hotel promotions, or about Accor partners. You can choose to unsubscribe from our Email Newsletters service by clicking a link in one of our email newsletters.

e. To improve our Accor services, including:
   - To conduct surveys and analyze guests' questionnaires and comments and activity patterns;
   - To manage guests' complaints;
   - To let you benefit from our loyalty program.

f. To secure and improve Your use of Accor Internet websites, including:
   - To improve website navigation;
   - To implement security and fraud prevention means.

g. To comply with local regulations (e.g. retention of business or accounting documents).

Sharing of Your Personal Information

As a global company, we strive to offer You the same level of service and hospitality all around the world. To this end, subject to Your rights set forth in section 13 below, we may have to share Your PI with internal or external recipients in the following ways:

a. The Accor Group: we may share Your PI with any Accor entity authorized individuals who need to access Your PI to provide You with the requested services or in the context of an action as a consequence of You providing such PI:
   - Hotel Staff;
   - Reservation Staff using Accor reservation tools;
   - Information Technology,
   - Commercial partnership and marketing departments;
   - Medical services, if any;
   - Legal Department, if necessary.

b. Any relevant individuals of the Accor Group entities for specific categories of data. External ser vice providers and partners: we may share Your PI with third parties for providing You with the requested services and improving Your stay with us:
   - Third party service providers: IT subcontractors, international call centres, banks, credit card providers; outside counsels, mailing service providers, printing companies;
   - Commercial Partners.

c. Local authorities – internal investigations: we may also share information with local authorities if required by local law or as part of internal investigations within the Accor Group in compliance with local regulations.

International Transfers

We may transfer for the purposes set forth in Article 7 of this Hotel Guest Privacy Policy Your PI to recipients, internal or external, which may be located in countries with different levels of PI protection.

Therefore, in addition to the implementation of the present Hotel Guest Privacy Policy, Accor implements,, appropriate measures, including contractual clauses, to secure transfer of Your

PI to any Accor entity or external recipient located in a country with a level of protection different from the one existing in the country in which the PI is collected.

Data Security

Accor takes appropriate technical and organisational measures, in accordance with local law requirements, to protect Your PI against accidental or unlawful destruction or accidental loss, alteration, unauthorized disclosure or access. To this end, we have implemented technical measures such as firewalls and organisational measures such as a login/efficient password system, physical protection, etc.

You may have to enter Your credit card details to complete Your reservations; in such event, Accor uses Secure Socket Layer (SSL) technology to encrypt such PI.

Session Cookies/External Links

Accor uses persistent cookies to manage Your session on Accor's websites and to personalize Your online experience (automatic recognition, list of Your favourite hotels, etc.).

We also collect technical information on Your computer each time You open a page during Your visit to our sites. This information includes Your IP (Internet Protocol) address, the operating system used, the type of browser, the screen resolution and the origin website address, as needed. We collect this information to improve the quality of Your visit to our site and do not sell or transfer this information to third parties. These temporary cookies are a built-in feature of the technology used. Most browsers automatically accept these cookies, but You can delete them or have them automatically refused. As each browser is different, You should refer to the "Help" section on Your browser toolbar to find out how to set Your preferences regarding cookies. However, You may not be able to use certain features on our site if You choose not to accept cookies.

We may offer You advertising or links to third-parties' websites which may collect PI about You when You view or click on their advertising or content through the use of cookies. Accor cannot control this collection of information and accepts no responsibility for this collection, use or disclosure of Your PI by third-party companies. You should contact these advertisers or content providers if You have any questions about their use of the PI they collect. Your visit to these third-parties' websites is in no way subject to this Hotel Guest Privacy Policy. Accor takes no responsibility for any privacy policies or practices of any third-parties' web sites accessible from Accor's websites.

Data Storage

We will store Your PI only for the time necessary for the purposes stated in this Hotel Guest Privacy Policy, or as permitted by the applicable law.

Access and Modification

You have the right to access, modify or delete Your PI. You can also object to the processing of Your PI as described in this Hotel Guest Privacy Policy provided that You have legitimate reasons. However, please note that if You object, we may in certain circumstances be unable to provide You with the service requested.

Hotel Service for Overnight Rooms

Bed and Breakfast

A bed and breakfast (or B&B) is a small lodging establishment that offers overnight accommodation and breakfast, but usually does not offer other meals. Typically, bed and breakfasts are private homes with fewer than 10 bedrooms available for commercial use.

Overview

Generally, guests are accommodated in private bedrooms with private bathrooms, or in a suite of rooms including an en suite bathroom. Some homes have private bedrooms with a bathroom which is shared with other guests. Breakfast is served in the bedroom, a dining room, or the host's kitchen. B&Bs and guest houses may be operated either as a secondary source of income or a primary occupation. Usually the owners themselves prepare the breakfast and clean the room etc., but some bed and breakfasts hire staff for cleaning or cooking. Although some bed and breakfast owners hire professional staff, a property which hires professional management is usually no longer considered a bed and breakfast, but enters the category of inn or hotel.

Some B&Bs operate in a niche market. Floating bed and breakfasts for example are a concept originating in Seattle in which a boat or houseboat offers B&B accommodation.

Regional Differences

Australia

Despite the cultural similarities and a population more than twenty times greater, there are far fewer B&Bs in the whole of Australia than there are in just the South Island of New Zealand.

Since the 1960s the average per capita disposable income of Australians has been greater than that of New Zealanders and this has mitigated the powerful incentive to let out rooms in their homes to travellers. Another factor may be that Australia has, apart from City States such as Singapore, the greatest concentration of city dwellers anywhere on the globe and these cities are amply supplied with budget hotels and motels.

British Isles

B&Bs, and frequently guest houses, are a budget option where owners often take pride in the high service levels, local knowledge and personal touch that they are able to offer.

There tend to be concentrations of B&Bs in seaside towns where, historically, the working classes holidayed such as County Down, Northern Ireland, and Blackpool, England, and isolated rural areas such as the Highlands of Scotland and Connemara where there is not the year-round concentration of travellers that would sustain an hotel. They are present in most towns and cities, and their numbers vary on trade such as for business travellers and tourists: York and Edinburgh for example both have several hundred establishments known as either B&Bs or guest houses. In very busy areas, B&Bs may display a sign saying "VACANCIES" (rooms available) or "NO VACANCIES", to save both the hosts and potential guests the trouble of them having to enquire within. Breakfast is usually cooked on demand for the guest and is usually some kind of full breakfast, but some offer a continental breakfast.

In recent years B&Bs in the UK have struggled against budget hotel chains such as Premier Travel Inn and Travelodge. Traditionally, business travellers used B&Bs but many of these clients now tend to stay in budget hotel chains. However, in holiday areas the B&B and guest house still prevail. Unlike the hotel chains, they provide a more comprehensive service and breakfast is included in the price, and some who stay regularly may simply like knowing their hosts. B&Bs tend to place their bedrooms within three different categories:

- *Deluxe*: This standard of B&B accommodation in Ireland is considered to be very high and deluxe rooms would be available in high end B&Bs and guesthouse accommodation. Deluxe rooms would often have additional furniture or Jacuzzis in the bathroom. Check the description.
- *En-Suite*: There is a private bathroom within the bedroom. This will always contain a WC and washbasin, and a shower or bath or both.
- *Standard*: There is not a bathroom within the bedroom. In this case there will be shared bathroom facilities in another room on the corridor. Usually there will be a washbasin within the room.

Cuba

In Cuba, which opened up to tourism in the 1990s after the financial support of the Soviet Union ended, a form of B&B called *casa particular* ("private home") became the main form of accommodation outside the tourist resorts.

Israel

The Israeli B&B is known as a *zimmer* (German for *room*). All over the country, but especially in the north of the country and the Galilee, *zimmers* have become an alternative to hotels for romantic weekends or family vacations.

Italy

In Italy, regional law regulates B&Bs.

India

In India, the government is promoting the concept of bed & breakfast. The government is doing this to increase tourism, especially keeping in view the expected demand for hotels during the 2010 Commonwealth Games in Delhi. They have classified B&B in 2 categories-Gold & Silver B&B. All B&B will be approved by the Ministry of Tourism who will then categorize it as Gold or Silver based upon the pre-defined criteria.

Kyrgyzstan

The tourism industry in Kyrgyzstan includes some B&Bs. One group, called CBT, organises homestays with people who own homes and rent rooms by the night. They help tourists and travellers in Kyrgyzstan find places to stay.

New Zealand

As in the USA, bed and breakfasts in New Zealand tend to be more expensive than motels and often feature historic homes and furnished bedrooms at a commensurate price.

North America

Many B&Bs in North America try to create a historical ambiance, with old properties turned into guesthouses decorated with antique furniture. For example, the Holladay House in Orange, Virginia is an 1830s Federal-style brick building that has been converted into a bed and breakfast. In the last ten years, B&B and Inn owners have been launching upscale amenities to improve business and move "up-market." It is not uncommon now to find free wireless Internet access, free parking, spa services, or nightly wine and cheese hours. Due to the need to stay competitive with the rest of the lodging industry, larger bed and breakfast inns have expanded to offer wedding services, business conference facilities, and meeting spaces as well as many other services a large hotel might offer.

The custom of opening one's home to travellers dates back the earliest day of Colonial America. Lodging establishments were few and far between in the 1700s, and apart from a limited number of coaching inns (a few of which survive as inns today), wayfarers relied on the kindness of strangers to provide a bed for the night. Hotels became more common with the advent of the railroad, and later, the automobile, and most towns had at least one prominent hotel.

During the Great Depression, tourist homes provided an economic advantage to both the traveller and the host. Driving through town (no Interstates then), travellers stopped at houses with signs reading Tourists or Guests, indicating that travellers could rent a room for the night for about $2. The money generated needed income for the home owner and saved money for the traveller.

After World War II, middle-class Americans began travelling in Europe in large numbers, many experiencing the European-style B&Bs (Zimmer frei in Germany, chambres d'hotes in France) for the first time. Some were inspired to open B&Bs in the U.S.; tourist home owners updated their properties as B&Bs. The interest in B&Bs coincided with an increasing interest in historic preservation, spurred by the U.S. Bicentennial in 1976 and assisted by two crucial pieces of legislation: the National Historic Preservation Act of 1966, and the Tax Reform Act of 1976, which provided tax incentives for the restoration and reuse of historic structures.

Through the 1980s and 1990s, B&Bs increased rapidly in numbers and evolved from homestay B&Bs with shared baths and a simple furnishings to beautifully renovated historic mansions with luxurious decor and amenities. The next big change started in the mid 1990s when the Internet became a major marketing force, making it affordable for innkeepers to promote their properties worldwide. Email marketing, in particular, serves as a useful tool for the Bed & Breakfast industry, for it proactively builds relationships with the existing guests after their stay. This helps increase the likelihood for more repeat bookings and also guest referrals in the future. At present, travellers research and book B&B online, checking out detailed photos, videos, and reviews. B&Bs are found in all states, in major cities and remote rural areas, occupying everything from modest cottages to opulent mansions, and in restored structures from schools to cabooses to churches.

Spain

In Spain, B&Bs are often run by people who place personal or family needs ahead of wealth and profit maximization. The business attracts numerous entrepreneurs with predominantly lifestyle motives, yet challenges them in specific ways. Spain does not have a B&B culture like Great Britain. As anything "modern" rules, locals usually shake their head at tourists visiting B&Bs when they could stay at a "proper hotel" for the same money or less. A study of the years 1997–2000, using a sample of 1131 Spanish firms, suggests that marketing must be done over the medium to long term to be effective.

Regulations

Regulations and laws vary considerably between jurisdictions both in content and extent and in enforcement. The most common regulations B&Bs must follow pertain to safety. They are usually required by local and national ordinances to have fire resistance, a sufficient fire escape plan in place, and smoke detectors in each guest room. Kitchens and equipment used to serve meals are also often required to be monitored for hygienic operation, but there are significant national and local differences.

In Hawaii, it is illegal to open a new bed & breakfast on Oahu as of 1989. The reason for the moratorium is to force home owners with extra room to rent out their extra space to low income residents who otherwise cannot afford housing on crowded Oahu.

Professional and Trade Associations

Many inns and bed and breakfasts are members of professional associations. There are international, national, regional, and local associations, all of which provide services to both their members and the travelling public. Many require their members to meet specific standards of quality, while others simply require a lodging establishment to pay dues. These associations also facilitate marketing of the individual B&Bs and provide a stamp of approval that the business in question is reputable.

While various local governments have regulations and inspect lodging establishments for health and safety issues, membership in a state/provincial/national bed and breakfast association can indicate a higher standard of hospitality. Associations sometimes review their members' properties and tend to have additional standards of care.

In the US for example, each state has an innkeeping association (usually non-profit) that exists to promote the industry and tourism. However, many state associations, have rigorous inspection criteria that often exceed government requirements for safety and cleanliness.

In Australia, the industry is represented by the Bed & Breakfast, Farmstay and Accommodation Australia Ltd (BBFAA).

Organizations such as the Automobile Association also provide periodical inspections of B&B inns.

In the British Isles the national approval boards set up by governments are far more stringent than others, while in Ireland there is an association that will only use the national tourist board's approved members (Almara Accommodations Dublin).

Studies

Tourism Queensland Study

In January 2003 Tourism Queensland conducted a review of current research to gain a better understanding of the Bed & Breakfast (B&B) market:

Key needs that must be met for people staying at bed and breakfast style accommodation include: pampering and personalised service in an attractive location in an attractive house, opposed to more 'standard' hotelrooms.

The following attributes are also appealing:

- Homely or wholesome atmosphere (older segments) or luxurious/heritage surrounds
- Home style meals
- Area for conversing with other guests
- Ability to tap into local knowledge of attractions and activities in local area.

Guests at B&Bs were asked to identify the features and factors which motivated them to choose the establishment they were staying at. The friendliness of the host was the most important factor, followed by easy access to other places, the site being the most appealing place in the region. Usually B & B's are privately owned, and therefore very different from standard commercial hotels.

Bed & Breakfasts provide mutual benefits for both the visitor and the operator. Visitors have the opportunity for a relaxing break in a homely environment. Operators have the opportunity to develop a profitable business, make new friends and contacts, understand the cultures andlifestyles of others, and to educate guests about their way of life.

Income and leisure time have changed so that shorter breaks with greater choice of leisure activities are sought. Changing work patterns have increased the popularity of shorter breaks that minimize the absence from work and the effect of absences on workflow and involvement.

Bed & Breakfast holidays tend to be short break holidays and could benefit from the increased popularity of short breaks, sought by people who aim for authenticity and personal service.

Motel

Entering dictionaries after World War II, the word motel, a portmanteau of *motor* and *hotel* or *motorists' hotel*, referred initially to a type of hotel consisting of a single building of connected rooms whose doors faced a parking lot and, in some circumstances, a common area; or a series of small cabins with common parking. As the United States highway system began to develop in the 1920s, long distance road journeys became more and the need for inexpensive, easily accessible overnight accommodation sited close to the main routes, led to the growth of the motel concept.

History

Auto camps predated motels by a few years. Unlike motels, auto camps and tourist courts typically provided bed and breakfast or hotel style service, usually with stand-alone cabins. After the invention of the motel, auto camps continued in popularity through the Depression years and after World War II, their popularity finally starting to diminish with the construction of freeways and changes in consumer demands. Examples include the Rising Sun Auto Camp in Glacier National Park and Blue Bonnet Court in Texas. Such facilities were "mom-and-pop" facilities on the outskirts of a town that were as quirky as their owners. They attracted the first "road warriors" as they crossed North America in their new automobiles. The 1935 City Directory for San Diego, CA lists "motel" type accommodations under Tourist Camps.

In contrast, though they remained "Mom and Pop" operations, motels quickly adopted a homogenized appearance and were designed from the start to cater purely for motorists. The motel concept originated with the Motel Inn of San Luis Obispo, constructed in 1925 by Arthur Heineman. In conceiving of a name for his hotel Heineman abbreviated *motor hotel* to *motel*.

Motels are typically constructed in an 'I'-or 'L'-or 'U'-shaped layout that includes guest rooms, an attached manager's office, a small reception and, in some cases, a small diner. Post-war motels sought more visual distinction, often featuring eye-catching neon signs which employed themes from popular culture, ranging from Western imagery of cowboys and Indians to contemporary images of spaceships and atomic era iconography.

Motels differ from hotels in their common location along highways, as opposed to the urban cores favoured by hotels, and their orientation to the outside (in contrast to hotels whose doors typically face an interior hallway). Motels almost by definition include a parking lot, while older hotels were not built with automobile parking in mind.

With the 1952 introduction of Kemmons Wilson's Holiday Inn, the mom-and-pop motels of that era went into decline. Eventually, the emergence of the interstate highway system, along with other factors, led to a blurring of the motel and the hotel, though family-owned motels with as few as five rooms may still be found, especially along older highways.

Long-term

Motels/hotels with low rates sometimes serve as housing for people who are not able to afford an apartment or have recently lost their home and need somewhere to stay until further arrangements are made. Motels catering to long-term stays often have kitchenettes.

Short-time

In most countries of Latin America and some countries of East Asia, motels are also known as short-time hotels, offering a short-time or "transit" stay with hourly rates, primarily intended for people having sexual liaisons and not requiring a full night's accommodation. In Mexico, love hotel equivalents are known as "Motel de paso" (Passing Motel), even if they are actually meant mostly access. In Argentina, these establishments are called *albergue transitorio* ("temporary lodging"), though known as *telo* in vesre-slang. In Panama, love hotels with individual garages are known as Push Buttons (referring to the button that you push to close the garage door and the other button that grants access to the room). In Paraguay, similarly to Brazil and Colombia, motels may charge only by the hour and are also popularly known as *reservados*. In Singapore, cheap hotels often offer a slightly more euphemistic "transit" stay for short-time visitors. In Manila, a campaign against the hotels, believed by religious conservatives to contribute to social decay in the predominantly Roman Catholic country, ended with the city banning hotels from offering stays of very short duration. As of December 2006, there are still many short time hotels in operation. In Belgium and France, these establishments are known as *hotels de passe*. In Chile, they are known as *motels parejeros* (coupling motels), and many of them offer hourly rates.

In the United States and Canada, some ordinary motels in low income areas—often called *no-tell motels* or *hot sheet motels*—play a similar role to love hotels.

Sustainable Competitive Advantage

Sustainable competitive advantage is the focal point of your corporate strategy. It allows the maintenance and improvement of your enterprise's competitive position in the market. It is an advantage that enables business to survive against its competition over a long period of time.

Todays' Era of Hypercompetition

Hypercompetition is a key feature of the new economy. New customers want it quicker, cheaper, and they want it their way.

The fundamental quantitative and qualitative shift in competition requires organizational change on an unprecedented scale. Today, your sustainable competitive advantage should be built upon your corporate capabilities and must constantly be reinvented.

Distinctive Capabilities

Distinctive capabilities are the basis of your competitive advantage. According to the new resource-based view of the company, sustainable competitive advantage is achieved by continuously developing existing and creating new resources and capabilities in response to rapidly changing market conditions.

Among these resources and capabilities, in the new economy, knowledge represents the most important value-creating asset.

In the twenty-first-century landscape, firms must compete in a complex and challenging context that is being transformed by many factors, from globalization, technological development, and increasingly rapid diffusion of new technology, to the development and use of knowledge. This new landscape requires firms to do things differently in order to survive and prosper. Specifically, they must look to new sources of competitive advantage and engage in new forms of competition.

This, in turn, requires a clear understanding of the nature of competition and competitive dynamics.

One popular approach to understanding competitive dynamics is the resource-based view of the firm. According to this view, the explanation for why some firms ultimately succeed and others fail can be found in understanding their resources and capabilities.

A firm's resources and capabilities influence both the strategic choices that managers make and the implementation of those chosen strategies.

To understand why certain competitive strategies are more effective than others, one must consider the distribution of resources in competing firms. Although a given firm may possess more or less of any particular resource, only those resources that are rare, valuable, and difficult to imitate provide a sustainable competitive advantage. When the strategies employed are successful in leveraging the firm's rare, valuable, and difficult-to-imitate resources, that firm is likely to gain an advantage over its competitors in the marketplace and thus earn higher returns. Competitive advantages that are sustained over time lead to higher performance.

If a firm could modernize its plant, or develop a more efficient distribution process, or access cheaper credit, it could compete successfully and prosper. But firms employ both tangible and intangible resources in the development and implementation of strategies, and as the nature of work and competition changes, intangible resources are becoming more important.

Examples of intangible resources are reputation, brand equity, and—for our purposes the most important of these—human capital. In fact, in any competitive landscape it has been argued that intangible resources are more likely to produce a competitive advantage because they often are truly rare and can be more difficult for competitors to imitate.

Among a firm's intangible resources, human capital may be the most important and critical for competitive advantage because it is the most difficult to imitate.

Tourism Academics

Taking important lessons within the confines of a classroom is the first and foremost way of augmenting knowledge and it is altogether certain that knowledge can be gained by reading books, talking to people and also by opting for other means of communication. However, in the present times, apart from these popular methods of acquiring knowledge, traveling to foreign locations and enrolling in short term courses in those countries is getting popular as an effective method of gaining knowledge in a specific subject/field. What is interesting is that while visiting a foreign country on an educational trip, the visitor also gets to know the culture and history of its people, the tidbits on people's lifestyle and architecture.

This is exactly the educational tourism phenomenon that is attaining universal popularity and jumping on the bandwagon, people from far-flung corners of the world are especially considering India as an important destination for their educational tours. These tours are especially focused on having a share of the educational experiences available in the country and also to enhance knowledge on the rich Indian history and culture.

The various aspects of educational tourism include an educational program in which the participants chose to travel to a region or country in specific groups with the aim of learning something from the visited region. In specific terms, educational tourism is all about visiting and then staying in a foreign country for more than 24 hours and not more than one year in a row for the purpose of availing short term language classes, education in school/universities, vocational and other specialized courses.

Apart from being a mystic beauty India is also known for its strong educational system which offers broad range of educational scopes here. The striking fact associated with the ever-increasing popularity of educational tourism in India is that short term courses are available in Indian universities and other educational institutions at a very nominal fee compared to other universities and this is hugely attracting foreigners to partake in the Indian educational system.

One of the premier Indian universities, the Delhi University offers cheap courses lasting for a period of around 4 months in subject areas such as Introduction to Sanskrit Language, Indian Economy After Independence, Indian Music, Indian Philosophy and Culture et al and various other related topics.

Foreigners are hugely attracted by the cost-effectiveness of these courses and as these courses throw light on different aspects of Indian culture and history, the tourists studying them are introduced to the variegated facets of Indian cultural experience in an effective manner.

However, likewise to the University of Delhi, the University Of Madras also offers short term training/courses on subjects such as Folk Music of India, Folk Dances of India, Indian Music and Bharatanatyam, Women and Environment in India, Travel Medicine et al. The educational tourism sector is also mushrooming in the Indian subcontinent due to the use of highly standardized English in various educational institutions across the country, cost-effectiveness of courses available here and a higher degree of academic standards. a Moreover, a range of study tours and student exchange programs are also facilitated by Indian universities welcoming students from different parts of the world, this too has led to a tremendous growth in the educational tourism industry in India.

Most importantly, comprehensive educational tourism packages are offered by the Indian universities which are prepared in a way that it is possible for the tourist to gain a firm hold on the specific subject matter. Further, as the people visiting India in search of wholesome learning experience gain ample scope to educate themselves on the history and culture of the country, wildlife and ecology, flora and fauna of the nation in addition to gaining expertise in their own course material, the number of visitors looking for educational opportunities in India has increased tremendously making India the nerve centre of global educational tourism.

Visitors opting for Educational Tourism in India are entitled to the following services:

- Internationally approved courses at top-rated Indian universities/colleges/other educational institutions.
- Comprehensive educational packages at cheap rates
- Standardized fooding and lodging facility for all foreign students
- Flights and visa arrangement at the earliest.
- Special security cover is available for girl students at all universities and colleges.

5

Hotel Management and Catering

Mobile Catering

A mobile caterer serves food directly from a vehicle or cart that is designed for the purpose. Mobile catering is common at outdoor events (such as concerts), workplaces, and downtown business districts.

Event Catering

Event ranges from box-lunch drop-off to full-service catering. Caterers and their staff are part of the food service industry.

When most people refer to a "caterer", they are referring to an event caterer who serves food with waiting staff at dining tables or sets up a self-serve buffet. The food may be prepared on site, i.e., made completely at the event, or the caterer may choose to bring prepared food and put the finishing touches on once it arrives.

The event caterer staff are not responsible for preparing the food but often help set up the dining area. This service is typically provided at banquets, conventions, and weddings. Any event where all who attend are provided with food and drinks or sometimes only hors d'oeuvres is often called a *catered event*.

Many events require working with an entire theme or color scheme. A catering company or specialist is expected to know how to prepare food and to make it attractive. As such, certain catering companies have moved toward a full-service business model commonly associated with event planners. They take charge of not only food preparation but also decorations, such as table settings and lighting.

The trend is towards satisfying all the clients senses with food as a focal point. With the correct atmosphere, professional event caterers with experience can make an event special and memorable.

Beautifully prepared food alone can appeal to the senses of taste, smell, and sight-perhaps even touch, but the decorations and ambiance can play a significant part in a successfully catered event. Catering is often sold on a per-person basis, meaning that there is a flat price for each additional person. However, things like lighting and fire permits are not scaled with the guest count, so per-person pricing is not always appropriate. It is necessary to keep the cost of the food and supplies below a price margin in order to make a profit on the catering.

As many others in the food service industry, caterers and their staff work long hours. It is not uncommon for them to work on holidays or 7 days a week during holiday event seasons.

A comprehensive, formal full-service catering proposal is likely to include the following elements:

Time-line matters: rental arrival time, staff arrival time, bar open time, meal serve time, bar close time, rental pickup, out-of-venue time. Each of these factors affects the catering price.

For example, a rental quote for an "anytime" weekday delivery is usually much more economical than an "exact-time" delivery.

- General menu considerations: Clients may have specific dietary or religious needs to consider. these include Halal, Kosher, Vegetarian, Vegan and food allergy requests. Increasingly, clients are interested in food sustainability and food safety.
- Hors d'oeuvres: it should be clear if these are passed or stationary. Most caterers agree that three or four passed items are appropriate for the one-hour period prior to a meal.
- Meal Rentals: May include tables, chairs, dance floor, plants, tabletop (china, flatware, glassware, linens, chargers), bar glassware, serving equipment, salt/peppers, etc. It should be clear whether table and chair setup and take-down is included. Most rental companies do not automatically include setup and take-down in the rental charges.

- Labour: Verbiage varies from caterer to caterer, but generally speaking, an event will have a Lead/Captain/ Event Manager, a Chef, perhaps a Sous Chef or Kitchen Assistant, Wait staff and Bartenders. The labour on a plated dinner is generally much higher than the labour on a buffet, because a plated dinner involves double the china, and usually a minimum of three served courses, plus served coffee. Simply put, there's a lot more to do. To do it properly requires roughly 10 to 50% more staff. On a large event, this can be substantial, especially if overtime or doubletime applies.
- Service Charge: Sales Tax, Some quotes will include lighting, fire permits, draping, florals, valet and coat check. Many venues discreetly get a "cut" of the catering bill. Caterers are contractually committed to not disclose this fee specifically in their contracts with the clients. Therefore, catering will sometimes cost substantially more at one venue versus another.Also, caterers must compete with illegal operators. A legitimate caterer will have a business license and a health permit both showing the address of the place from which they do business.

Catering Officers on Ships

Merchant ships often carry Catering Officers-especially ferries, cruise liners and large cargo ships. In fact, the term "catering" was in use in the world of the merchant marine long before it became established as a land-bound business. The "Careers Scotland" website gives the following definition of a Catering Officer's duties:

Merchant Navy catering officers oversee the purchase, preparation and serving of food and drink to crew members and passengers. They are also responsible for accommodation services, including the provision of linen, bedding and laundry. They may be in overall charge of administration, organising record keeping, wage payment, and the interpretation of customs and immigration records that apply while the ship is in port.

On larger ships, responsibilities may be shared with the purser, who looks after passengers' comfort and facilities such as banking and shopping, while the catering officer concentrates on organising stores, overseeing the preparation of menus and meals and generally managing dining rooms and services. On a cruise liner, catering officers may be known as 'hotel services managers'.

Merchant Navy officers sometimes work in difficult and uncomfortable conditions. They spend long periods of time away from family and friends.

Airline Meal

An airline meal or in-flight meal is a meal served to passengers on board a commercial airliner. These meals are prepared by airline catering services.

The first kitchens preparing meals in-flight were established by United Airlines in 1936.

These meals vary widely in quality and quantity across different airline companies and classes of travel. They range from a simple beverage in short-haul economy class to a seven-course gourmet meal in long-haul first class.

Contents

The type of food varies depending upon the airline company and class of travel. Meals may be served as "one tray" or in multiple courses with no tray and with a tablecloth, metal cutlery, and glassware (generally in first and business classes).

The airline dinner typically includes meat (most commonly chicken or beef) or fish, a salad or vegetable, a small bread roll, and a dessert.

Caterers usually produce alternative meals for passengers with restrictive diets. These must usually be ordered in advance, sometimes when buying the ticket. Some of the more common examples include:

- Cultural diets, such as French, Italian, Chinese, Japanese or Indian style.
- Infant and baby meals. Some airlines also offer children's meals, containing foods that picky children will enjoy such as baked beans, mini-hamburgers and hot dogs.
- Medical diets, including low/high fiber, low fat/cholesterol, diabetic, peanut free, non-lactose, low salt/sodium, low-purine, low-calorie, low-protein, bland (non-spicy) and gluten-free meals.

- Religious diets, including Kosher, Halal and Hindu, Buddhist and Jain vegetarian (sometimes termed Asian vegetarian) meals.
- Vegetarian and vegan meals. Some airlines do not offer a specific meal for vegetarians; instead, they are given a vegan meal.

Cutlery

Before the September 11th attacks in 2001, first class passengers were often provided with full sets of metal cutlery. Afterward, common household items were evaluated more closely for their potential use as weapons on aircraft, and both first class and coach class passengers were restricted to plastic utensils (also known as "Sporks"). This restriction has since been relaxed in many countries.

Other Non-food Items

Condiments (typically salt, pepper, and sugar) are supplied in small sachets. For cleanliness most meals come with a napkin and a moist towelette. First and business class passengers are often provided with hot towels, proper salt and pepper shakers, free movies, drawing for various electronics not limited to laptop computers and various other forms of electronics.

Breakfast

During morning flights a cooked breakfast or smaller continental-style may be served. On long haul flights and (short/medium haul flights within Asia) breakfast normally includes an entrée of pancakes or eggs, traditional fried breakfast foods such as sausages and grilled tomatoes, and often muffins or pastry, fruits and breakfast cereal on the side. On shorter flights a continental-style breakfast, generally including a miniature box of breakfast cereal, fruits and either a muffin, pastry, or bagel. Coffee and tea are offered as well, and sometimes hot chocolate.

Quality

Food on board the flight ranges in price from free (many airlines, especially those in Asia and all airlines on long-distance flights) to as much as ten dollars (Midwest Airlines). Quality may also fluctuate due to shifts in the economics of the airline industry, with private jet passengers receiving the equivalent of five-star food service.

On the longest flights in first class and business class, most Asian and European airlines serve multicourse gourmet meals, while airlines based in the US tend to serve large, hearty, meals including a salad, steak or chicken, potatoes, and ice cream.

Some long-haul flights in first class (from mostly Asian carriers) offer such delicacies as caviar, champagne, and sorbet. The cost and availability of meals on US airlines has changed considerably in recent years, as financial pressures have inspired some airlines to either begin charging for meals or abandon them altogether in favour of small snacks (Southwest Airlines).

Eliminating free pretzels saved Northwest $2 million annually. The carrier lost nearly $3.3 billion since 2001. Air China has reported that each domestic flight's meal requires RMB50 (US$7.3) while international flights require RMB70 (US$10). However. Air China is also minimizing costs by loading only 95% of all meals to reduce leftovers and storing non-perishable foods for emergencies.

Taste

Meals must generally be frozen and heated on the ground before takeoff, rather than prepared fresh. Guillaume de Syon, a history professor at Albright College who wrote about the history of airline meals, said that the higher altitudes alter the taste of the food and the function of the taste buds; according to de Syon the food may taste "dry and flavourless" as a result of the pressurization and passengers, feeling thirsty due to pressurization, many drink alcohol when they ought to drink water.

History

In 1958 Pan Am and several European airlines went into a legal dispute over whether certain airline food sandwiches counted as a meal.

Food Safety

Food safety is paramount in the airline catering industry. A case of mass food poisoning amongst the passengers on an airliner could have disastrous consequences. For example, on February 20, 1992, shrimp tainted with cholera was served on Aerolineas Argentinas Flight 386. An elderly passenger died and other passengers fell ill.

Technical Crew Meals

Food safety with technical crew meals (pilots and flight engineers) is sometimes even stricter than for passengers. Many foodstuffs are banned completely from crew meals, including all egg products and often any dairy that has not been ultra-heat treated. The meals supplied on some airlines are labeled with the position of the crew member for whom they are intended, and no technical crew member eats any of the same products as his or her colleague. This ensures that each pilot eats a different meal to minimize the risk of all pilots on board being ill. This situation was a key part of the plot of the movie "Airplane!"

Catering and Customer

Effective customer relations is one of those hidden cogs that can help keep a catering business turning smoothly. From marketing of catering services to event planning to post-party follow-up, an open pipeline of communications and an underlying commitment to customer service are the foundation of some of the most successful catering operations.

At Harvard Univ., where catering underwent a complete overhaul five years ago, the motto—and operational creed—of the upscale Crimson Catering division is "Excellence Measured By Your Satisfaction."

Harvard Express, the lower-ticket, self-service arm, is no less committed to customer service. It promises nothing less than "A Simple Guarantee: 100% Satisfaction."

The strategy appears to be working—the two catering operations generate combined sales of approximately $1.3 million, 75% of it from Crimson Catering.

The top challenge: "Our biggest challenge is maximizing business from existing customers," says Elaine Smart, asst. dir. for catering and residential dining services, who was brought in five years ago to create a new identity for the Harvard catering business.

"We strive for the highest possible degree of customer satisfaction, rather than trying to build the number of customers."

All marketing materials, for both divisions, have been carefully designed to be as user-friendly as possible, she points out. Crimson Catering menus and brochures are updated four times a year to keep fatigue from setting in among regular clientele. "We consider our menu to be our best marketing piece. Each is individually and professionally designed, in full colour with seasonal themes. They're very nicely done, so they won't get lost on people's desks."

Thank-yous count: To ensure client retention, Smart or one of her staff contacts each customer personally after every event to thank them for their business. Customers receive handwritten thank-you notes with a personalized gift such as a logoed coffee mug and a tin of homemade brownies and cookies.

Included is an easy-to-use Function Evaluation Form, a tri-fold, postage-paid self-mailer soliciting feedback on everything from the pre-function planning experience to the presentation of food and linen. Negative evaluations warrant a phone call to discuss what went wrong and what correctional steps might be made in the future.

"Harvard may be big, but it's a closed environment," explains Smart. "Because we don't have exclusivity on-campus, we're up against everyone in the city. We believe that our customers are entitled to the best. And in order to get the business, we have to be the best."

As image-builder: For Scott County Food Service Catering, in Georgetown, KY, catering is only as good as the image of the foodservice department in the local community—an image fed Eleanor Hall works hard at constantly.

"Initially, administration did not want us catering, so we had to work hard to gain their trust," notes Hall, who now counts sales of $15,000-$20,000 a year from catering.

Employees involved in catering throughout the 10-school district are cross-trained in presentation and prep and encouraged to apply new standards of quality to school lunch. When the district first got involved in catering she also gave classes on garnishing and sent someone from each school to a cake-decorating class to help develop their talent.

"I encourage people to garnish school lunch, because I want the quality of school foodservice to be as good as the catering," explains Hall. "We have a lot of talent here and I want to keep developing it. We did a reception for the Chamber of Commerce where everybody gave it their all, and the guests were very surprised that school foodservice could do the things we do. This is a good way for people in town to see what we're capable of."

25 meeting areas: Technology helps catering manager Joseph Swinski stay in touch with customers at GTech Corp. in West Greenwich, RI. With 25 different conference and meeting areas and sales of more than $200,000 a year—approximately one-quarter of it involving visiting high-level dignitaries being courted for orders of lottery systems and supplies—the company needs efficient, cost-effective catering that is also highly flexible.

For convenient ordering of day-to-day catering functions, Swinski created standard self-service menus and pricing, and an easy-to-use Function Request Form which is available on the in-house e-mail system.

An administrative assistant can simply pull up the menus and forms, fill them out and send them in, receiving same-day confirmation and the assurance that catering is one less thing to worry about in the course of a busy workday. The Request Form is linked to a program that calculates prices, schedules the room, and integrates with ordering functions, as well.

This system allows Swinski and his staff to concentrate more time and energy on the high-profile, custom-designed work. (In a typical week, GTech hosts as many as half-a-dozen groups from around the world who are coming to view the systems—and purchase them.) The company has taken the unusual step of creating a marketing position to coordinate every aspect of the multiple-day visitor events, from booking hotels to planning the agenda. Anna Ragosta acts as the ultimate "client," making the complex, often sensitive planning process easier and more comfortable for the host team.

Organizational Forms in the International Hotels

Organizational Form Variation in the Hotel Industry There are three organizational modes under which a given hotel can operate. These differ along two dimensions. First, they vary in the level of the central firm's equity involvement; and second, they vary in the extent to which the firm retains operational control. The three organizational forms are:

Firm owned and operated Here, the hierarchical firm is the equity owner and full residual claimant. Hotel managers are employees of the hotel company. Management contracts In this case, the hotel is owned by an outside group of investors, who have hired the firm to run the hotel under its brand. The contracts are fairly long term, lasting up to and sometimes beyond 10 years. Employees of the hotel firm administer the unit as though it were owned and operated, but the firm is recompensed via management fees. These are generally a percentage of gross revenues, sometimes supplemented by guaranteed annual minimum or lump-sum payments. Franchised In this case, the hotel is owned and run by a separate entity, which pays fees to the firm in exchange for the rights to use the brand for some period of time. The contract also specifies that the franchisees must adhere to certain guidelines set by the company to ensure that it meets certain quality thresholds. Like the management contracts, franchising arrangements tend to be long-term.

These different forms give hotel firms flexibility in how they respond to incentive issues and the regulatory environment, making the industry a particularly suitable context to consider how firm boundaries are affected by institutions.

Institutions and Equity

Like the telecommunications, manufacturing and energy industries that have been the mainstay of the literature on institutions' economic impact (e.g. Henisz & Zelner (2001); Smarzynska & Wei (2002); Gutierrez (2003)), the hotel industry is characterized by large, up-front capital investments.

In the case of large resorts, these up-front costs may routinely be as much as $100 million (Contractor & Kundu (1998a)). Super-premium facilities can cost even more. For example, the recently constructed Wynn Las Vegas is reported to have cost $2.7 billion. Furthermore, hotel firms are also susceptible to government intervention and hold-up problems after construction. For example, a hotel's operating expenses can be modified by governmental manipulation of the costs of obtaining operating licenses, or meeting sanitary and safety standards.

These issues, combined with the relative lack of alternative uses for its assets, make the hotel industry vulnerable to ex-post policy changes. While cases of outright asset expropriation are uncommon, the international business press is full of stories about sudden changes in the regulation of hotels. For example, in June 2006, the United Arab Emirates' Economic Department decreed that all hotels and hotel apartments required licenses to "serve alcohol, and open bars, nightclubs and restaurants which show artistic programmes." Such changes in regulation can have profound impacts on the profitability of operating hotels in affected markets. Indeed, major hotel chain operators like Accor and Marriott explicitly talk about political risk, economic uncertainty, and/or the impact of regulatory changes in their discussion of strategy and financial outlook in their annual reports.

Institutions and the Incentive to Maintain Control

The strength of a brand, and thus the benefit of being associated with a well-known brand, critically depends on the capacity of the brand owner to deliver what customers expect. This in turn crucially depends on the behavior and hard work of local managers and their ability and willingness to abide by firm policies. In the context of an industry such as lodging, and others where firms operate chains of outlets, the physical distance between headquarters and local operations makes it difficult to observe the behavior of employee managers.

The agency theoretic solution to this problem is that the firm should devise a high-powered incentive contract for its local managers. This, in fact, is what franchising achieves: by making the local operator a residual claimant, the firm obtains higher effort from its managers, and thus greater output locally. This solution is expected to be especially valuable when local effort has a large impact on output, and when it is particularly difficult to observe the provision of such effort.

While franchising an outlet, or hotel, addresses the "incentive to shirk" problem, it creates another type of incentive problem, however. As residual claimants, franchisees bear the burden of maintaining quality and abiding with company policies valued by customers, but because they operate under a common brand, they share the benefits of these behaviours with other franchisees.

Lafontaine & Raynaud (2002)). As noted by Brickley & Dark (1987) and Brickley (1999), freeriding on the brand is especially likely to be a problem in non-repeat industries such as lodging, where customers cannot discipline local operators because they rarely frequent the same outlet.

Lafontaine & Raynaud (2002) argue that franchisors address this problem of franchisee freeriding by including a number of clauses in their contracts that impose constraints on the behavior of franchisees, such as, for example, specific operations procedures, input sourcing requirements, minimum advertising requirements. Whether or not the franchisee abides by these rules is observable to the franchisor, at least in more transparent contexts, and the franchisee who is found in violation of such rules can be terminated on this basis. Combined with franchisee rents from local operations, these rules and the opportunity to terminate non-complying franchisees yield a selfenforcement mechanism. In other words, the franchisee who wishes to continue to earn the rents associated with being part of the franchise chooses to abide by the requirements in the contract and does not free-ride. Lafontaine & Raynaud (2002) argue that such a mechanism complements the residual claims in franchise contracts as they address the free-riding problem generated by franchisee ownership of local outlets.

While the self-enforcing aspect of franchise contracts can be relied upon to address free-riding, it relies critically on the capacity of the franchisor to observe certain aspects of local operations and interpret them correctly. It also requires that the terms of the contract be enforceable, and that non-complying franchisees can be terminated. In more volatile environments, however, these conditions may not be satisfied.

One well-known example of a franchisee in a repeat industry who chose to ignore company standards and policies in an international context was Raymond Dayan, the owner of the exclusive territorial rights for Paris, France for McDonald's. By 1982, Dayan had 12 restaurants in operation in Paris, but: McDonald's in Paris was considered a "QSC [Quality, Service, Cleanliness] wasteland" by everyone else in the system. The company's strict specifications on food products had been blatantly ignored. Hamburgers were prepared without all of the standard ingredients. Food was held so long and served so cold that McDonald's managers inspecting the stores found it difficult to eat Veteran managers insist that they have never seen McDonald's units maintained in a filthier state: cooking oils were rancid and black, layers of grease covered the floors and walls, litter was strewn about the store, and grease dripped from the vents into cups hung from the ceiling. In fact, the stores were so unclean that McDonald's franchisees elsewhere around the world began hearing complaints about them from their own local customers who had seen Dayan's units while visiting Paris.

When McDonald's tried to terminate Dayan's license, Dayan sued in Illinois court, arguing that McDonald's was just trying to take back from him what turned out to be a very profitable market. The judge in this case ruled in McDonald's favor, and McDonald's was able to terminate Dayan's license. In other cases and other contexts, however, local courts have been the locus of the suits, and they have favoured the local franchisee to the detriment of the franchisor or the chain. Where free-riding is expected to be particularly problematic, for example when the brand is very valuable, or when outlets are very large and thus more likely to generate more externalities, or in markets where enforcement is difficult, the cost of franchisee free-riding is high. In those cases, firms may opt for a contract that does not generate local incentives to free-ride, namely a contract that does not make the manager's welfare dependent on the profits of the local unit. Consistent with this argument, Lafontaine & Shaw (1999), for example, find evidence that franchisors with more valuable brands, and those whose outlets are larger, indeed operate more of their outlets corporately.

A number of discrete choice variables are used to capture different aspects of the Company's choice of organizational form for a given outlet. The first takes the value of 1 if an outlet is franchised or under a management contract and thus indicates whether the Company has chosen an equity involvement. The second takes the value of 1 if the hotel is company-owned or operated under a management contract, indicating whether or not the Company manages the unit itself. A third variable is coded as 0 if a given hotel is company owned and operated, 1 if operated under a management contract, and 2 if franchised.

The impacts of the market development variables represent something of a puzzle. Market size (proxied using the log of population and the log of per capita GDP) increases the likelihood that the company takes an equity stake in the business, which was not a prediction that emerged from our model. These two variables also increased the probability that the Company controls an outlet using its own employees as predicted, though this effect is never statistically significant. These results suggest that there may be rents to owning a hotel in larger markets that the Company cannot gain access to except by owning the outlet.

Finally, the results for hotel size and monitoring cost variables on the probability that the Company uses employee managers are generally consistent with our model's predictions. As hypothesized, larger outlets are more likely to be operated with employee managers as are hotels in culturally similar countries. Physical distance has a negative but insignificant impact. Interestingly, the Company's experience in the host country has a negative and significant impact on the likelihood that the Company's employees manage a given hotel. This may suggest that the Company needs time to find franchisees it trusts not to degrade the value of its brands, or that increased experience in a country make it easier for the Company to obtain and interpret information about local operations, making franchising more feasible.

Globalization in the Hotel and Catering Sector

The influence of global processes on the development of economy is reflected in the intensity and directions of tourist flows, and, therefore, in the development strategies of tourist companies. The fast progress in information technology, economic growth of developing countries and political changes in many countries of the world, traffic development etc. have been the main factors for accelerating the growth of global tourist market. Due to the process of globalization and offensive strategies in the last few decades, multinational companies are able to penetrate and expand their business activity more easily on the once inaccessible markets. During this period, no other social and economic phenomenon has had such an impressive development as international tourism. There have been significant quantitative, quality, structural, economic, geographical, sociological and other changes in the sphere of demand as well as that of offer. Therefore, nowadays there is almost no country in the world that is not involved in different aspects of tourist flow and business trips to a higher or lower extent.

These trends have been manifested in the hotel industry, as an economic activity and material basis for tourism. According to them, world's tourist flows have been influencing the intensity of growth and the structure of accommodation capacities, the level of hotel concentration, or dispersion in space. In that sense, monitoring the quantitative dimension of hotel industry development includes the analysis of spatial and structural expansion of hotel capacities, as the basis for understanding the development and modern tendencies in the world's hotel industry.

Basic indicators of hotel industry development in the world framework can be seen through the dynamics of the growth of accommodation capacities, territorial distribution of accommodation facilities, new organizational forms of business, improvement of material basis by applying technical and technological innovations, diversification processes, that is, establishing a significant number of types on one hand, and product standardization processes in the function of obtaining a recognizable market identity, on the other hand.

The Concept and Development of Hotel Chains

The traditional form of hotel industry consisting of small hotels individually owned is changing every day and is starting to resemble the form of other industries where large companies increase their share on the market. These companies in the accommodation industry are most often called hotel chains. "A hotel chain implies establishing a business system from a number of objects under the same name, which function in the narrower and wider business environment'.

The nucleus of every hotel is related to stepping out of the business framework of a single object, that is, to the purpose of establishing the technical, technological and organizational business concept which is checked and affirmed and the style of business which is recognizable, by implementing the existing facilities into the system or by constructing new ones on chosen locations. In the initial phase of development, it is a smaller number of accommodation capacities and the narrower zone of influence. The further development of a hotel chain implies the increase in capacities as well as territorial expansion by taking into account the basic principles and following global trends in tourism on the world market.

Since the 1950s, the expansion of the demand for hotel service in the world has been directly influenced by the increase in traveling, that is, the increase in tourist, as well as business and other trips variously motivated. The development of hotel chains has also been influenced by traveling within the borders of countries, which has also had the tendency towards increasing. However, during the 20th century, the development of business regarding hotel chains was not continuous. Therefore, according to the means and characteristics of market dealings in the development of international hotel chains, two periods can be detected.

The first period lasted until the 1970s and was characterized by intensive traffic development, above all air and road traffic, the appearance of new tourist destinations and the expansion of tourism in general. During this period, there was an occurrence of gradual internationalization of dealings in hotel business. The carriers of the growth and development were primarily hotel companies in the USA. During this period, some of the most famous hotel chains in the world, such as InterContinental, Hilton, Holiday Inns etc. were established.

The second period was marked by the increase in the number of international hotel chains and their capacities abroad, greater versatility in business dealings, gradual abandoning of the concept of one (unique) brand and introducing new, multiple (multiplied) brands. By introducing more brands, multinational hotel companies differentiated their services according to the needs of a greater number of segments, above all tourist and business trips. Adapting to the above mentioned changes is evident both in the policy of distribution and of location: apart from resort centres, the main orientation is towards large cities as business centres and towards international communication, particularly airports and highways.

An important feature of this period is the appearance of new ways of providing the growth and development of international hotel chains, as well as significant engaging of capital and companies from other branches of economy into hotel business. Unlike other companies involved in hotel business, hotel chains have defined standards in all business areas, their own philosophy and marketing strategy, a unique booking system, human resource education etc., all of which make them not only recognizable on the market but also the main carriers of tourism development in the future. The pronounced domination of hotel chains from the

USA is gradually reducing and the share of British, French, Japanese and German, and in the last few years Chinese companies, is increasing.

The Capacities of International Hotel Chains

According to the estimation of the World Tourism Organization, the overall accommodation capacities are over 20 million rooms. International Hotel and Restaurant Association (IHRA) keeps records of over 300 hotel chains different in size, ownership structure, types of business connections, the quality of hotel capacities, business concepts, prices etc. According to the information for 2008, 300 ranked hotel chains in 54.400 hotels had over 7.2 million rooms at their disposal. In other words, business systems that operated as hotel chains comprised one third of the world's accommodation capacities. Ten leading hotel companies in 2008 managed over 4.1 million rooms, which comprised 56.6% of ranked hotel chains capacities. The top five leading hotel companies alone had 2.8 million rooms, or 38% of the complete recorded offer of hotel chains. This shows a high degree of the so-called corporation concentration. If considered according to the company's origin country, an absolute domination of the USA and European countries is evident, with over 90% of the world's offer of hotel chains.

For the last twenty years, a more intensive increase in Asia, the Pacific, Africa etc. is noted in terms of the growth dynamics of capacities and their spatial distribution. The carriers of the capacities increase in these regions, apart from companies from the USA and Europe, are national hotel chains from China, Japan, Singapore, UAE, JAR, Egypt, etc. The leading Asian and the thirteenth hotel chain in the world for its accommodation capacities is Jin Jiang from Shanghai, which had about 80 thousand rooms at its disposal. The increase in accommodation capacities in other parts of the world leads to the mitigation of unevenness in the offer of hotel capacities.

Factors in Forming Hotel Chains

Numerous factors have influenced the formation of international, specialized hotel chains, that is, their beginnings and development. There are various connections and relations among these factors; therefore it is very difficult to determine which were dominant in forming a particular hotel chain. They can be divided into two main groups: external and internal factors.

External factors include general circumstances that served the establishment and expansion of international hotel chains. External factors which have influenced the occurrence of this type of hotel enterprises are: a) the expansion in the demand for hotel services in the world (driving factors of tourist traveling and business trips) and b) the need to accelerate the economic growth of certain regions in the world.

Strong economic growth, enabled by exceptional technological improvements and the increase of work productivity under changed market conditions, with simultaneous significant political and social changes in the world, have had significant influence on the fact that in the last few decades the most important driving factors of tourist travel have been revealed.

The most important factors of the increase in the size of tourist travel are: the level of urbanization and industrialization, the standard of living, the quality of work and living environment, available free time, advertising, traffic development, prices etc. Significant political and social changes, as well as the world market liberalization, have brought about the large increase in business trips. It is estimated that this segment of traveling comprises around 25% of overall realized catering consumption in the world. In the USA, in the overall structure of hotel guests, the share of passing business travellers is dominant with 29% as well as participants in conferences and meetings with 25%.

The need to accelerate the economic growth of certain regions of the world is considered to be the main factor in the appearance of some of the most famous international hotel chains. A typical example is InterContinental Hotels Group (IHG). This hotel chain was founded by the airline company Pan American World Airways (Pan Am) in 1946, for the purpose of improving tourism and increasing accommodation capacities in Latin America. The first hotel was bought in 1949 in Brazil. According to the information for 2008, 4.186 hotels were part of the IHG hotel chain.

Hilton Hotels Corporation is the second most famous American chain whose international expansion is explained by the need for economic growth of less developed areas. Namely, Conrad Hilton, the founder of the corporation, provided a contract in 1948 re garding the management of the first large hotel in Puerto Rico, which was built by the Commonwealth as a part of the economic growth program. The success of the Hilton's hotel was the basis for the tourist "boom" of Puerto Rico, and, consequently, the improvement of the economic situation in the Carrribean. According to the information for 2008, Hilton Corporation is ranked as the fourth international hotel chain in the world regarding the number of rooms, which, in 2008, managed 3.265 accommodation facilities in 78 countries on the world.

Distinction should be made between this kind of forming of famous hotel chains and engaging many others in numerous underdeveloped areas, which are attractive and perspective for tourism and business, for the purpose of spreading the already existing international activities, using the advantage, expanding their share of the market etc. It is necessary to distinguish between the phase of forming and later developmental stages of international hotel chains.

Internal factors are closely connected with external factors, and are thus necessary to be viewed through their interdependence. Internal factors are: certain brand and quality guarantee as well as greater efficiency in business (diversification of offer). Each hotel chain is trying to offer services which are different form other chains' services in certain segments, but which present significant experience for the client, that is, present a level of satisfaction that the consumer experiences while staying at a particular hotel.

Therefore, those hotel chains that offer to their consumers a certain brand and guaranteed quality will have the competitive advantage. Their brand (or brands) is recognizable among customers by its quality, price, means of providing service and other features of the particular chain. Service quality is an extremely important factor, through which it becomes internationally recognized (Best Western, Hilton, Holiday Inn, Hyatt and other corporations). That is why one of the important elements of market performance are promo slogans, for example, the Hilton hotel chain has a slogan "When an American does business, the way of the American's business ends in the Hilton", the Marriott hotel chain "When Marriott does it, it does it right" etc.

International business provides greater efficiency. Through diversification of their offer, hotel chains reduce the risk of business through product variety and geographical diffusion. It enlarges the range of their complete offer and encourages the creation of new units abroad. The combination of expansion and diversification as the direction of growth has enabled the world's most famous hotel chains to enter international hotel business, that is, to grow from national into international companies; thus, for instance, Holiday Inn started its business with motels, and Marriott as a restaurant etc.

According to all this, the advantage of hotel chains is in their size, that is, more rational and efficient business dealings, or saving due to economies of scale. One should bear in mind that efficient business can be done by individual hotels with large capacity, but the complete profitability is accomplished by large hotel groups. The more efficient business dealings of hotel chains are reflected in: saving in finance and marketing, saving when purchasing various products and services, saving related to management, technical saving as well as that related to risk diversification. Apart from that, large hotel chains manage accommodation capacities of different ranges, and are able to offer a product with a different price range: a complete service in a luxury hotel, luxurious suites for everybody, mid-range hotels for a wider circle of consumers, moderate prices with limited service, resort hotels, economic motels etc.. On the other hand, hotel chains, as any other large company, have problems in communication, supervision and expenses.

The Process of Territorial Expansion of Hotel Chains

The development of international tourism in the last few decades has brought significant changes in business orientation of hotel chains, out of which the process of territorial expansion has a special role. The quantitative growth of hotel chains inevitably leads to their territorial expansion towards certain macro tourist regions of the world and permanent increase in accommodation capacities. The process of geographical expansion of hotel chains appears as a concrete manifestation of the growth strategy. The development and business behavior of companies in the modern world economy can be manifested through four orientations: ethnocentric, polycentric, regiocentric and geocentric.

In the first, ethnocentric phase, a company is by its vision and orientation focused on the domestic market. In its business dealings, the company relies on the national market and its resources, as well as national culture in thinking, deciding and taking action. This orientation is a characteristic of smaller hotel companies which observe internationalization from the point of the possibility of implementing their ethnocentric business orientation abroad. That is why such companies choose markets that are geographically and ethnographically close, for example, Canada for companies from the USA.

The polycentric business orientation represents the beginning of geographic diversification and internationalization of business, by creating branches and representative offices in another country. Stepping onto the international market changes the business philosophy and leads to adjusting the business to the economic conditions of new countries, while the culture in behavior and decision-making is domestic. The strategy of these companies is "to adjust all branches to the economic conditions of those countries in which they do business, and through their growth relatively independent parts-divisions are created."

Regiocentric orientation in business implies higher ambitions in terms of territorial growth, but within the region. Business activities of a company are directed to consumers and resources of one or more areas and their integration into the local economy. Besides that, the culture in business behavior is regional, consumers in those areas are target groups, people from the region are used in business dealings, and financial sources are redistributed within the area of business. Hotel chains that operate on the territory of Europe within tourist macro regions can serve as an example.

Geocentric orientation in hotel chain business looks at the world as a potential market. With this business orientation, national, regional and intercontinental barriers are surpassed and a business strategy is created with the aim of competitiveness on the global market. The majority of hotel chains that are nowadays multinational –global passed through the above-mentioned three phases on their way of development. Each hotel enterprise is potentially oriented towards international business.

One of key indicators of geocentric and global orientation of international hotel chains is seen in their territorial prevalence in the world. Territorial prevalence is expressed through the number of countries in which international hotel enterprises are present with accommodation facilities with their name. Therefore, along with accommodation capacity, territorial prevalence is also an important indicator of the growth strategy in international hotel business.

The biggest international hotel chain, according to the number of rooms and guests, IHG (InterContinental Hotels Group), is present with its hotel capacities in 100 countries of the world. Within this hotel giant, which in 4.400 hotels has over 180 million tourist days, seven world brands operate, the most famous being Holiday Inn Hotels & Resorts and Holiday Inn Express. Therefore, hotel brands – chains which symbolize hotel business in the USA, operate today within the English company with its headquarters in Windsor. Although InterContinental Hotels Group is formally a European company, its largest hotel branch is made of typically American hotels. This indicates its global orientation in business and permanent territorial expansion towards new markets with different levels of hotel development. For the USA market, due to certain tax releases, there is a characteristic increase in the shares of catering companies by companies primarily dealing with real estate. Among such companies is Starwood Hotel & Resort Worldwide, which became the corporation of global importance after purchasing Sheraton Westin hotel chain. In 2008 this company had accommodation facilities in 97 countries.

French Accor is present in 95 countries, thus confirming its international business orientation, and also Best Western International in 80 countries, as well as hotel chains Hilton Hotels Corp. and Carslon Hotels Worldwide operating in 78 and 74 countries respectively. The second place on the list of leading hotel corporations, Wyndham Hotel Group (previously Cendant Corporation), was formed as a global service with diversified business activities in 1977. This hotel chain appeared with its accommodation capacities outside the North American continent in 1999. Although Wyndham corporation has over 7.000 hotels and accommodation capacities in 66 countries of the world, its business orientation is still directed towards the USA market. The example of Wyndham shows that size does not necessarily imply international orientation. This corporation, for example, had only

100 hotels outside North America in 1998. However, the process of its internationalization has intensified by signing business arrangements with foreign partners, primarily from Eastern and Central Europe, so that today this company is leading in the number of hotels around the world.

Some big companies accelerate their territorial expansion towards new markets using the strategy "centre and cog", developed by airline companies. Namely, in order to compete with independent hotels, hotel chains first build luxurious brand hotels in big cities, and then spread towards surrounding smaller towns with secondary brands. The best example of this strategy is the American hotel chain Marriott International, which is expanding on the Russian market through Moscow and St. Petersburg, as primary and strategic centres, and the towns of Nizhniy Novgorod, Samara, Kazan and Yekaterinburg as secondary markets.On the global level, hotel chains more often achieve better results than independent hotels. However, on some markets, such as Hong Kong, Singapore, Sao Paolo, Sydney, Budapest, Amsterdam etc., independent hotels are more booked. The ever discriminating demand, when high quality in the domain of basic service is understood, forces hotel chains to find new ways of animating their clients. One of the ways of improving accommodation capacities is building the so-called theme hotels, which represent an independent tourist attraction with its architecture, decor and atmosphere.

"Imitating the already affirmed tourist attractions is used as the most powerful means of achieving this aim, through historical eclecticism in architecture, appropriate interior design and decor." The most spectacular example is Las Vegas, where there are many mega hotels with casinos exploiting various themes (Egypt, Paris, New York, Rome, Venice): Venetion/Palazzo with 7.128 rooms, MGM Grand with 5.044 rooms, Luxsor with 4.048 rooms etc. The leading hotel chain regarding the number of theme mega hotels is MGM Mirage with around 50.000 rooms in 17 objects (Las Vegas, Makao, Rino etc.).

Types of Hotel Chains in the World

As a consequence of harsh competition and for the purpose of obtaining the best possible position on the international market, the process of enlarging international hotel chains and forming new companies including renowned hotel chains is present. The aim of forming new hotel companies is providing necessary financial resources for maintaining and improving their business standards. Hotel chains as a part of such companies continue their activities using their recognizable trademarks, but they also carry the trademark of the new founded company, for which it represents certain publicity on the global level. Apart from that, there is differentiating between hotel chains on the market (from budget to luxurious) in the sense of business orientation, according to various segments and target groups of clients. According to the methodology of the international magazine "Hotels", there are three types of hotel chains: corporate chains, management companies and voluntary chain associations.

Corporate chains are recognized by their brand or hotel brands, or a well-known trademark. The biggest corporate chains develop many brands-trademarks, which in the best way show the service type and quality. Business activities on the national and international scales are done in different ways, therefore, franchising contracts, management contracts, various sale norms while including companies from other branches of economy and other means are used. Accommodation capacities of leading hotel chains in the world are enormous: accommodation capacities of IHG (InterConinental Hotels Group) in 2008 were over 585.000 rooms in over 4.100 hotels, Wyndham Hotel Group 550.000 rooms in over 7.000 hotels etc.

Management companies are companies (operators) that manage various hotel brands of corporate chains or their parts, their own brands, as well as independent hotels (hotels outside the chains), which do not have their own brand. In hotel business, a management contract represents a way of business cooperation based on providing special, professional services by specialized companies. There can be different types of contracts between hotel chains-hotel owners and management companies:

- Joint investments contract (when the management company – operator is an equal partner in the joint ownership over a hotel, and, thus in profit);
- Lease contract (when the management company temporarily, or for a certain period of time rents an object and pays a certain amount of money for that);

- Management contract (when the management company can, but does not have to be an investor, but manages a hotel for agreed compensation);
- Franchise contract (when the management company takes the franchise from the franchise receiver).

Management companies are much smaller in size and capacity than corporate chains. Accommodation capacities with a smaller number of rooms dominate their structure, so the differences in the average size of objects are significantly smaller than with corporate chains.

The largest number of management companies manages objects of famous hotel chains in the USA, such as: Holiday Inns, Sheraton, Best Western etc. In the USA, big corporate chains have in their structure management companies who control different hotels. For example, corporate chain Marriott International, apart from the hotels in its ownership, on various grounds also manages around 900 hotels which are not in its ownership. The biggest management companies that do not own hotels are: Extended Stay Hotels (manages around 700 hotels), Interstate Hotels&Resorts (manages around 230 hotels) etc. Unlike corporate chains, management companies are less oriented towards the international hotel business.

A special form of activities in hotel business is franchising. The franchising system in national and international framework is used by the largest corporate chains. To hotel enterprises (or entrepreneurs) which receive a franchise, this system provides work technology according to the standards of the franchiser, thus achieving appropriate service quality and control; using the brand name of the franchiser, which makes him recognizable on the market, enables various kinds of help with bookings, sales, promotion, human resource training etc. However, the biggest advantage of the franchise receiver lies in the fact that, by entering the business system of a large hotel chain, it avoids the risks and problems of providing the market for their services.

The advantage of a hotel company that gives a franchise is the fact that it provides a significant number of selling points in their own and other countries without large investments. The company spreads on the market with minimum financial risk. Leading corporate hotel chains are the biggest givers. The best examples are corporate chains: Wyndham Hotel Group (out of 7.043 hotels, 7.016 are franchised), Choice Hotels International (all the hotels are franchised), InterContinental Hotels Group (86% are franchised) etc.

Voluntary chains (associations) base their activities on providing service of global marketing and reservations to independent hotels and corporate chains, particularly those of national character. These voluntary chains are also called consortiums. Consortiums are voluntary associations of a group of independent hotels, national and international chains, whose main aim is to animate the demand and enlarge their offer on the international market.

The origin of voluntary chains is related to internationalization and globalization of hotel business. Hotel enterprises join voluntary chains when they are not able to follow the expansion in business activities both in the material sense and in human resources. Activities of voluntary chains are related to: sales and reservations, advertising and other promotional activities, cooperation with airline companies, providing other services etc. In 2008, 25 biggest voluntary chains covered sales, promotion and other activities in 26.000 hotels and around 2.9 million rooms. The number of rooms was expanded by 5% in comparison to 2007. The biggest voluntary chain in the world is British Utell, an affiliate of the company Pegasus from the USA. According to the information for 2008, this chain served 11.900 hotels with around 1.380.000 rooms. The chain, in comparison to 2007, increased its services by another 400 hotels.

According to the information for 2008, the largest number of voluntary chains was based in Europe. Unlike big voluntary chains, which are mainly related to the European market, management companies are more numerous on the USA market.

Conclusion

Economic globalization, readily available markets, traffic development and advancements in information and other technologies have all caused an increase in the number of tourist, business and other kinds of trips, thus deeply influencing the transformation of hotel business. One of the most important transformations and one of the most important characteristics of business dealings in hotel enterprises is included in business integrations and connections as well as territorial expansion. High concentration of accommodation capacities in certain parts of the world (the USA, the Mediterranean, the Alps etc.) forces hotel chains to find new destinations for their enlargement and territorial expansion. That is why the end of the 20th and the beginning of the 21st century have been marked with changes in spatial distribution and more intense increase in accommodation capacities in the areas of former socialist countries, Asia, the Pacific and Africa.

Internationalization provides hotel chains the improvement of their position on the global market. In order to obtain better positions on the international market, huge financial transactions have appeared recently, leading to changes in the ownership structure and the formation of new companies, both on the national as well as international (global) level. In this way, financial resources are obtained, as well as increased influence on the market, maintenance and innovations in business standards. Besides carrying the trademark of a newly founded company, hotel chains continue doing their business under their own recognizable trademark-brand. The branded name of a hotel chain has numerous advantages, such as greater marketing power, ensured product quality originating from established standards, help in management, easier approach to financial institutions etc. However, the mass usage of hotels by clients with different buying powers will maintain a wide range of objects as well as prices.

Importance and Usage of Dress Code

Clothing is an aspect of human physical appearance, and like other aspects of human physical appearance it has social significance. All societies have dress codes, most of which are unwritten but understood by most members of the society. The dress code has built in rules or signals indicating the message being given by a person's clothing and how it is worn. This message may include indications of the person's social class, income, occupation, ethnic and religious affiliation, attitude, marital status, sexual availability and sexual orientation. Clothes convey other social messages including the stating or claiming personal or cultural identity, the establishing, maintaining, or defying social group norms, and appreciating comfort and functionality.

For example, wearing expensive clothes can communicate wealth, the image of wealth, or cheaper access to quality clothing. All factors apply inversely to the wearing of inexpensive clothing and similar goods. The observer sees the resultant, expensive clothes, but may incorrectly perceive the extent to which these factors apply to the person observed. (cf. conspicuous consumption). Clothing can convey a social message, even if none is intended.

If the receiver's code of interpretation differs from the sender's code of communication, misinterpretation follows. In every culture, current fashion governs the manner of consciously constructing, assembling, and wearing clothing to convey a social message. The rate of change of fashion varies, and so modifies the style in wearing clothes and its accessories within months or days, especially in small social groups or in communications media-influenced modern societies. More extensive changes, requiring more time, money, and effort to effect, may span generations. When fashion changes, the messages communicated by clothing change.

History

Europe

In the Middle Ages the European nobility used a dress code to differentiate themselves from the other classes.

The Americas

The indigenous peoples of the Pacific Northwest Coast had a complex social structure, including slaves, commoners, and nobles, and dress codes to indicate these social distinctions. John R. Jewitt, an Englishman who wrote a memoir about his years as a captive of the Nuu-chah-nulth people in 1802-1805, describes how, after some time living there, Maquina and the chiefs decided that he must now be "considered one of them, and conform to their customs".

Jewitt resented the imposition of this dress code, finding the loose untailored garments very cold, and attributed to them a subsequent illness of which he almost died. He was not allowed to cut his hair, and had to paint his face and body as a Nootka would.

Signifier

Gender: Various traditions suggests that certain items of clothing intrinsically suit different gender roles. In particular, the wearing of skirts and trousers has given rise to common phrases expressing implied restrictions in use and disapproval of offending behavior. For example, ancient Greeks often considered the wearing of trousers by Persian men as a sign of effeminacy.

Social Status

In many societies, people of high rank reserve special items of clothing or decoration for themselves as symbols of their social status. In ancient times, only Roman senators could wear garments dyed with Tyrian purple; only high-ranking Hawaiian chiefs could wear feather cloaks and palaoa or carved whale teeth. In China before the establishment of the republic, only the emperor could wear yellow.

Occupation

Military, police, and firefighters usually wear uniforms, as do workers in many industries. School children often wear school uniforms, while college and university students sometimes wear academic dress. Members of religious orders may wear uniforms known as habits. Sometimes a single item of clothing or a single accessory can declare one's occupation or rank within a profession.

Ethnic and Political Affiliation

In many regions of the world, national costumes and styles in clothing and ornament declare membership in a certain village, caste, religion, etc. A Scotsman declares his clan with his tartan. A French peasant woman identified her village with her cap or coif.

Clothes can also proclaim dissent from cultural norms and mainstream beliefs, as well as personal independence. In 19th-century Europe, artists and writers lived *la vie de Boheme* and dressed to shock: George Sand in men's clothing, female emancipationists in bloomers, male artists in velvet waistcoats and gaudy neckcloths. Bohemians, beatniks, hippies, Goths, Punks and Skinheads have continued the (countercultural) tradition in the 20th-century West.

Religious Affiliation

A Sikh or Muslim man may display his religious affiliation by wearing a turban and other traditional clothing. Many Muslim women wear head or body covering that proclaims their status as respectable women and as considered a means for covering the Awrah. A Jewish man may indicate his observance of Judaism by wearing a yarmulke.

Marital Status

Traditionally, Hindu women wear *sindoor*, a red powder, in the parting of their hair to indicate their married status; if widowed, they abandon *sindoor* and jewellery and wear simple white clothing. However this is not true of all Hindu women; in the modern world this is not a norm and women without sindoor may not necessarily be unmarried.

In many Orthodox Jewish circles, married women wear head coverings such as a hat, snood, or wig. Additionally, after their marriage Jewish men of Ashkenazi descent begin to wear a Tallit during prayer. Men and women of the Western world may wear wedding rings to indicate their married status, and women may also wear engagement rings when they are engaged.

Laws and Social Norms

In New Guinea and Vanuatu there are areas where it is customary for the men to wear nothing but penis sheaths in public-this is uncommon in more developed areas. Women wear string skirts. In remote areas of Bali, women may go topless. In India, Hindu contemporary daily dress like saris tend to often show bare stomachs, but the feeling of culture and tradition covers such exposure.

In the United States, a few businesses or restaurants display dress code signs requiring shoes and shirts, claiming to be there on account of a health code, although no such health codes exist,. these signs have remained popular since businesses looked for ways to reduce the number of hippies in their facilities. Also, it is common belief that there are laws against driving barefoot, however, no such laws exist. It is quite uncommon for people to be nude in public in the United States, however, there are a few private beaches and resorts that cater to such a population.

Private Dress Codes

Dress codes may be enforced by private entities, usually imposing a particular requirement for entry into a private space. "Dress code" may also refer to a social norm.

- By religious law or tradition
- For employees, pupils/students, etc.-sometimes a uniform; sometimes depending on the day, see Casual Friday;
- For customers, e.g. for a disco, nightclub, casino, shop or restaurant
- In special parties; sometimes a specific costume is requested
- Fetish clubs often require patrons to dress in fetish clothing
- As social rules in general.

Schools worldwide also have dress code. Dress code prevents people from wearing clothing deemed inappropriate by social custom.

Dress codes function on certain social occasions and for certain jobs. A school or a military institution may require specified uniforms; if it allows the wearing of plain clothes it may place restrictions on their use. A bouncer of a disco or nightclub may judge visitors' clothing and refuse entrance to those not clad according to specified or intuited requirements.

Some dress codes specify that tattoos have to be covered.

A "formal" or white tie dress code typically means tail-coats for men and full-length evening dresses for women. "Semi-formal" has a much less precise definition but typically means an evening jacket and tie for men (known as black tie) and a dress for women. "Business casual" typically means not wearing jeans or track suits, but wearing instead collared shirts, and more *country* trousers (not black, but more *relaxed*, including things such as corduroy). "Casual" typically just means clothing for the torso, legs and shoes. "Wedding Casual" defines yet another mode of dress, where guests dress respectfully, but not necessarily fancily. Basically, no jeans and T-shirts.

Transparent or semi-transparent clothing can play with the boundaries of dress-codes regarding modesty. Dress codes usually set forth a lower bound on body covering. However, sometimes it can specify the opposite, for example, in UK gay jargon, *dress code,* means people who dress in a militaristic manner. *Dress code* nights in nightclubs, and elsewhere, are deemed to specifically target people who have militaristic fetishes (e.g. leather/skinhead men).

Work Place

White collar work place clothing has changed through the years. In a corporate office, appropriate clothes are clean, formal clothes such as a shirt, necktie, and suit, or other similar outfits. Previous business dress code eras (the 1950s in the U.S.) featured standardised business clothes that strongly differentiated what was acceptable and unacceptable for men and women to wear while working. Today, the two styles have merged; women's work clothes expanded to include the suit (and its variants) in addition to the usual dresses, skirts, and blouses; men's clothes have expanded to include garments and bright colours.

Casual wear entered corporate culture with the advent of the Silicon Valley, California, technology company featuring informal work clothes on the job. Additionally, some companies set aside days — generally Fridays ("dress-down Friday", "casual Friday")— when workers may wear informal clothes. The clothing a company requires its worker to wear on the job varies with the occupation and profession.

Some businesses observe that anti-discrimination law restricts their determining what is appropriate and inappropriate workplace clothing. Yet, in fact, most businesses have much authority in determining and establishing what work place clothes they can require of their workers. Generally, a carefully drafted dress code applied consistently does not violate anti-discrimination laws.

Business Casual

Business casual dress, also "smart casual", is a popular work place dress code that emerged in white-collar workplaces in Western countries in the 1990s, especially in the United States and Canada. Many information technology businesses in Silicon Valley were early adopters of this dress code. In contrast to formal business wear such as suits and neckties (the international standard business attire), the business casual dress code has no generally-accepted definition; its interpretation differs widely among organizations and is often a cause of sartorial confusion among workers. The job search engine Monster.com offers this definition: *In general, business casual means dressing professionally, looking relaxed, yet neat and pulled together.* A more pragmatic definition is that business casual dress is the mid ground between formal business clothes and street clothes. Examples of clothing combinations considered appropriate for work by businesses that consider themselves as using the business-casual dress code are:

- for men: a shirt with a collar (tennis shirt) and cotton trousers, "khakis": in American English
- for women: a tennis shirt and trousers Generally, neckties are excluded from business casual dress, unless worn in untraditional ways. The acceptability of blue jeans and denim cloth clothing varies — some businesses disallow them as sloppy, not casual, yet tolerate men wearing blue jeans with a sports coat. Long sleeve shirts are also deemed appropriate. however this MUST be worn with a tie.

A survey was conducted to investigate the nature and use of employee dress codes of organizations that market professional services. The study sample consisted of personnel administrators employed in selected service organizations that are members of the American Society of Personnel Administrators; the total sample included 1000 administrators. The analysis of responses revealed that dress is important in marketing services and that compliance to a dress code is a criterion for employee performance evaluation. While most administrators agreed that dress is a significant factor in their companies' success, few organizations had formal written dress codes; dress codes are most often communicated orally. Traditions in the professions, the expectations of customers, Chief Executive Officers of the organizations, and past experiences were the factors that dominate the development of dress codes. On the question of dress code requirements for male vs. female employees, the study revealed that more service organizations specify dress for males than for females. For traditional business attire, comparing the dress codes of the different service organizations revealed several significant relationships.

In recent years much emphasis has been placed on the importance of dress and appearance for professional success. Often organizations make an effort to manage dress and appearance so as to communicate to the client/customer in the most effective manner. Such controls have traditionally been manifested in policies called "dress codes." The responsibility for the administration of dress codes has conventionally been treated as a personal function.

"Proper" business dress has long been a part of the norms of professional services practitioners such as bankers, accountants, stock brokers and management consultants. However, it is interesting to note that in the marketing literature there is little attention devoted to dress as it relates to the marketing of professional services. This is particularly interesting when one considers the growth of professional service industries as a part of the U.S. economy and the broadscale increases in attention focused on services marketing by practitioners and academicians.

The marketing literature does, however, address the issue of personal appearance as it relates to the personal sales interview. It is well documented from a behavioural standpoint that dress has a significant impact upon perception and image formation as a part of the interpersonal communication process. Peak (1986) discovered that when personality traits are correlated with clothing styles, persons who wear conservative clothing are perceived as being more intelligent, mature, generous, sincere, trustful, understanding and dependable than those wearing more "daring" styles. According to Premeaux and Mondy (1987), dress establishes a level of respect and authority. This is often necessary to get the work done. In a study on occupation and grooming (Littrell and Verger, 1986) it was found that less positive characteristics are attributed to those who were groomed "poorly" than to those well groomed.

There is an essential difference between the professional salesperson and the professional service practitioner which underlies the justification of this study. Sales personnel are designated as the "front-line" customer contact persons for an organization which markets goods. Management, as well as salespersons themselves, are not only aware of the role of personal appearance and dress in interpersonal communication, but have employed the resources necessary to incorporate dress codes into promotion and marketing strategies. On the other hand, it is argued that professional service practitioners see themselves as "doers" rather than, sellers" (Bloom, 1984). Therefore, it is felt by some that these employees do not focus the necessary attention on those behavioural factors important in selling or marketing as would designated marketing personnel (Bloom, 1984). As Denny (1981) states:

One of the fundamental misconceptions many accountants have about marketing is that...someone else can bring in the new clients and then they can take over and do the work. Unfortunately they are wrong...It takes an accountant to sell accounting services.

The literature dealing with services marketing lends support to the premise that the dress behavior of employees could be a salient attribute of the buyer when involved in the purchase process of a professional service. Two commonly cited characteristics of services, intangibility and inseparability, give credence to this postulate, as discussed below (Zeithaml, 1985).

Because services are intangible in nature, perceptual and communication problems exist during the exchange process which make the true quality of the service difficult to evaluate and distinguish (Nickels, 1984). Pricing and valuation problems result, leading the buyer to feel uncertainty (Lovelock, 1981). With complex technical services such as legal, financial or consulting research, the problem is magnified because of the lack of knowledge of the buyer (Bloom, 1984). It can be argued that because the buyer cannot see (touch, smell or feel) the true quality of the service for evaluation that he might use surrogate criteria such as the behavior of the practitioner, the physical appearance of the facility or other tangible cues. Dress behavior, then, can become a tangible evaluative criteria for the buyer, regardless of the relationship dress has to the skills of the practitioner or quality of the service performed.

Another theoretical argument offered which distinguishes services from goods is that of inseparability. Often production and consumption of services cannot be separated temporally or spatially (Chase, 1978). Consequently, personal contact exists between the producer and consumer, allowing the buyer to have the perceptual exposure necessary to observe behavioural and physical characteristics of the seller.

The premise set forth as the rationale for this study is that through their behavior, each practitioner in a service organization which has customer/client contact plays a role in marketing that organization's service. Since dress is an important aspect of that behavior which plays a role in the communication process during this interaction, dress behavior can be a salient factor in the exchange process. If this premise is accepted, and dress is perceived to be important in marketing of professional services, then the question of management or control of employee dress arises. One would assume that organizations would make an effort to manage appearance so as to communicate to the client/customer in the most effective manner.

Results

The personnel administrators responding to the questionnaire clearly indicated that appearance of professional employees was a significant factor when a potential client or customer evaluated their company's services.

Of the 304 responding personnel administrators, 73% indicated that a dress code, either formally or informally communicated, had been established for their service organizations. Among those respondents whose organizations employed any type ot dress code, 67% noted that individual employee compliance to the code was a criterion for employee performance evaluation. Eighty-five percent of the respondents indicated that compliance to a dress code was either absolutely necessary or very important when employers underwent performance evaluation.

6

Hotel Resource Management in Hospitality and Tourism

Resource Management: An Introduction

Basic Idea

You have acquired a set of resources, but for you to be effective, you need you to come up with a scheme to use these resources. Remember that you may not have the resources "forever," as it the case with dynamic resources, so you are best advised to make the best of what you have for as long as you have them. Even if the resources are dedicated resources, you still would need a way to ensure high utilization. Resource managers are needed for you to achieve this goal. A typical resource manger uses some sort of a scheduler to ensure proper usage or resources by increasing their utilization. Scheduling is the concept of sharing a scarce resource amongst users without starving any of the users, and at best gives the impression that every user has access to all of what that resource has to offer. This poses a challenge when the numbers of users increase dramatically or the duration of the jobs varies greatly. What makes this challenge even greater is that scheduling problems are mostly NP-Complete, with a very limited number of scenarios that are considered to fall under the P-type problem domain.

Single criterion scheduling are problems where the user is interested in maximizing or minimizing only one thing or criterion (minimize the flow, time, or the completion time). Many scenarios, machine shop or otherwise, require more than criteria to be optimized. For example, on a multi-processing machine, you want to minimize startup time and at the same time minimize completion time of all the tasks. There are times where these two criterions conflict; in other words, you might need to suspend a task, thus delaying its completion time, to start a newly arrived task. The point is that "sacrifices" must be made, and that is the point of heuristic-type algorithms; they aim to minimize the overall sacrifice one has to make to optimize everything near-perfectly. This does not always work, however, but considering the problem domain, it is a very good attempt at solving the unsolvable. As you might expect, scheduling shares a number of ideas from optimization theory.

Quality of Service (QoS) for Grid computing has a special meaning because it no longer applies only to network resources. Compute, data, and network resources together need to be managed and there needs to be a mechanism that provides a quantifiable way of dictating QoS across all three domains. Scheduling systems thus need to take QoS guarantees into account when scheduling tasks across resources and administrative domains. The concept of QoS and data scheduling is further complicated when talking about globally distributed and/or dense systems where scheduling becomes more difficult; therefore, meeting QoS guarantees becomes even more complex.

Think of an operating system and how it schedules various threads or processes on the CPU. As the number of CPUs increase, the problem becomes more difficult, but the concept is still the same. These are a number of different scheduling algorithms, but I will not cover them in this article. The main focus here is to break down a resource manager into its core components, and talk about how these components work together to achieve a single goal: high resource utilization.

Resource Manager Components

Conceptually speaking, the resource manager is very simple:

- Queue incoming tasks
- Keep a record of available resources
- Match resources with the incoming tasks (scheduler)
- Queue results.

I am not saying that it is easy to design or write a resource manager, however, but from a conceptual standpoint it is a simple enough design that you can relate to. There are a number of ways that this architecture can be realized, but the one thing you need to keep in mind here is that network queuing theory plays a major role here. If you have an influx of tasks that is greater than the speed that your processing engine is able to off-load, the client queue will get backed up and you will start to lose tasks. This is the same behavior if you were to talk about a router placed in a network with large amounts of data transfer. Congestion control is implicit in the case of a resource manager as the resources will only be ready and request to process the next task when the current task has already been completed. This makes our understanding of the environment a little easier as if we were seeing a backlog of tasks waiting to be processed, this is a clear indication that we need only to add more resources to assist with the heavy load of the incoming tasks.

Your goal in this article is not to build a resource manager, but rather have a clear and better understanding of how one actually works and what its main components are. Focus a bit on the overall flow. You will delve into the details in the subsequent sections.

The flow is something like the following:

1. Resources log on to the Grid resource manager.
2. Basic resource information is sent to the resource manager such as OS type, amount of free memory, number of CPUs, and a number of other parameters based on the Resource Manager involved.
3. Data and any updates as synchronized between the resource manager and the resource.
4. Resource goes in to a waiting queue ready to be assigned a task.
5. The resource manager updates the table of available resources with the new resource.
6. The scheduling engine assigns a task to the resource if and when a new task is available.
7. The resource gets the task and the data, loads the appropriate service, and executes the task.
8. The task result is sent back to the client.
9. The resource is ready for another task.

Changes in Asian HRM

Ten years ago, Human Resource Management was almost an unknown term in Asia. Training, selection, and performance appraisal were given very short shrift, and staff specialists, when they existed, were known as Personnel Managers, or had a dual role of Administration Manager with a "Personnel" tag thrown in for good measure.

Back in those days, Asian companies were not aware of how effective management of the human resource had a major bearing on the bottom line. The educational sector gave little support. Professional associations were fledgling to say the least. A "personnel" position was often something in which you ended up in after failing to make sales, and seen as a dead end position. The National University of Singapore, the government anointed showcase of an Asian university did not offer one unit in psychology. China funded anything to do with science and technology, but soft sciences such as management and HRM were ignored.

Part of this was due of course to the culture of staffing of Asian business. *Guanxi* reigned supreme in staffing decisions, with family controlled companies meaning promotion was often the sole prerogative of family members. Cash reigned supreme as a way of evaluating jobs, where opportunities for professional development, training, and knowledge acquirement played very much the second fiddle to the salary level and perks. Objective rating of performance in many companies was therefore irrelevant, even if there was the competence to perform it well.

The bubble economy decade, where for many companies profits and growth were assured despite the competence (or incompetence) of management, effectively masked the growing malaise of Asian organizations. The signs were there, as a review of the past items on the Chao Phraya River Rat would attest. Over five years, the Rat's column drew attention to monstrous staff turnover rates, which meant that any investment in development or training was to naught anyway, as staff were likely to leave any time for a job which paid a few dollars extra, and often in an industry or function totally unrelated. We referred to the unsustainability of professional and management salaries, and salary packages and perquisites so over valued and out-of-kilter with other economies that warning bells about an Asian crisis should have re sounded well before that fateful day in June.

In the meantime, interest in MBA and professional qualifications was increasing, and appealed to many for the prestige and authority they bestowed on the holder. However, these qualifications rarely integrated well with individual and organizational career and skills development, and were valued as status symbols rather than an experience that "added value" to the real worth of an individual to an organization. The race for the MBA merely added costs to a companies payroll (in having to pay extra for the perceived value of an MBA, or sponsoring studies) with limited real benefit to the bottom line.

This week's election of articles that focus on Human Resource Management however, demonstrate that things are indeed changing. Companies and researchers are looking seriously at how effective Human Resource Management and Human Resource Development can build more substantial organizations than those that stumbled badly during the Asian crisis, where poor attendance to training, staff development, selection, and performance appraisal finally wrought it's savage consequences.

Some of the best articles this week, focus on the difference between effective Human Resource Management in Asia compared to the West, where many of the principles were conceived and developed.

Causes of Organizational Change

This is a time of unprecedented change in our society. The changes one experiences are happening at faster and faster rates. As examples, the telephone, radio, TV, and microwave weren't even in use decades ago, and today these gadgets are commonplace, along with the computer, Internet, and fax machine.

In just a few months, the technology that an organization uses on an everyday basis may be outdated and replaced. That means an organization needs to be responsive to advances in the technological environment; its employees' work skills must evolve as technology evolves. Organizations that refuse to adapt are likely to be the ones that won't be around in a few short years. If an organization wants to survive and prosper, its managers must continually innovate and adapt to new situations.

Every organization goes through periods of transformation that can cause stress and uncertainty. To be successful, organizations must embrace many types of change. Businesses must develop improved production technologies, create new products desired in the marketplace, implement new administrative systems, and upgrade employees' skills. Organizations that adapt successfully are both profitable and admired.

Managers must contend with all factors that affect their organizations. The following lists internal and external environmental factors that can encourage organizational changes:

- The external environment is affected by political, social, technological, and economic stimuli outside of the organization that cause changes.
- The internal environment is affected by the organization's management policies and styles, systems, and procedures, as well as employee attitudes.

Typically, the concept of organizational change is used to describe organization-wide change, as opposed to smaller changes such as adding a new person, modifying a program, and so on. Examples of organization-wide change might include a change in mission, restructuring operations (for example, restructuring to self-managed teams or due to layoffs), new technologies, mergers, or new programs such as Total Quality Management, re-engineering, and so on.

Managers should note that all changes should be implemented as part of a strategy to accomplish an overall goal; these transformations should not take place just for the sake of change.

Solving Operational Problems in Performance Management Schemes

This essay identifies some common difficulties in performance management schemes.

Firstly, we will analyse root cause of these problems so as to gain a deeper insight into its complexity. This is followed by some suggestions for solving these problems. The problems are selected from various stages of the performance management cycle so as to provide an overview of the functioning of the performance management scheme.

The six problems discussed are as follows:-

- The problem of employees' opposition and rejection to the performance management scheme.
- The problem of non-involvement of the CEO during implementation of the scheme.
- Difficulties caused by unstable strategic goals in employees' appraisal and reward determination.
- Difficulties in the operations of performance appraisal.
- Weakness in the feedback mechanism.
- Weaknesses in the performance-related pay scheme.

Various forms of performance management schemes are commonly prescribed for the modern organisation with the objective of effecting continuous performance improvement. However, the studies of Bevan and Thomson (1996) as well as Guest and Peccei (1994) have failed to show conclusive evidence that the use of performance management schemes have actually resulted in performance improvement. Granted it is difficult to demonstrate the cause-effect between performance management and performance improvement. Other factors, both intrinsic and extrinsic, exert their influences on the organisation's performance. However, the lack of verifiable results does cause one to question the theory. Another possibility for the lack of clear success could be the faulty or half-hearted implementation of the scheme in the work place.

A common difficulty encountered during the introduction of performance management scheme is the employees' opposition and rejection of the performance management scheme.

The introduction of performance management scheme represents a radical change to the organisation. Not only does it seek to change the organisational culture, it also alters the employee's psychological contract. In practice, performance management schemes which are hastily introduced often fail because of lack of cooperation from the employees.

Cummings and Worley (1993) tells us that generally most employees do not support change as it entails moving from the known to the unknown. However, the employees may support the change if they perceived there are good reasons for them to do so.

To ensure effective integration and acceptance of the performance management scheme into the organisation, there is a need to prepare the mindset of both management and employees before launching the scheme. Firstly, senior and middle management should invest sufficient time to research and understand the full intricacies of the scheme. A study on the potential effects of the scheme on the workforce and also operations would be useful for anticipating problems later. Ultimately, the management team, especially the CEO, must be truly converted to the benefits of the scheme, or else they would be unable to convince the rest of the organisation.

As the employee dislike moving into the unknown, providing them information on the scheme through training and seminars will allay their fears and doubts. The training for both management and employees should cover skills such as setting objectives, measuring performance, appraising performance, giving feedback, motivating, coaching and counseling.

Another difficulty faced by some organisations is the non-involvement of the CEO during traumatic period of implementation. As the performance management scheme changes the work culture and the psychological contract, the employees may feel disorientated and demoralized.

Studies conducted by Sparrow and Hiltrop (1994) showed that 90% of senior management have not received performance appraisals in the last two years. The non-participation of senior management in the process, which supposedly they endorsed, sends out the wrong signal to employees on the importance of the scheme.

In practice, the CEO may moot the idea of a performance management scheme. However, the personnel department (sometimes with the assistance of an external consultant), are often given the task of designing the scheme. Therefore, ownership of the performance management scheme remains solely with the personnel department. Implementation of the scheme is delegated to line managers, who lack the know-how, commitment, authority and enthusiasm to get the scheme to work.

The employee's perception of the CEO's commitment is vital for the acceptance of the scheme within the organisation. The CEO should be highly visible in his role as champion of the scheme. The emphasis on performance should continually be reiterated in the CEO's daily dealings with his employees. If the employees sense that their CEO is uncertain about the scheme, some of them will attempt to undermine its implementation.

Most employees are not naturally motivated toward high performance as it entails much effort. Therefore, if performance is to become ingrained into the work culture, the CEO must lead the rest of the organisation towards improvement.

The CEO, due to his privileged position at the top of the organisation hierarchy, can inspire, motivate, assure and move his followers to accept difficult changes. He is able to silence sceptics, promote speedy adoption of the scheme and instil the required discipline for the maintenance of the scheme.

The unstable nature of strategic goals can cause difficulties in employee's appraisal and reward determination

To ensure alignment of an individual's performance objectives with the overall organisation strategic plans, Beardwell and Holden (2001) propose that performance objectives be cascaded from overall business strategy.

Stiles et al. (1997)'s research shows that linking performance objectives to strategic goals can result in performance objectives having a short-term focus. Strategic goals are becoming increasingly unstable as the organisation responds to the changes in the external environment. Therefore, performance targets or even the objectives themselves may be changed midpoint due to the change in business strategy.

Appraising the employee's performance and calculating the reward becomes complicated. The employee may have put in effort to achieve the obsolete performance objective. However, as the business strategy has changed, his effort did not contribute to organisational performance. In practice, many organisations will not pay out reward for the employee's effort.

I believe that fair play must always prevail, or the employees will be disillusioned and loose faith in the scheme. Before setting new performance objectives, the manager should make an assessment of the employee's achievement thus far in relations to the obsolete performance objective. A fair amount of incentive should be paid to the employee in recognition of his effort. The manager should then re-negotiate the new performance objectives, targets and expected rewards.

In my opinion, senior management should realize that there are costs incurred whenever the business strategy is changed midpoint. It would not be fair to ask the employee to bear even a small portion of this cost

There are difficulties in the operation of performance appraisal.

Lawler et al. (1984) described performance appraisal as an unpleasant activity, which is despised by managers and supervisor. While Napier and Latham (1986) suggested employees often see no value in the performance appraisal interview and feel that it does not have a significant influence on their performance or development.

I consider the above-mentioned perceptions to be overly severe. In contrary, performance appraisal continues to be the most popular method of assessing employee's performance. Most managers and employees approach it with a sense of anticipation and high expectation as it effects the pay packet.

However, due to a major flaw in its construct, many managers and employees alike may have some doubts about its effectiveness. The performance appraisal has two main objectives which are in conflict.

The performance appraisal's first objective is to assess the employee's past performance for the purpose of determining rewards or promotions, while the second objective is to plan for the development and improvement of the employee. McGregor (1957) rightfully pointed out that the appraiser is often unable to resolve the conflicting roles of "disciplinary judge" and "helpful counsellor".

It is difficult to perform the first role (disciplinary judge) well without affecting the other. In his first role, the appraiser may have to give a negative but fair assessment of the employee's performance. However, he risks ruining the good working relationship he has with the employee. A good working relationship build on trust is vital for the appraiser to be effective in his second role of "helpful counsellor". Additionally, most employees are reluctant to report serious problems at work during the appraisal. Understandably, there is genuine fear that the work problems may be construed as the employee's weaknesses or poor performance. In practice, appraisers often compromise on the evaluations in a futile attempt to fulfil both objectives.

I concur with Randell (1973) who argues that the reward review should be separated from the performance review in terms of operation and documentation. Therefore, the solution is a re-design of the performance appraisal. Two separate reviews with a different focus to resolve the appraiser's dilemma of conflicting roles.

The developmental review focuses on improving the work performance of the employee. It should be held regularly, at least once a month, between the employee and his direct manager. During the review, the manager will provide the necessary coaching and counselling to the employee.

Feedback on the work performance is both requested for and given to the employee. Training and developmental issues are discussed with the employee. The employee's performance targets and successes to date are reviewed. Notable accomplishment are recognized and recorded in the meeting. A small incentive payment can be made immediately to motivate the employee.

The reward review may be held less frequently or once a year. It is held to decide on the employee's annual increment, bonuses or promotion. I propose that the appraiser for the reward review be the manager's immediate superior.

The manager's presence in the reward review shall be to support the employee's case for the reward. He confirms the accomplishments of the employee during the previous year. The manager's new role placed him on the same side as the employee. This arrangement promotes openness, strengthens working relationship and increases mutual respect between employee and manager.

There is an inherent weakness in the feedback mechanism of a performance management scheme. Feedback is an indispensable control mechanism for performance management. In practice,

Folger and Cropanzano (1998) pointed out that most managers dislike giving negative feedback during the performance appraisal interview and are not skilled in providing it.

The lack of skill in giving feedback causes the following problems in the workplace. Feedback is often too positively biased and therefore inaccurate. Work problems remain unsolved as managers avoid passing negative feedback to the employee. Consequently, the employee remains unaware of his own weaknesses and mistakes.

On the other hand, a poorly delivered criticism can cause the employee to be severely de-motivated. Disagreement over the feedback can result in tension or poor working relationship between the manager and the employee.

There are contradictory views on feedback and its effect on the motivation. Hackman and Oldham (1980) suggest that performance feedback increase job satisfaction and motivation. However, Bratton and Gold (1999) disagree and state that feedback has a definite influence in the de-motivation of employees. In my opinion, both the perspectives can be correct depending on the circumstances. However, I am an optimist leaning more towards Hackman and Oldham's perspective.

My suggestions for improving the feedback mechanism are as follows. Training in effective communications, motivation and human relation skills should be given to all managers.

Additionally, there should be two separate reviews, which is the reward review and developmental review. Feedbacks given during developmental reviews are more likely to be received positively, as the manager is playing the role of "helpful counsellor".

Lastly, I wish to suggest a few practical methods on giving feedback. One way is to re-phrase the feedback as suggestions for improvement. Another method is to guide the employee using non-threatening questions to discover the problem by himself. However, if the manager's relationship with the employee is excellent, the direct approach would always be preferred.

Performance-related pay scheme in its most common form has the following weaknesses: long time delay between performance and reward, unable to reinforce positive behaviour patterns and non-sustainable use of pay rise as reward.

Performance-related pay seems to be the most common remuneration scheme for an organisation implementing performance management. In performance-related pay the employee's financial rewards are link to the achievement of performance targets. In the ensuing paragraphs I will suggest some practical improvement to this remuneration scheme.

In practice, most organisations mete out rewards (such as promotions, salary increase or bonus payment) or punishment (such as demotion, salary freeze, no bonus or reprimand) after the annual performance appraisal.

Although significant accomplishments and critical failures are recorded throughout the year, reward and punishment are delayed until the end of the year.

My criticism is that this delay weakens the employee's perception of a link between measured performance and reward. According to Mabey and Salaman (1995), the employee's perception of the link between measured performance and reward are crucial to the success of the performance management system.

The reward or punishment meted out reinforces the overall contribution of the employee, which is an aggregation of both accomplishments and failures for the year. My criticism is that this arrangement is unable to provide the direct link between positive behaviour patterns to the reward.

According to Torrington and Hall (1998), an organisation using pay rise to motivate employee may be facing an escalating financial burden. The organisation faces the danger of an "inflationary spiral" as it takes an ever-increasing quantum of pay increase to maintain the same level of high performance.

My criticism is that the use of pay rise as reward is not sustainable in the long term. An organisation cannot afford to pay high staff overheads in a sluggish economy.

In most schemes, even poor performers will get a pay adjustment to counter inflation. The employee is often not told the percentage of the pay rise, which is inflation related. My criticism is that the link between performance and pay rise (reward) becomes obscured. The problem is compounded by the fact that each employee's pay and quantum of pay rise are considered private and confidential information. Therefore an employee is unable to justify or compare his reward against that of his colleague.

I would like to suggest some changes to the performance-related pay scheme. In the re-designed scheme, the manager is allocated an annual budget for his department's reward payments. The manager and his superior shall negotiate the amount of the reward budget during the setting of the department's performance objectives. The manager shall be given the authority to disburse the budget amount with the intention of motivating performance in his department.

However, the amount that is eventually utilized for the year must correlate to department's success in meeting its performance objective. If the department is deemed to have achieve 50% of the set target, then 50% of the budget can be disburse as rewards to the employees. Amount not used at the end of the year may be distributed as bonus payments to deserving employees.

When an employee accomplishes significant success, the manager shall record the accomplishment in the developmental review and immediately reward the employee with an incentive payment. Applying Thorndike's Law of Effect, the immediate reward will reinforce the employee's positive behaviour pattern.

The re-designed performance-related pay scheme offers the following advantages.

Firstly, since reward is given immediately upon recording performance, a clear link between performance and its corresponding reward is established.

Secondly, correct behavior patterns that lead to success are positively reinforced.

Thirdly, the financial costs for the reward scheme are pre-determined and non-escalating.

Fourthly, it can be assumed that the manager will ensure effective distribution of the incentives so as to achieve the best possible performance.

Fifth, the autonomy given to the manager to reward will increase the manager's authority and control over his department.

However, the re-designed scheme is not able to remove the subjectivity that is inherent in performance-related pay schemes. The manager's decision on the distribution of reward can be subjective.

Therefore, some employees may complaint of favouritism and unfairness. A possible solution is to have the manager's superior verify any reward decision. Ultimately, the manager is forced to demonstrate fairness, as a demoralized department will not meet its performance targets.

From our analysis above, we have learnt the following.

Firstly, the employees' rejection and opposition to the introduction of a performance management scheme can be reduced by providing training and seminar before the launch of the scheme.

Secondly, the CEO plays an important role during the implementation of the scheme.

Thirdly, the employee should be rewarded for his effort should the performance objectives be changed midpoint.

Fourthly, the effectiveness of the performance appraisal can be improved by having separate reviews for reward and employee development.

Fifthly, training in effective communications, motivation and human relation skills can improve the effectiveness of the feedback mechanism.

Lastly, the performance-related pay scheme can be improved by paying immediate reward when achievement is recorded. Cash incentives are more viable as reward compared to pay rise which is not sustainable over the long term.

HR Professionals in Managing Performance of Hotel

The management of people is the most critical component of an organisation's ability to implement its strategy effectively and compete in an increasingly complex and dynamic global economy.

For organisations, and HR departments in particular, understanding the international context in which you and your company operate is more important now than ever before with reorganisation demands driven by the marketplace. HR must ensure they are in a position to manage a more globally dispersed workforce and support international business growth within their organisation.

To succeed in the global marketplace, HR must act at a strategic business partner with a thorough understanding of the organisation's big picture and be able to influence key decisions and policies. Recruiting in different talent markets; implementing a global reward strategy; and ensuring effective talent and performance management are just some of the challenges facing HR, not to mention complying with local employment law and practice.

The lodging industry, routinely dealing with employee turnover rates as high as nearly 160 percent for some employees, has also had to deal with the downturn in revenues attributed to the economy's sluggishness and the terrorist attacks. As a result, hotel companies across the spectrum—from resort complexes to moderately priced facilities-have to work harder to win travellers' business.

Booking beds comes down to quality of service, according to HR professionals in the hotel industry. "We're only as good as our staff," says Nicola Thomson, director of management, recruiting and selection for Toronto-based Four Seasons Hotels & Resorts. "If we don't have people who want to serve and are good at it, we are not successful."

To foster a service orientation in lower-paid employees—and to keep the best people and reduce costly turnover—hotel companies are adopting incentives that range from bonuses, recognition and transportation assistance to programs that offer training and advancement.

The First Steps

Retaining good employees, industry observers say, depends on recruiting and hiring the most suitable job candidates. Although the applicant pool has expanded during the current economic slowdown, it's still not necessarily easy to find the right people for the jobs, particularly for low-skill, entry-level spots such as housekeeping. In the hospitality industry, unlike other businesses, job competency isn't enough. Hotels require employees to be, well, hospitable. Expressing an opinion shared by many HR professionals for hotel companies, Welzel says: "You can teach skills—how to make a bed, how to answer the phone—but you can't teach people to smile. The single best indicator of whether someone will work here is: Are they friendly? If so, we hire them and will work with them to attain specific skills."

A proven approach in recruiting is a referral program. Under a program that Welzel introduced at Classic Hospitality, an employee who refers someone who is hired and stays on the job for six months gets an extra week's salary.

Another way to attract job candidates is to highlight a hotel's attributes. For example, at the new Washington Terrace Hotel, a downtown property that used to be a Doubletree and that underwent a $14-million renovation, General Manager Peter Carroll has hired many of the former Doubletree employees. He increased service demands but didn't have to increase pay. "It's a matter of pride for the employees" to be able to say they work at the Washington Terrace, he says.

In Denver, one of the hospitality industry's fastest-growing markets, strong competition for workers prompted the Denver Marriott to get creative in its recruiting.

The hotel started "partnering with local schools for interns and trainees, doing alternative advertising [such as on buses that serve low-income neighborhoods] and recruiting people with disabilities," a traditionally underemployed segment of the population, says Rebecca Peralta, PHR, director of human resources.

Although hotels in more remote locations usually don't have those kinds of community resources to tap, they can take advantage of their strengths.

The Woolverton Inn, a small, upscale property near Stockton, N.J., and not far from Pennsylvania s Bucks County attractions, highlights its pastoral setting as a pleasant place to work. "We are not near a big city, so we can't attract a big number of people" says coowner Matthew Lovette, who handles HR for the business.

"We make it a point to do public relations in the community. We run local ads and get the local papers to do articles on us so we get out in front of potential employees. Our strategy has worked.

We literally have people walking up the hill and asking for jobs because they've heard about us'

Although a remote location can he a headache for attracting job candidates, devising a solution for the problem can prove to be a plus for retaining good employees. When the Four Seasons organization opened its Scottsdale, Ariz., resort three years ago, inadequate public transportation virtually ruled out workers who didn't have cars.

"The bus from Phoenix took 45 minutes and dropped people off about two miles from the hotel," explains corporate recruiting director Thomson, who helped open the property. "What we wound up doing is arranging our own bus service to pick up employees in Phoenix and take them to our door," she says.

That solution not only filled jobs but also launched new Four Seasons careers. "Many people who came to work with us were Croatian refugees, who have stayed and worked their way up to supervisory positions," Thomson says.

Keeping the Best

Four Seasons promotes internally when possible, Thomson notes, and that's believed to be a major reason that the company has some of the industry's lowest turnover rates—25 percent for all Four Seasons employees, 19 percent for managers. Turnover rates throughout the industry, according to the American Hotel & Motel Association, are 158 percent for front-line employees and 129 percent for managers.

Carol Etheridge, HR director for Bermuda-based Orient-Express Hotels Ltd., which owns or runs 41 leisure properties in 16 countries, and who currently serves as acting HR director of Charleston Place in Charleston, S.C., says, "When we find great employees and we find out they want to stay, well, we do everything we can to make that happen."

A retention program at Charleston Place, called Trading Places, enables employees to train in other departments at full pay for three weeks. Delores Collins, who started as a housekeeper at the hotel in 1993, expressed interest in working at the front desk and entered the program. Six months after completing her training, she was hired for ajob in reservations.

For Orient-Express, anecdotal evidence—stories such as Collins' and those of other employees—has added up. Etheridge now travels to all Orient-Express locations in North America to ensure that each property has strong retention programs in place. "Every property is different, so we don't expect them to duplicate what we did at Charleston Place;' she says. "But we do expect every property to have a component like it."

It's Not Always About Salary

With lodging industry revenues under pressure, many hotel companies say they can't afford to use salary increases as a retention tool. "We can only go so high in terms of what we pay housekeepers," says the Woolverton Inn's Lovette. "We've come up with other ideas of ways to recognize people, like our Room Check program."

At Charleston Place, Etheridge established the WOW! Program, which encourages co-workers to recognize outstanding service. Employees give one another WOW! certificates, which ultimately add up to companywide recognition, a gala and travel prizes.

Informal recognition is important, too. "I'm a big believer in empowerment," says Etheridge. "I always tell employees, 'I'm the HR expert; you're the expert at what you do.' I put the power in their hands and say 'I trust you.

That pays off." Etheridge cites an instance in which a housekeeper overheard two guests talking about how they were celebrating their anniversary at the hotel. The housekeeper had a complimentary bottle of champagne sent to their room as a congratulatory gesture on behalf of the hotel. "It cost that housekeeper nothing," Etheridge says. "She made a $50 tip, and she made the hotel look great."

Classic Hospitality throws an annual holiday party for employees. "It's important to us that spouses and children come too, so that everyone feels included in this hotel family," says HR director Welzel. She believes that the company's emphasis on a personal connection between employees and the hotels is the prime reason retention rates are so strong. Forty-three percent of employees have been with the organization for three or more years, for example. "We have several housekeepers, beverage servers and engineers who have worked for us for over 20 years," she adds.

Bringing employees together also goes a long way in keeping them with the hotel. "Every year we do something special to show them and their families how much we appreciate their work," says the Woolverton Inn's Lovette. Recently the company took its staff to New York for dinner and a Broadway show. Overall, the Woolverton's multiple retention efforts have paid off: The inn has had no employee turnover in the past 12 months.

"Treat people the way you expect hotel guests to be treated," says Thomson. "Do that and you will attract great employees and keep most of them."

Hotel and Restaurant Law

The hospitality industry is affected by the law in a multitude of ways, whether one operates a restaurant, hotel, resort, or hotel and restaurant destinations. To be successful in the hospitality industry, business managers must make informed decisions, engaging in preventative management by knowing how to avoid legal problems in carrying out their duties.

7

Hospitality and Tourism Management Systems

Hospitality and Tourism Management (HTM) is a multidisciplinary field of study with the purpose of preparing people with the expertise, commitment, and skills for management, marketing, and operations positions in the expanding industry that provides food, accommodations, and tourism services to people away from home. As a field of study, Hospitality and Tourism Management is interdisciplinary. It draws upon a wide range of basic disciplines to provide the fundamental knowledge and skills that are required to fulfill the diverse demands placed upon individuals in management positions within the hospitality industry.

Tourism and Hospitality

Tourism and Hospitality in India

As per the Travel and Tourism Competitiveness Report 2009 by the World Economic Forum, India is ranked 11th in the Asia Pacific region and 62nd overall, moving up three places on the list of the world's attractive destinations. It is ranked the 14th best tourist destination for its natural resources and 24th for its cultural resources, with many World Heritage sites, both natural and cultural, rich fauna, and strong creative industries in the country. India also bagged 37th rank for its air transport network. The India travel and tourism industry ranked 5th in the long-term (10-year) growth and is expected to be the second largest employer in the world by 2019.

India has been ranked the "best country brand for value-for-money" in the Country Brand Index (CBI) survey conducted by FutureBrand, a leading global brand consultancy.

India also claimed the second place in CBI's "best country brand for history", as well as appears among the top 5 in the best country brand for authenticity and art & culture, and the fourth best new country for business. India made it to the list of "rising stars" or the countries that are likely to become major tourist destinations in the next five years, led by the United Arab Emirates, China, and Vietnam.

Contribution to the Economy

According to the Travel & Tourism Competitiveness Report 2009 brought out by the World Economic Forum, the contribution of travel and tourism to gross domestic product (GDP) is expected to be at US$ 187.3 billion by 2019.

The report also states that real GDP growth for travel and tourism economy is expected to achieve an average of 7.7 per cent per annum over the next 10 years.

Export earnings from international visitors and tourism goods are expected to generate US$ 51.4 billion (nominal terms) by 2019. The travel and tourism sector which accounted for 6.4 per cent of total employment in 2009 is expected to generate 40,037,000 jobs i.e. 7.2 per cent of total employment by 2019.

Foreign Tourist Arrivals

Estimates of foreign tourist arrivals (FTAs) and foreign exchange earnings (FEE) are important indicators of the tourism sector.

According to the latest data released by the Ministry of Tourism, FTAs during January 2010 were 491,000 as compared to 422,000 in January 2009, an increase of 16.4 per cent. FEE in US$ terms during January 2010 were US$ 1.21 billion as compared to US$ 941 million in January 2009, a growth of 29.1 per cent.

Moreover, to give a further boost to the tourist arrivals, the Indian Association of Tour Operators (IATO) has drawn up plans to hold roadshows in the US, UK, European Union nations and Australia in 2010 to hard sell India as a tourist hub.

Government Initiative

The campaign 'Visit India Year 2009' was launched at the International Tourism Exchange in Berlin, aimed to project India as an attractive destination for holidaymakers. The government joined hands with leading airlines, hoteliers, holiday resorts and tour operators, and offered them a wide range of incentives and bonuses during the period between April and December, 2009.

Euromonitor International's Travel And Tourism in India report states that the Government of India increased spend on advertising campaigns (including for the campaigns 'Incredible India' and 'Ahithi Devo Bhava'-Visitors are like God) to reinforce the rich variety of tourism in India.

The ministry promoted India as a safe tourist destination and undertook various measures, such as stepping up vigilance in key cities and at historically important tourist sites. It also deployed increased manpower and resources for improving security checks at key airports and railway stations.

Medical Tourism

Despite the economic slowdown, medical tourism in India is the fastest growing segment of tourism industry, according to the market research report "Booming Medical Tourism in India". The report adds that India offers a great potential in the medical tourism industry. Factors such as low cost, scale and range of treatments provided in the country add to its attractiveness as a medical tourism destination.

In addition to the existence of modern medicine, indigenous medical practitioners are providing their services across the country with more than 3,000 hospitals and 726,000 registered practitioners catering to the needs of traditional Indian healthcare. A number of Indian hotels will tie up with professional organisations in a range of wellness fields to enter the wellness services market.

According to a report by RNCOS, medical tourism will grow at a CAGR of over 27 per cent in the period 2009–12 to generate revenues worth US$ 2.4 billion by 2012. The number of medical tourists is anticipated to grow at a CAGR of over 19 per cent to reach 1.1 million by 2012. The report adds that India's share in the global medical tourism industry will climb to around 2.4 per cent by the end of 2012.

Hospitality

The Indian hotel industry is adding over 90,000 more rooms across the country in the next five years to meet the demand. The contribution of the hotel industry to the country's GDP was 6.1 per cent in 2008-09.

- Carlson Group, the global hospitality chain, is bringing its luxury hotel brand Regent to India and has signed an agreement with real estate firm, Pioneer Urban Land and Infrastructure, which will invest US$ 49.97 million for building the first Regent hotel in Gurgaon that will open in 2013.
- The Leela plans to open six more properties by 2013, taking the total number of hotels to 12.
- ITC Ltd expects to add 8-10 hotels in India in the next 3-5 years to the existing 110 that it currently operates.
- The Thailand-based hospitality major, Amari, plans to foray into the Indian market by setting up seven four-star hotels near major airports in the country.

The Road Ahead

According to the latest Tourism Satellite Accounting (TSA) research, released by the World Travel and Tourism Council (WTTC) and its strategic partner Oxford Economics in March 2009:

- The demand for travel and tourism in India is expected to grow by 8.2 per cent between 2010 and 2019 and will place India at the third position in the world.
- India's travel and tourism sector is expected to be the second largest employer in the world, employing 40,037,000 by 2019.
- Capital investment in India's travel and tourism sector is expected to grow at 8.8 per cent between 2010 and 2019.
- The report forecasts India to get capital investment worth US$ 94.5 billion in the travel and tourism sector in 2019.
- India is projected to become the fifth fastest growing business travel destination from 2010-2019 with an estimated real growth rate of 7.6 per cent.

- Preparing for the 2010 Commonwealth Games in Delhi, the Tourism Ministry is exploring the provision of tented accommodation to tourists in Faridabad and Surajkund in nearby Haryana.

According to *World Travel and Tourism Council,* India will be a tourism hotspot from 2009-2018, having the highest 10-year growth potential. The *Travel & Tourism Competitiveness Report 2007* ranked tourism in India 6th in terms of price competitiveness and 39th in terms of safety and security. Despite short-and medium-term setbacks, such as shortage of hotel rooms, tourism revenues are expected to surge by 42% from 2007 to 2017.

Tourism by State

Andhra Pradesh

Andhra Pradesh has a rich cultural heritage and a variety of tourist attractions. The state of Andhra Pradesh comprises scenic hills, forests, beaches and temples. Also known as *The City of Nizams* and *The City of Pearls,* Hyderabad is today one of the most developed cities in the country and a modern hub of information technology, ITES, and biotechnology. Hyderabad is known for its rich history, culture and architecture representing its unique character as a meeting point for North and South India, and also its multilingual culture, both geographically and culturally.

Andhra Pradesh is the home of many religious pilgrim centres. Tirupati, the abode of Lord Venkateswara, is the richest and most visited religious centre (of any faith) in the world. Srisailam, the abode of Sri Mallikarjuna, is one of twelve Jyothirlingalu in India, Amaravati's Siva temple is one of the Pancharamams, and Yadagirigutta, the abode of an avatara of Vishnu, Sri Lakshmi Narasimha. The Ramappa temple and Thousand Pillars temple in Warangal are famous for some fine temple carvings. The state has numerous Buddhist centres at Amaravati, Nagarjuna Konda, Bhattiprolu, Ghantasala, Nelakondapalli, Dhulikatta, Bavikonda, Thotlakonda, Shalihundam, Pavuralakonda, Sankaram, Phanigiri and Kolanpaka.

The golden beaches at Visakhapatnam, the one-million-year old limestone caves at Borra, picturesque Araku Valley, hill resorts of Horsley Hills, river Godavari racing through a narrow gorge at Papi Kondalu, waterfalls at Ettipotala, Kuntala and rich biodiversity at Talakona, are some of the natural attractions of the state. Visakhapatnam is home to many tourist attactions such as the INS Karasura Submarine museum (The only one of its kind in India), Yarada Beach, Araku Valley, VUDA Park, Indira Gandhi Zoological Gardens.

The weather in Andhra Pradesh is mostly tropical and the best time to visit is in November through to January. The monsoon season commences in June and ends in September, so travel would not be advisable during this period.

Assam

Assam is the central state in the North-East Region of India and serves as the gateway to the rest of the Seven Sister States. Assam boasts of famous wildlife preserves – the Kaziranga National Park and the Manas National Park, the largest river island Majuli, and tea-estates dating back to time of British Raj.

The weather is mostly sub-tropical. Assam experiences the Indian monsoon and has one of the highest forest densities in India. The winter months (October to April) are the best time to visit.

Assam has a rich cultural heritage going back to the Ahom Kingdom which governed the region for many centuries before the British occupation. Other notable features include the Brahmaputra River, the mystery of the bird suicides in Jatinga, numerous temples including Kamakhya of Tantric sect, ruins of palaces, etc. Guwahati, the capital city of Assam, boasts many bazaars, temples, and wildlife sanctuaries.

Bihar

Bihar is one of the oldest continuously inhabited places in the world with history of 3000 years. The rich culture and heritage of Bihar is evident from the innumerable ancient monuments that are dotted all over this state in eastern India. This is the Place of Aryabhatta, Great Ashoka, Chanakya and many more.

Bihar is one of the most sacred places of various religions such as Hinduism, Buddhism, Jainism, Sikhism & Islam. Famous Attraction includes Mahabodhi Temple, a Buddhist shrine and UNESCO World Heritage Site is also situated in Bihar, Barabar Caves the oldest rockcut caves in India, Khuda Bakhsh Oriental Library the Oldest Library of India.

Delhi

Delhi is the capital city of India. A fine blend of old and new, ancient and modern, Delhi is a melting pot of cultures, religions. Delhi has been the capital of numerous empires that ruled India, making it rich in history.

The rulers left behind their trademark architectural styles. Delhi currently has many renowned historic monuments and landmarks such as the Tughlaqabad fort, Qutub Minar, Purana Quila, Lodhi Gardens, Jama Masjid, Humayun's tomb, Red Fort, and Safdarjung's Tomb. Modern monuments include Jantar Mantar, India Gate, Rashtrapati Bhavan, Laxminarayan Temple, Lotus temple and Akshardham Temple.

New Delhi is famous for its British colonial architecture, wide roads, and tree-lined boulevards. Delhi is home to numerous political landmarks, national museums, Islamic shrines, Hindu temples, green parks, and trendy malls.

Goa

Goa is one of the most famous tourist destinations in India. A former colony of Portugal, Goa is famous for its excellent beaches, Portuguese churches, Hindu temples, and wildlife sanctuaries. The Basilica of Bom Jesus, Mangueshi Temple, Dudhsagar Falls, and Shantadurga are famous attractions in Goa. Recently a Wax Museum (Wax World) has also opened in Old Goa housing a number of wax personalities of Indian history, culture and heritage.

The Goa Carnival is a world famous event, with colorful masks and floats, drums and reverberating music, and dance performances. The celebrations run three days culminating in a carnival parade on fat Tuesday.

Himachal Pradesh

Himachal Pradesh is famous for its Himalayan landscapes and popular hill-stations. Many outdoor activities such as rock climbing, mountain biking, paragliding, ice-skating, and heli-skiing are popular tourist attractions in Himachal Pradesh.

Shimla, the state capital, is very popular among tourists. The Kalka-Shimla Railway is a Mountain railway which is a UNESCO World Heritage Site. Shimla is also a famous skiing attraction in India. Other popular hill stations include Manali and Kasauli.

Dharamshala, home of the Dalai Lama, is known for its Tibetan monasteries and Buddhist temples. Many trekking expeditions also begin here.

Jammu and Kashmir

Jammu and Kashmir is the northernmost state of India. Jammu is noted for its scenic landscape, ancient temples, Hindu shrines, castles, gardens, and forts. The Hindu holy shrines of Amarnath and Vaishno Devi attract tens of thousands of Hindu devotees every year. Jammu's natural landscape has made it one of the popular destinations for adventure tourism in South Asia. Jammu's historic monuments feature a unique blend of Islamic and Hindu architecture styles.

Tourism forms an integral part of the Kashmiri economy. Often dubbed "Paradise on Earth", Kashmir's mountainous landscape has attracted tourists for centuries. Notable places are Dal Lake, Srinagar Phalagam, Gulmarg, Yeusmarg and Mughal Gardens etc. However, the tourism industry is severely affected by the insurgency.

In recent years, Ladakh has emerged as a major hub for adventure tourism. This part of Greater Himalaya called "moon on earth" comprising of naked peaks and deep gorges was once known for the silk route to High Asia from the subcontinent. Leh is also a growing tourist spot.

Karnataka

Karnataka has been ranked as fourth most popular destination for tourism among states of India. It has the second highest number of protected monuments in India, at 507.

Kannada dynasties like Kadambas, Western Gangas, Chalukyas, Rashtrakutas, Hoysalas and Vijayanagaras, ruled Karnataka particularly North Karnataka. They built great monuments to Buddhism, Jainism, Shaivism. The monuments are still present at Badami, Aihole, Pattadakal, Hampi, Lakshmeshwar, Sudi, Hooli, Mahadeva Temple (Itagi), Dambal, Lakkundi, Gadag, Hangal, Halasi, Galaganatha, Chaudayyadanapura, Banavasi, Belur, Halebidu, Shravanabelagola, Sannati and many more.

Notable Islamic monuments are present at Bijapur, Bidar, Gulbarga, Raichur and other part of the state. Gol Gumbaz at

Bijapur, has the second largest pre-modern dome in the world after the Byzantine Hagia Sophia. Karnataka has two World heritage sites, at Hampi and Pattadakal, both are in North Karnataka.

Karnataka is famous for its waterfalls. Jog falls of Shimoga District is one of the highest waterfalls in Asia. This state has 21 wildlife sanctuaries and five National parks and is home to more than 500 species of birds. Karnataka has many beaches at Karwar, Gokarna, Murdeshwara, Surathkal. Karnataka is a rock climbers paradise. Yana in Uttara Kannada, Fort in Chitradurga, Ramnagara near Bangalore district, Shivagange in Tumkur district and tekal in Kolar district are a rock climbers heaven.

Kerala

Kerala is a state on the tropical Malabar Coast of southwestern India. Nicknamed as one of the *"10 paradises of the world"* by National Geographic, Kerala is famous especially for its ecotourism initiatives. Its unique culture and traditions, coupled with its varied demography, has made it one of the most popular tourist destinations in India. Growing at a rate of 13.31%, the tourism industry significantly contributes to the state's economy.

Kerala is known for its tropical backwaters and pristine beaches such as Kovalam.

Madhya Pradesh

Madhya Pradesh is called the *"Heart of India"* because of its location in the centre of the country. It has been home to the cultural heritage of Hinduism, Islam, Buddhism, Sikhism, Jainism. Innumerable monuments, exquisitely carved temples, stupas, forts and palaces are dotted all over the State.

The temples of Khajuraho are world-famous for their erotic sculptures, and are a UNESCO World Heritage Site. Gwalior is famous for its forts, the Tomb of Rani Lakshmibai, and the Palace of Tansen.

Madhya Pradesh is also known as *Tiger State* because of the tiger population. Famous national parks like Kanha, Bandhavgadh, Shivpuri, Sanjay, Pench are located in MP. Spectacular mountain ranges, meandering rivers and miles and miles of dense forests offering a unique and exciting panorama of wildlife in sylvan surroundings.

Maharashtra

Maharashtra is the second most visited state in India by foreign tourists, with more than 2 million foreign tourists arrivals annually. Maharashtra boasts of a large number of popular and revered religious venues that are heavily frequented by locals as well as out-of-state visitors.

Ajanta Caves, Ellora Caves and Victoria Terminus are the three UNESCO World Heritage sites in Maharashtra and are highly responsible for the development of Tourism in the state.

Mumbai is the most cosmopolitan city in India, and a great place to experience modern India. Mumbai famous for Bollywood, the world's largest film industry. In addition, Mumbai is famous for its clubs, shopping, and upscale gastronomy. The city is known for its architecture, from the ancient Elephanta Caves, to the Islamic Haji Ali Mosque, to the colonial architecture of Bombay High Court and Victoria Terminus.

Maharashtra also has numerous adventure tourism destinations, including paragliding, rock climbing, canoeing, kayaking, snorkelling, and scuba diving. Maharashtra also has several pristine national parks and reserves. The Bibi Ka Maqbara at Aurangabad the Mahalakshmi temple at Kolhapur, the cities of Nashik, Trimbak famous for religious importance and the city of Pune the seat of the Maratha Empire and the fantastic Ganesh Chaturthi celebrations together contribute for the Tourism sector of Mahrashtra.

Orissa

Orissa has been a preferred destination from ancient days for people who have an interest in spirituality, religion, culture, art and natural beauty. Ancient and medieval architecture, pristine sea beaches, the classical and ethnic dance forms and a variety of festivals. Orissa has kept the religion of Buddhism alive. Rock-edicts that have challenged time stand huge and over-powering by the banks of the river Daya. The torch of Buddhism is still ablaze in the sublime triangle at Udayagiri and Khandagiri Caves, on the banks of river Birupa. Precious fragments of a glorious past come alive in the shape of stupas, rock-cut caves, rock-edicts, excavated monasteries, viharas, chaityas and sacred relics in caskets and the Rock-edicts of Ashoka. Orissa is also famous for its well-preserved Hindu Temples, especially the Konark Sun Temple. Orissa is the home for various tribal communities who have contributed uniquely to the multicultural and multilingual character of the state. Their handicrafts, different dance forms, jungle products and their unique life style blended with their healing practices have got world wide attention.

Puducherry

The Union Territory of Puducherry comprises four coastal regions viz-Puducherry, Karaikal, Mahe and Yanam. Puducherry is the Capital of this Union Territory and one of the most popular tourist destinations in South India. Puducherry has been described by National Geographic as "a glowing highlight of subcontinental sojourn". The city has many beautiful colonial buildings, churches, temples, and statues, which, combined with the systematic town planning and the well planned French style avenues, still preserve much of the colonial ambience.

Punjab

Punjab is one of India's most beautiful states. The state of Punjab is renowned for its cuisine, culture and history. Punjab has a vast public transportation and communication network. Some of the main cities in Punjab are Amritsar, Chandigarh, and Ludhiana.

Punjab also has a rich religious history incorporating Sikhism and Hinduism. Tourism in Punjab is principally suited for the tourists interested in culture, ancient civilization, spirituality and epic history. Some of the villages in Punjab are also a must see for the person who wants to see the true Punjab, with their beautiful traditional Indian homes, farms and temples, this is a must see for any visitor that goes to Punjab.

Rajasthan

Rajasthan, literally meaning *"Land of the Kings"*, is one of the most attractive tourist destinations in Northern India. The vast sand dunes of the Thar Desert attract millions of tourists from around the globe every year.

Attractions:

- Jaipur-The capital of Rajasthan, famous for its rich history and royal architecture.

- Jodhpur-Fortress-city at the edge of the Thar Desert, famous for its blue homes and architecture.
- Udaipur-Known as the "Venice" of India.
- Jaisalmer-Famous for its golden fortress.
- Barmer-Barmer and surrounding areas offer perfect picture of typical Rajasthani villages.
- Bikaner-Famous for its medieval history as a trade route outpost.
- Mount Abu-Is the highest peak in the Aravalli Range of Rajasthan.
- Pushkar-It has the first and one of the very Brahma temples in the world.
- Nathdwara-This town near Udaipur hosts the famous temple of Shrinathji.
- Ranthambore-Situated near Sawai Madhopur, this town has one of the largest and most famous national parks in India.

Sikkim

Originally known as Suk-Heem, which in the local language means "peaceful home", Sikkim was an independent kingdom till the year 1974, when it became a part of the Republic of India. The capital of Sikkim is Gangtok, located approximately 185 kilometers from New Jalpaiguri, the nearest railway station to Sikkim. Although, an airport is under construction at Dekiling in East Sikkim, the nearest airport to Sikkim would be Bagdogra. Sikkim is considered as the land of Orchids and mystic cultures and colorful traditions. Sikkim is well known among trekkers and adventure lovers, as West Sikkim has a lot to give them.

Places near Sikkim include Darjeeling also known as the Queen of hills and Kalimpong. Darjeeling, other than its world famous "Darjeeling tea" is also famous for its refined "Prep schools" founded during the British Raj. Kalimpong is also famous for its flora cultivation and is home to many internationally known Nurseries.

Tamil Nadu

Tamil Nadu lies in the southern Indian peninsula, on the shores of the Bay of Bengal. Many great rulers including the

Cholas, Pallavas, Pandyas and the Vijayanagara Empire ruled over parts of Tamil Nadu. The state is known for its cultural heritage and temple architecture.

Attractions include Mahabalipuram, famous for its Shore Temple, Kanyakumari, the southernmost tip of India, Auroville, an International Utopian city, Mudumalai Wildlife Sanctuary, Ooty and Kodaikanal, two famous hill stations. The Nilgiri Mountain Railway is a Unesco World Heritage Site

Uttarakhand

Uttaranchal is the 27th state of the Republic of India. It contains glaciers, snow-clad mountains, valley of flowers, skiing slopes and dense forests, and many shrines and places of pilgrimage. *Char-dhams*, the four most sacred and revered Hindu temples: Badrinath, Kedarnath, Gangotri and Yamunotri are nestled in the Himalayas. Haridwar which means *Gateway to God* is the only place on the plains.

It holds the watershed for Gangetic River System spanning 300 km from Satluj in the west to Kali river in the east. Nanda Devi (25640 Ft.) is the second highest peak in India after Kanchenjunga (28160 Ft.). Dunagiri, Neelkanth, Chaukhamba, Panchachuli, Trisul are other peaks above 23000 Ft. It is considered the abode of *Devtas, Yakashyas, Kinners,* Fairies and Sages. It boasts of some old hill-stations developed during British era like Mussoorie, Almora and Nainital.

Uttar Pradesh

Situated in the northern part of India, Uttar Pradesh is important with its wealth of monuments and religious fervour. Geographically, Uttar Pradesh is very diverse, with Himalayan foothills in the extreme north, the Gangetic Plain in the centre, and the Vindhya Mountain Range towards the South.

It is also home of India's most visited site, the Taj Mahal, and Hinduism's holiest city, Varanasi.

The most populous state of the Indian Union also has a rich cultural heritage, and at the heart of North India, Uttar Pradesh has much to offer. Places of interest include Varanasi, Agra, Mathura, Jhansi, Prayag, Sarnath, Ayodhya, Dudhwa National Park and Fatehpur Sikri.

West Bengal

Kolkata, one of the many cities in the state of West Bengal has been nicknamed the City of Palaces. This comes from the numerous palatial mansions built all over the city. Unlike many north Indian cities, whose construction stresses minimalism, the layout of much of the architectural variety in Kolkata owes its origins to European styles and tastes imported by the British and, to a much lesser extent, the Portuguese and French. The buildings were designed and inspired by the tastes of the English gentleman around and the aspiring Bengali Babu (literally, a *nouveau riche* Bengali who aspired to cultivation of English etiquette, manners and custom, as such practices were favourable to monetary gains from the British). Today, many of these structures are in various stages of decay. Some of the major buildings of this period are well maintained and several buildings have been declared as heritage structures.

From historical point of view, the story of West Bengal begins from Gour and Pandua situated close to the present district town of Malda. The twin medieval cities had been sacked at least once by changing powers in the 15th century. However, ruins from the period still remain, and several architectural specimens still retain the glory and shin of those times. The Hindu architecture of Bishnupur in terracotta and laterite sandstone are renowned world over. Towards the British colonial period came the architecture of Murshidabad and Coochbehar.

Historic Monuments

The Taj Mahal is one of India's best-known sites and one of the best architectural achievements in India. Located in Agra, it was built between 1631 and 1653 by Emperor Shah Jahan in honour of his wife, Arjumand Banu, more popularly known as Mumtaz Mahal. The Taj Mahal serves as her tomb.

The Golden Temple is one of the most respected temples in India and the most sacred place for Sikhs. The Golden Temple is located in Amritsar, Punjab, India.

The Bahai temple in Delhi, was completed in 1986 and serves as the Mother Temple of the Indian Subcontinent. It has won numerous architectural awards and been featured in hundreds of newspaper and magazine articles.

The Victoria Terminus in Mumbai was built by the British and is a UNESCO World Heritage Site.

The Taj Mahal Palace is an icon of Mumbai.

The Victoria Memorial in Kolkata.

Nature Tourism

India has geographical diversity, which resulted in varieties of nature tourism.

- Water falls in Western Ghats including Jog falls (highest in India).
- Western Ghats
- Kerala backwaters
- Hill Stations
- Wildlife reserves.

Wildlife in India

India is home to several well known large mammals including the Asian Elephant, Bengal Tiger, Asiatic Lion, Leopard and Indian Rhinoceros, often engrained culturally and religiously often being associated with deities. Other well known large Indian mammals include ungulates such as the domestic Asian Water buffalo, wild Asian Water buffalo, Nilgai, Gaur and several species of deer and antelope.

Some members of the dog family such as the Indian Wolf, Bengal Fox, Golden Jackal and the Dhole or Wild Dogs are also widely distributed. It is also home to the Striped Hyaena, Macaques, Langurs and Mongoose species. India also has a large variety of protected wildlife.

The country's protected wilderness consists of 75 National parks of India and 421 Sanctuaries, of which 19 fall under the purview of Project Tiger. Its climatic and geographic diversity makes it the home of over 350 mammals and 1200 bird species, many of which are unique to the subcontinent.

Some well known national wildlife sanctuaries include Bharatpur, Corbett, Kanha, Kaziranga, Periyar, Ranthambore and Sariska. The world's largest mangrove forest Sundarbans is located in southern West Bengal. The *Sundarbans* is UNESCO World Heritage Site.

Hill Stations

Several hill stations served as summer capitals of Indian provinces, princely states, or, in the case of Shimla, of British India itself. Since Indian Independence, the role of these hill stations as summer capitals has largely ended, but many hill stations remain popular summer resorts. Most famous hill stations are:

- Pachmarhi, Madhya Pradesh-It is also known as The Queen of Satpura.
- Araku, Andhra Pradesh
- Gulmarg, Srinagar and Laddakh in Jammu and Kashmir
- Darjeeling in West Bengal
- Munnar in Kerala
- Ooty and Kodaikanal in Tamil Nadu
- Shillong in Meghalaya
- Shimla, Kullu in Himachal Pradesh
- Nainital in Uttarakhand
- Gangtok in Sikkim
- Mussoorie in Uttarakhand.

In addition to the bustling hill stations and summer capitals of yore, there are several serene and peaceful nature retreats and places of interest to visit for a nature lover. These range from the stunning moonscapes of Leh and Ladhak, to small, exclusive nature retreats such as Dunagiri, Binsar, Mukteshwar in the Himalayas, to rolling vistas of Western Ghats to numerous private retreats in the rolling hills of Kerala.

Beaches

Elephants and camels rides are common on Indian beaches. Shown here is Havelock Island, part of the Andaman and Nicobar Islands. India offers a wide range of tropical beaches with silver/ golden sand to coral beaches of Lakshadweep. States like Kerala and Goa have exploited the potential of beaches to the fullest. However, there are a lot many unexploited beaches in the states of Andhra Pradesh, Gujarat, Maharastra, Tamil Nadu and Karnataka. These states have very high potential to be develop them as future destinations for prospective tourists. Some of the famous tourist beaches are:

- Beaches of Vizag, Andhra Pradesh
- Beaches of Puri, Orissa
- Beaches of Digha, West Bengal
- Beaches of Goa
- Kovalam Beach, Kerala
- Marina Beach, Chennai
- Beaches of Mahabalipuram
- Beaches in Mumbai
- Beaches of Diu
- Beaches of Midnapore, West Bengal
- Andaman and Nicobar Islands
- Lakshadweep Islands.
- Adventure Tourism
- River rafting and kayaking in Himalayas
- Mountain climbing in Himalayas
- Rock climbing in Madhya Pradesh
- Skiing in Gulmarg or Auli
- Boat racing in Bhopal
- Paragliding in Maharashtra.

The Indian Tourism and Hospitality Industry

Tourism and Hospitality Industry

- Hospitality, as an industry segment in itself, is a US$ 3.5 trillion service sector within the global economy.
- In India, the tourism and hospitality industries are witnessing a period of exponential growth; the world's leading travel and tourism journal, "Conde Nast Traveller", ranked India as the numero uno travel destination in the world for 2007, as against fourth position in 2006.
- The year 2007 also marked the fifth consecutive year during which India has witnessed double-digit growth in foreign tourist arrivals.
- Along with the rise in foreign tourist arrivals, foreign exchange earnings have shown a robust growth of 25.6% during January-October 2007 to touch US$ 6.32 billion as against US$ 5.03 billion during January-October 2006.

- Tourism has now become a significant industry in India, contributing around 5.9 per cent of the Gross Domestic Product (GDP) and providing employment to about 41.8 million people.
- As per the World Travel & Tourism Council, the tourism industry in India is likely to generate US$ 121.4 billion of economic activity by 2015 and Hospitality sector has the potential to earn US$ 24 billion in foreign exchange by 2015.
- Additionally, India is also likely to become a major hub for medical tourism, with revenues from the industry estimated to grow from US$ 333 million in 2007 to US$ 2.2 billion by 2012, says a study by the Confederation of Indian Industry (CII) and McKinsey.
- The booming tourism industry has had a cascading effect on the hospitality sector with an increase in the occupancy ratios and average room rates. While occupancy ratio is around 80-85 per cent – up nearly 10 percent from three years back, the average increase in room rates over the last one year has hovered around 22-25%.
- It is pertinent to mention in this context, that according to recent estimates, there are a total of 110,000 rooms in India, as against a total requirement of approximately 250,000 – demonstrating the untapped potential that continues to exist in this industry.
- With a view to stimulating domestic and international investments in this sector, the government has implemented the following initiatives:
    i. 100% FDI under the automatic route is now permitted in all construction development projects including construction of hotels and resorts, recreational facilities and city and regional level infrastructure.
    ii. 100% FDI is now permitted in all airport development projects subject to the condition that FDI for upgradation of existing airports requires FIPB approval beyond 74%.
    iii. A five year tax holiday has been extended to Companies that set up hotels, resorts and convention

centres at specified destinations, subject to compliance with the prescribed conditions.

iv. Plans for substantial upgradation of 28 regional airports in smaller towns and the privatization and expansion of Delhi and Mumbai airports

- The aforementioned initiatives have resulted in increasing FDI inflows being witnessed by this industry. For the period April 2000 to November 2007, a total of US$ 636 million in foreign direct investments was channelised towards development of hotels and tourism.
- The hospitality industry has also been receiving increasing interest from the Private Equity Sector – investments have tripled from US$ 60 million in 2004-05 to over US$ 180 million in 2006-07.
- It is estimated that the hospitality sector is likely to see a further US$ 11.41 billion in inbound investments over the next two years.
- Several global hospitality majors such as Hilton, Accor, Marriott International, Berggruen Hotels, Cabana Hotels, Premier Travel Inn (PTI) and InterContinental Hotels group have already announced major investment plans in India in recent years.

Food and Tourism

The concept of 'ethnic food tourism" may have relevance in present days due to increase in tourist industry in the Himalayas. Movement and interaction of people, sense of respect to traditional value and culture will serve to intricately link the enjoyment of dinning to locale, making this the standard of food culture of the region. France attracts the greatest number of tourists worldwide as estimated in 1998 reaching 70 million, which even exceeds the existing population of 58 million. The secret to this appeal is nothing but the delicious food and wine of France, served in inexpensive traditional restaurants that offer the delicious agricultural produce of the region which allows one to experience enjoyment and friendship. Finding enjoyment in eating the produce of the region while in that region – herein lies the essence of a food culture that gives confidence in life, pride to the people of the region and ultimately, enjoyment and friendship. Further, it imparts meaning to the act of travel and bestows happiness upon the traveller. The promoters have to focus on the specific food culture of a region in a presentable form where tourists can find local cuisine in menu.

Ethnic food culture harnesses the cultural history of particular community, their indigenous knowledge of food production, vast nutritious qualities, microbial diversity associated with fermented foods as genetic resources, source of income generation related to tourism and enjoyment of dining.

- Food tourism includes all unique and memorable food experiences, not just four star or critically acclaimed restaurants. Price is not necessarily indicative of quality. According to industry research, true food tourists are perfectly happy at a roadside cafe in the middle of nowhere, as long as there is something memorable about their visit.
- Tourist consumers were asked to list aspects that make a place a good food destination.

Activities

In addition to sampling local food and dishes, food tourists are also likely to engage in the following activities during their holiday:

- Visit museums
- Go shopping
- Attend music and/or film festivals
- Participate in general outdoor recreation.

Accommodation Preferences

- In an in-depth survey of 11 consumers regarding their perception of restaurants and destination, 91% of respondents indicated they choose their accommodation based on the availability of restaurants in the area. One consumer revealed this was because it was less restrictive price-wise, (i.e. more choice), while others mentioned the benefits of proximity, and being able to walk to and from restaurants.
- One consumer did not consider the availability of restaurants to be an important factor in their accommodation decision. This was because they simply

expected most city-located accommodation to be situated near restaurant facilities.

Travel Party

Of the total domestic visitors who ate out and/or visited restaurants during their overnight trip, 31% were travelling as part of an adult couple and 24% were travelling alone.

Family groups (ie, parents and children) and friends and/or relatives travelling together (without children) each accounted for a further 19%.

Information Sources

Travellers on holiday use the following sources of information when selecting a restaurant:

- Travel guides
- Brochures from travel agencies
- Newspaper articles
- Magazines
- TV programs
- Word of mouth
- The internet
- Consumer's own knowledge
- Menu shopping.

Length of Trip

Domestic visitors who engaged in the activity of eating out and/or dining at restaurants stayed for an average of 4.5 nights on their trip. By comparison, the average length of stay for all domestic visitors was 4.0 nights.

Barriers

- Many who attempt to define food and culinary tourism immediately think of wineries and fine restaurants. These are two components of the niche, but by no means a definitive list. Food tourism can occur at a farmers' market, or even in the home of a friend or relative.
- Travellers do not often choose their holiday destination based on the food tourism experiences they anticipate to encounter, but still end up remembering their holiday to

a certain extent on the quality of the food they experienced at the destination. This creates a conundrum in that many tourists choose holiday destinations based on one perceived aspect (e.g. beaches, accommodation etc.), but their actual satisfaction will be based on aspects (ie, food) they did not consider in their original holiday choice.

- According to research conducted into what aspects of food tourism consumers find appealing, 73% said that a variety of eating options was an important consideration in their destination choice. This automatically biases tourist consumers towards more developed destinations that receive a sufficient volume of visitors to support a diverse food industry. Only 36% of respondents mentioned regional food as being important.

Opportunities

- The food tourism niche market presents a new aspect of destination marketing, which can enhance the attractiveness of a destination without necessarily involving extensive new product development. Food tourism can essentially be viewed as a subset of cultural tourism, with the local cuisine being a product of the local culture and the natural environment. Therefore, regions that possess unique dishes and food products as a result of their culture and environment may be transformed into food tourism destinations with minimum marketing and product development.
- In terms of regional aspects, food tourism can be divided into a rural and an urban/city experience. The urban/city experience usually presents travellers with a wide variety of food tourism products, and convenience in the form of restaurant precincts and culturally distinct cuisine. Rural food tourism on the other hand is not usually considered as a developed tourism product. Activities such as visits to farms and farmers' markets, fruit picking and agricultural farm accommodation may provide important supplemental activities to struggling rural areas.
- Research suggests that in many instances, consumers attribute their lack of satisfaction with food on their holiday

to the reason their trip did not become an overall memorable holiday. Destinations could develop higher consumer satisfaction levels (and hence higher return and recommendation rates) if they could guide tourists to food products that provide memorable experiences (whether it is service, quality, value for money, or uniqueness). This may be achieved through either consumer marketing (e.g. a tourist restaurant/food tourism brochure) or through cooperative product development.

- No state or local food tourism associations currently exist in Queensland. The marketing and development of new food tourism products could be assisted and facilitated by the formation of such an organisation. Membership could also act as a strong indicator to consumers of quality tourism food product.

Marketing

- A large proportion of consumers emphasise a variety of food product as being important in their overall satisfaction with a destination. Therefore, promoting the variety of restaurants and food products available in a destination may enhance destination attractiveness.
- True food tourism visitors can be accessed via industry associations such as the International Culinary Tourism Association and consumer publications.
- It could be useful to include information relating to the following features in any materials prepared for marketing the food tourism product:
    - o the location (including proximity to other local attractions),
    - o access to the property (roads, signage),
    - o attractions on the property (gardens, views),
    - o leisure opportunities (games, crafts, recreational pursuits), and
    - o local area attractions (tourist drives, museums, events).

Culinary Tourism

Judging by the surge since 2001 in the number of times "culinary tourism" has appeared as a subject matter or in a session title in tourism industry conferences and programs, we can see that Culinary Tourism is valued by tourism industry professionals as one of the most popular niches in the world's tourism industry. This makes sense, given recent consumer focus on healthy and organic eating, culinary/food pedigrees, and the simple fact that all travellers must eat. Not every visitor goes shopping or visits museums, but all travellers eat. For anyone who doubts, look at the increase in cooking shows featured on The Travel Channel [Anthony Bourdain No Reservations] or travel shows featured on The Food Network [Rachel Ray's $40 a Day series], as examples.

Culinary Tourism is not just experiences of the highest caliber-that would be gourmet tourism. This is perhaps best illustrated by the notion that Culinary Tourism is about what is "unique and memorable, not what is necessarily pretentious and exclusive". Similarly, wine tourism, beer tourism and spa tourism are also regarded as subsets of culinary tourism.

Indian Food Tourism

The finest of *India's* cuisines is as rich and diverse as it's civilization. It is an art form that has been passed on through generations purely by word of mouth, from *guru* teacher) to *vidhyarthi* (pupil) or from mother to daughter.

The hospitality of the Indians is legendary. In *Sanskrit* literature the three famous words *'Atithi Devo Bhava'* or 'The guest is truly your god' are a dictum of hospitality in India. Indians believe that they are honoured if they share their mealtimes with guests. Even the poorest look forward to guests and are willing to share this meager food with guest.

Lassi-Punjab

Lassi, by far, is the most easiest Indian dish to prepare and is taken cold. It is a good way to beat the scorching heat and get refreshed.

It can prepared in two ways either sweet or salty.

Biryani-Hyderabad

Hyderabadi Biryani is a famous meat and rice dish of *Hyderabad*, India.

It is a traditional celebration meal made using goat meat and rice and is the staple of a die-hard Hyderabadi. The blending of *mughlai* and *Telangana* cuisines in the kitchens of the *Nizam* (ruler of the historic Hyderabad State), resulted in the creation of Hyderabadi Biryani.

Halwa-Tirunelveli

This sweet (pronounced locally as ulva) is made from wheat and sugar. *Halwa* is brown and semi-solid in texture and contains lots of *ghee/Vanaspati* which gives it the oily look. It tastes the best when fresh and hot. Tirunelveli Halwa is said to owe its peculiar taste due to the recipe of this region.

Two of the famous halwa stores are *Irutu Kadai halwa (Dark Store halwa),* situated near the *Nellayappar* temple and Shanthi Sweets. The name *Irutu Kadai* of the former store derives from the fact that the looks of the store had been kept unchanged from the date it was started. Till date, there is no bright electrical lamp or even a board display to show the shop name!

Pani Puri/Golgappa/Golgappe-Indian Street Snack

Panipuri or Gol Gappa or Gup chup is a popular street snack in the Indian sub-continent. It comprises a round, hollow *puri,* fried crisp and filled with a watery mixture of tamarind, chilli and potato. The name *panipuri* literally means "water in fried bread". The snack has three major ingredients-Puris, pani (water) and stuffing.

Pesarattu-Andhra Pradesh

Pesarattu is a thicker verison of *Dosa* made specifically in major towns of Andhra Pradesh.

Idly-Kancheepuram

The *idli* is a savory cake popular throughout South India. The cakes are usually two to three inches in diameter and are made by steaming a batter consisting of fermented black lentils (de-husked) and rice.

Kancheepuram Idli as the name goes is from Kancheepuram, a holy city in Tamil Nadu, India. History goes that Kancheepuram Idly is served as *prasadam* (offering) in *Varadharaja Perumal Temple,* a famous Hindu temple dedicated to Lord Vishnu, located in the

Kancheepuram. It is a huge Idli (Steamed Rice Cake) which is added with spices.

Why Food Tourism is Becoming more Important?

Today's tourist is more cultured than visitors of 20 years ago, is well travelled, is searching for new experiences, is concerned about the environment, is interested in taking part in a health/well-being lifestyle and wants to experience the local culture when he goes on holiday.

Trend analyst, Ian Yeoman writes that food is a significant aspect of the tourist's experience of a destination, driven by the growing trends of authenticity and the need to have a high-quality experience. Food tourism shapes gastro destinations such as France, Italy and California whereas in emerging destinations such as Croatia, Vietnam and Mexico food plays an important part of the overall experience.

What are the Trends Shaping our Interest in Food Tourism?

Trend 1: Disposable Income and Spending Patterns

All across world, growing affluence of the populations has a profound impact on consumer spending. Consumers spend a higher proportion of their income on prepared food, gourmet products, eating out and food items with some form of health or ethical benefits.

The key point is that according to Michael Silverstein writing in his book Trading Up: The New American Luxury the consumer has traded up where the product is aspiration or traded down when the product is only function. This is one reason why producers and retailers have focused on quality through products such as Tesco's finest range or ethical consumption, where the consumer will pay a premium for 'fair trade' product.

Trend 2: Demographics and Household Change

According to research by the Future Foundation families are also becoming increasingly democratic in food choice, as children get older they have more influence in what they eat and where the family eats. Children are also spending increasing amounts of time with their grandparents with over two-thirds of children born between 1978 and 1986 being looked after by their grandparents at least once a month, compared to one quarter of those born in 1937 or earlier.

This increase indicates a demand for venues offering facilities that appeal to differing age groups and generations. By 2015, those aged between 45 and 59 will be part of the most populous age group in the United Kingdom.

Households headed by those aged 50 plus will account for around 50% of all households, and this same age group will account for over 39% of all consumers spending on leisure goods and services. In 2004, the 50–64 age groups spent US $24.80 per household per week on restaurant meals, US $2.40 more than the national average — this will be a key market in the future.

Another consequence of longevity is 'lifestyle fragmentation', the idea that life is increasingly being experienced as a series of non-linear events with no set pattern. As characteristics of different age groups becomes blurred and diverse, more people will expect the places they visit to be adaptable to different aspects of their daily lives.

In other words, eating out opportunities suitable for whatever the situations requires — whether this is work, with children or simply eating alone. And finally, rising divorce rates are also good for food tourism, as Michael Silverstein observe that divorcees have to search for new partners and subsequently will take prospective partners out for dinner and away for romantic weekends.

Trend 3: Individualism

Individualism means uniqueness as tourists search out local, fresh and good quality cuisine that reflects the authenticity of the destination. The end of mass customisation has seen Starbucks fail in Australia as the brand is perceived as bland and lacking individuality. Gone are the days of the British tourist wanting 'egg and chips' in Ibiza or American's only eating Kentucky Fried Chicken when in Australia.

Trend 4: The Multi-Cultured Consumer

The whole process of globalization has significantly amplified the meaning of the term multi-culturalism within our social order.

Access to an even wider range of ideas and interests has never been easier. The Internet boom, the expansion in specialist and minority TV channels, the relentless growth in international tourism, etc., combine to stretch perceptions and eliminate that what we might call mono-culturalism; seeing the world through only one set of pre-ordained, inherited notions.

The consumer of today will watch the latest Bollywood film, consume a curry, purchase exotic spices for cooking and will read about Rajasthan in the latest edition of the Lonely Planet. Multiculturalism has now become an everyday concept in the daily life of the consumer; today curry is the United Kingdom's favourite dish.

Trend 5: The Role of the Celebrity Chef and Media

The media has substantial influence in determining food product selection. The influence of celebrity chefs is often referred to as the Delia effect' after the media chef Delia Smith, whose 1998 television programme 'How to Cook' resulted in an extra 1.3 million eggs being sold in Britain each day of the series. The phenomena of Gordon Ramsey with 'Hells Kitchen' and the 'F word' or Jamie Oliver campaign for good wholesome school dinners all drives our interest in good quality real food.

The emergence of the niche food programmes, TV channels and magazines means the food celebrity and expert has been created. Today, that celebrity chef shapes tourism products, whether it is a cookery course with Rick Stein in Padstow or Martin Yan's food cruises across China.

Trend 6: Well-Being and Food

Around 30% of adults say that they have been eating less fat and sugar compared to the previous year and 28% say they are eating less salt, whereas other food groups, notably vegetables, fruit and bread/cereal/pasta/potatoes are on the rise. These trends have transformed themselves into the food industry with Starbucks offering Soya milk, and McDonalds offering salads.

In New York, the city council has banned certain types of fats. The proportion of vegetarians has only increased slightly in the last 20 years, with just over 5% of UK adults reporting themselves to be vegetarian in 2004. However, the number of food venues offering vegetarian options due to its association with healthy eating has increased exponentially along with a perception that vegetarian food in restaurants is more than 'vegetable lasagne' or a 'cheese omelette'.

Restaurants are also aware of specialist diets, whether it is catering for gluten free or the Atkins diet. Consumers will even visit a food nutritionalist or advisor of seek opinion about 'food balance' or 'sensitivity towards certain foods'.

The specialist diet is becoming more mainstream with individuals avoiding certain foodstuffs like 'dairy products' or the promotion of detox diets to cleanse the body. Consumers are therefore becoming ever more demanding and cautious regarding the food they eat.

These concerns and fears can be exploited in order to maximise potential marketing of certain products. However, due to the volatile nature of demands and trends, these requirements are hard to predict. Food providers need to have 'quick response' mechanisms in place to enable them to keep up with dietary fads and health scares.

Trend 7: Food as an Oasis

When on holiday, food becomes the social occasion when busy people create a 'time oasis', but also to connect with family members and friends who may in general be less time-impoverished. Food becomes a human-space within frequently much harried lives; the notion of the meal as a 'time oasis' seems to be a very powerful theme. As the consumer desire for new experiences increases, the 'authentic' restaurant experience becomes more important. Authenticity is about food that is simple, rooted in the region, natural, ethical, beautiful and human — all of the making for a food tourism destination.

Trend 8: Internet Usage

The world is online whether through your computer or mobile phone. Online restaurant reviews are the norm and companies like www.5pm.co.uk use the easyJet principles of yield management allowing consumer's discounts, reviews, auctions for exclusive restaurants, reservations and for restaurants a distribution system for selling unused capacity.

Trend 9: The Desire for New Experiences and Cultural Capital

Food has an important position and role in the emerging experience economy whether in the preparation of it, knowledge of it or consuming it.

As British sociologist Gershuny notes when discussing the whole concept of cultural capital. We have various skills in different sorts of consumption and organisational participation — we play football, we organise social events for the synagogue or church or mosque, we cook food and give dinner parties, we listen to music.

All of these activities give us different sorts of satisfaction, and different degrees of social status, depending on how fully and effectively we are able to participate in them. So, the growing importance of cultural issues, as a leisure activity and as a point of differentiation, means it is an important trend in food tourism as it is the tourist's knowledge of food that distinguishes them.

This means the food tourist has a desire for new tastes, knowledge and concepts and therefore food creates its own cultural capital — which destinations need to capitalise on. As consumers become richer and more sophisticated, they are drawn to new tastes and more adventurous than previous generations.

Trend 10: The Science of Food

Food tourism is shaped by the geopolitical trends. Today, we have rejected science from the food chain resulting in falling yields per hectare as we have rejected GM foods. Food inflation is rising all over the world, for example milk has doubled in price in the last 12 months Farmers are planting crops for fuel rather than food in the rush for biofuels.

Climate change is more disruptive and unpredictable. Rising temperatures mean less water in parts of the world. Land is becoming more expensive due to the increase in urbanisation, therefore less land for food production.

Because of these reasons, will the world return to science in order to protect future food supplies and increase yields? Does this mean cuisine is going to return to Star trek pills and NASA vac packs? Who knows?

Trend 11: However, the Consumer is a Hypochondriac

Although there is evidence that healthy eating is on the rise, the importance of organic food and a desire to try local produce—the consumer can be viewed as a hypochondriac as what they say and actually do can be two different things.

For example, obesity levels have trebled in the USA since 1980 and the amount of vegetables that people consume has steadily dropped since the 1970s.

On one hand, the French campaign against the company, saying it is a symbol of American imperialism and aggression in the world; promotes an unhealthy lifestyle and there is nothing good about its cuisine, whereas on the other hand, the French love the Big Mac, eating three times as many per head of population compared to Spain, Germany and Italy.

Food Tourism Destinations

Some destinations have begun to realise that there is great potential for food tourism to offer a sustainable tourism product, whether it is the fine wines of California or the great cheeses of France. One of the best examples of food tourism has been the rise in prominence of Ludlow in the United Kingdom as a food tourism destination whether it is festivals, slow food or Michelin star restaurants.

Ludlow from the early beginning of a farmers market has prospered into a major food tourism destination with a density of high quality restaurants, an abundance of local food suppliers in the high street and food festivals and events to attract tourists. Ludlow as a food destination illustrates its success through:

- Using food as a means to create cultural capital and social cachet
- Creating a density of food and drink suppliers which results in a tourism eating and shopping experience
- Creating a local authentic promise based upon good quality and fair pricing
- Creating a unique product better than that found in other regional food destinations

- Producers seeing themselves as being involved in tourism
- Tourism providers focusing on food as a point of difference.

Conclusions

Today, the consumer is better educated, wealthy, has travelled more extensively, lives longer, and is concerned about his health and the environment. As a result food and drink has become more important and have a higher priority amongst certain social groupings.

Too the extent food is the new culture capital of a destination, as if culture has moved out of the museum to become a living experience of consumption. One thing is clear; food must be a quality product, whether it is slow food or fast food. Finally, if food is not for you, there is always the no-food movement which is all the rage in Japan where holiday-makers are flocking to the Arina Hotel in the idyllic Nagano Mountains for a fasting feast!

8

The Global Importance of Tourism

Creating Jobs and Wealth

Travel & Tourism is the world's largest industry and creator of jobs across national and regional economies. WTTC/WEFA research show that in 2000, Travel & Tourism will generate, directly and indirectly, 11.7% of GDP and nearly 200 million jobs in the world-wide economy. These figures are forecasted to total 11.7% and 255 million respectively in 2010.

Jobs generated by Travel & Tourism are spread across the economy-in retail, construction, manufacturing and telecommunications, as well as directly in Travel & Tourism companies. These jobs employ a large proportion of women, minorities and young people; are predominantly in small and medium sized companies; and offer good training and transferability. Tourism can also be one of the most effective drivers for the development of regional economies. These patterns apply to both developed and emerging economies.

Contributing to Sustainable Development

The 1992 United Nations Conference on Environment and Development (UNCED), the Rio Earth Summit, identified Travel & Tourism as one of the key sectors of the economy which could make a positive contribution to achieving sustainable development. The Earth Summit lead to the adoption of Agenda 21, a comprehensive program of action adopted by 182 governments to provide a global blueprint for achieving sustainable development. Travel & Tourism is the first industry sector to have launched an industry-specific action plan based on Agenda 21. Travel & Tourism is able to contribute to development which is economically, ecologically and socially sustainable, because it:

- has less impact on natural resources and the environment than most other industries;
- is based on enjoyment and appreciation of local culture, built heritage, and natural environment, as such that the industry has a direct and powerful motivation to protect these assets;
- can play a positive part in increasing consumer commitment to sustainable development principles through its unparalleled consumer distribution channels; and
- provides an economic incentive to conserve natural environments and habitats which might otherwise be allocated to more environmentally damaging land uses, thereby, helping to maintain biodiversity.

Providing Infrastructure

To a greater degree than most activities, Travel & Tourism depends on a wide range of infrastructure services-airports, air navigation, roads, railheads and ports, as well as basic infrastructure services required by hotels, restaurants, shops, and recreation facilities (e.g. telecommunications and utilities).

It is the combination of tourism and good infrastructure that underpins the economic, environmental and social benefits. It is important to balance any decision to develop an area for tourism against the need to preserve fragile or threatened environments and cultures.

However, once a decision has been taken where an area is appropriate for new tourism development, or that an existing tourist site should be developed further, then good infrastructure will be essential to sustain the quality, economic viability and growth of Travel & Tourism. Good infrastructure will also be a key factor in the industry's ability to manage visitor flows in ways that do not affect the natural or built heritage, nor counteract against local interests.

Challenge for the Future

Travel & Tourism creates jobs and wealth and has tremendous potential to contribute to economically, environmentally and socially sustainable development in both developed countries and emerging nations. It has a comparative advantage in that its start up and running costs can be low compared to many other forms of industry development. It is also often one of the few realistic options for development in many areas. Therefore, there is a strong likelihood that the Travel & Tourism industry will continue to grow globally over the short to medium term.

Of course, if Travel & Tourism is managed badly, it can have a detrimental effect-it can damage fragile environments and destroy local cultures. The challenge is to manage the future growth of the industry so as to minimise its negative impacts on the environment and host communities whilst maximising the benefits it brings in terms of jobs, wealth and support for local culture and industry, and protection of the built and natural environment.

Industry Initiatives for Sustainable Tourism Problems

10. Travel & Tourism takes many different forms-from a trip only a few hours away from home to long distance travel overseas. A common belief is that most Travel & Tourism involves large numbers of visitors from developed countries travelling by air to destinations in emerging countries. In fact, in most countries, the domestic tourism market is larger than the inbound market. Of course, the social and cultural impact of inbound visitors is often greater than that of domestic tourists. Whether tourism is domestic or international, it involves visiting a destination away from the area in which one lives and using the services available in that destination. Therefore, tourists' requirements are for travel services to reach their destinations and once there, for services such as shelter, water, food, sanitation and entertainment.

What makes tourism special is that, many of these different products and services are often supplied by different operators: usually small or medium sized businesses in local ownership. This makes tourism a highly fragmented and diverse industry and so coordinated, industry-wide action is difficult to achieve. The influence of Travel & Tourism's demand also extends far beyond traditional tourism companies, into upstream suppliers like aircraft manufacturers or food producers and into the downstream service providers for travellers, like retail shops.

Despite the difficulties caused by fragmentation and lengthy supply chains, there has been a steady growth in environmental good practice across the industry in recent years. There are examples of-airlines and airports reducing pollution and noise impacts; cruise liners practising marine conservation; hotels implementing energy consumption and waste disposal programs; car rental companies investing in increasingly fuel efficient fleets and railways sound proofing to dampen noise. The result is that there are a number of excellent initiatives in place designed to improve the environmental management of Travel & Tourism businesses. Of course, more needs to be done.

Solutions

Providing Leadership

WTTC with 105 members is the global business leaders' forum for the Travel & Tourism industry.

The WTTC have set in place an extensive strategy to promote a culture of sustainable development and have put in place a three-tiered structure for its achievement. This involves:

Policy

In 1996 the WTTC, the World Tourism Organization and the Earth Council, joined together to launch an action plan entitled "Agenda 21 for the Travel & Tourism Industry: Towards.

Environmentally Sustainable Development"-a sectional sustainable development program based on the results of the Rio Earth Summit in 1992. Since the launch of the document, the three organisations have begun a series of regional seminars to increase awareness of the conclusions, and to adapt the program for local implementation. The program has held regional seminars in London and Jakarta in 1997 and Victoria Falls and Dominica in 1998.

WTTC has recently introduced a major addition to the program– the "Alliance for Sustainable Tourism", which invites public and private sector Travel & Tourism organisations to record their

Agenda 21 based activities on a central web site and commit to co-operation with all other partners. In order to develop the program from global principles to community based action, WTTC is also discussing with the International Council for Local Environment Initiatives (ICLEI) on how the principles of "Agenda 21 for Travel & Tourism" can be built into Local Agenda 21 programs. Furthermore, WTTC is considering pilot projects in 5 cities around the world to serve as models for other destinations.

Practice

In 1994, WTTC initiated the *"Green Globe"*, an Agenda 21 based industry improvement program, which provides guidance material and a certification process linked to both ISO standards and Agenda 21 principles. There are now 500 *"Green Globe"* members in 100 countries dedicated to improving environmental practice. The first certification has commenced with hotels groups in Jamaica and Manchester (UK). *"Green Globe"* has also developed a specific Destination Program, which provides a methodology for Travel & Tourism destinations to implement sustainable development. The ultimate aim is that *"Green Globe"* will become the primary global standard of environmental commitment by the global Travel & Tourism industry and will be recognised by the public as such. Currently, *"Green Globe"* has the support of over 20 international industry organisations representing thousands of businesses worldwide and the support of the World Tourism Organization, the United Nations Environment Program and the Earth Council.

Information

WTTC have also developed "ECoNETT", a website containing advice and data on good practice and sources of help and advice. "ECoNETT" is increasingly recognised as a focal point for environmental information, good practice, new techniques and technologies.

The International Hotel & Restaurant Association (IH&RA), based in Paris, represents over 700,000 establishments in more than 150 countries. Its membership comprises some 50 national and international hotel and restaurant chains, over 110 national hotel and restaurant associations, independent hotel operators and restaurateurs, industry suppliers and 130 hotel schools. The IH&RA has offices in Asia-Pacific and Latin America. It is also the voice of the world's hotels and restaurants and plays a global role in representing, protecting, promoting and informing the industry to enable its members to achieve their business objectives.

Corporate Initiatives

The International Hotel Environment Initiative (IHEI), based in London, England, is a program of The Prince of Wales Business

Leaders Forum. Founded in 1992 by a consortium of chief executives from 10 multinational hotel groups, IHEI is an educational charity designed to encourage continuous improvement in the environmental performance of the global hotel industry. It does this through:

- raising environmental awareness in the hotel industry by promoting good practice internationally;
- developing hotel-specific guidance, enabling hotels of all sizes to implement environmental programs; and
- multiplying the reach and impact of IHEI by working with partners, including hotel associations, governments, NGOs, tourism bodies and businesses.

IHEI is a catalyst and conduit for hotels to pool their resources and to share experience via a noncompetitive platform. In 5 years it has evolved into an organisation with global impact. IHEI has worked in 111 countries, stimulating and assisting with the establishment of local initiatives such as

New Zealand's "Environmental Hotels of Auckland, the Asia Pacific Hotel Environment Initiative" and the Caribbean Action for Sustainable Tourism. Member hotels now represent over 1 million guest rooms and more than 8,000 hotels on 5 continents.

The Co-operative Research Centre for Sustainable Tourism, based in Australia, was established in 1997 to enhance the strategic knowledge available to the Travel & Tourism industry through:

- long-term high-quality scientific and technological research which contributes to the development of an internationally competitive tourism industry;
- strengthening the links between research and its commercial and other applications;
- promoting cooperative research; and
- stimulating education and training, particularly in graduate programs, through active involvement of researchers from outside the higher education system in educational activities, and of graduate students in major research programs.

Company Initiatives

The Kandalama hotel in Sri Lanka has been a recipient of the "GREEN GLOBE" award, 3 years in a row, for its commitment to environmental excellence. The hotel has undertaken measures in the following areas to ensure that its operations are more sustainable:

- cultural and social-hotel employment, providing community infrastructure and development;
- natural environment-soil erosion measures and planting forests;
- pollution-sewage, solid waste and noise pollution reduction programs; and
- environmental communication-construction of an Eco Park where all waste is treated within the park, a dry debris sorting centre, a lecture room to promote environmental awareness and a sustainable development library.

Canadian Pacific Hotels, the largest hotel conglomerate in Canada, has developed an environmental program, which is recognised as the most comprehensive in the North American hotel industry. Based on the results of a survey, employee suggestions and the recommendations of a professional environmental consultant, Canadian Pacific Hotels developed a list of 16 goals to be attained by all hotels.

In addition to individual projects implemented at each of the 26 hotels, the goals set for the chain as a whole were ambitious: (I) to reduce the amount of waste sent to landfill by 50% across the chain, by launching an extensive recycling program; (ii) to redesign purchasing policies to ensure that waste is reduced at source, and supplies used in the hotels are nature friendly.

Inter-regional level

The Caribbean Action For Sustainable Tourism (CAST) is an alliance for sustainable growth developed by the Caribbean Hoteliers Association with the support of the WTTC, the IHEI and the Caribbean Tourism Organisation. CAST has developed workshops, training courses and guidance material for its members on a wide range of environmental issues, including:

- setting up environmental management systems;
- energy efficiency;
- renewable energy; and
- waste water management.

Agents and Partnerships for Change

The public sectors, particularly national and local government, have an important role to play by setting the agenda and providing the framework in which action should take place. The regulatory environment also plays an important role in creating the conditions suitable for sustainable tourism. Self-regulation involving the agreement and co-operation of industry is always likely to be the most effective solution. Therefore, the role of trade associations and industry organisations in distributing information among their members and encouraging participation is essential.

The major partnerships to be formed are between:

- industry and the public sector-to ensure consistency with the framework;
- industry and the voluntary sector-to tap into the enormous resources of expertise and good will that this sector is able to generate; and
- industry and the public-both travellers themselves and the people who live in the places they visit to develop more sustainable forms of tourism.

Influencing Consumer Behaviour to Promote Sustainable Tourism Problems

At the 1998 World Travel Market, WTTC hosted, as a part of its Environmental Awareness Day, a

seminar entitled "Does the Consumer Care?" At this event, MORI presented the latest findings from their Business and the Environment survey-an annual UK survey devoted to public attitudes to the environment. The survey is now in its tenth year and illustrates the challenge facing the Travel & Tourism industry in influencing consumer behaviour to promote sustainable tourism.

According to this survey, Travel & Tourism is now more associated with environmental damage than it has been in the past. Despite this decline in perception, the industry's economic success is not dependent on its green record-public sensitivity to environmental problems on holiday/business trips has not increased and is no more of a deterrent to repeat travel than it was previously.

There is a downward trend in the public's willingness to pay extra for environmental protection and environmentally friendly products, including "green" Travel & Tourism. Awareness of companies making environmental commitments is only marginally up. Therefore, the challenge is to persuade the consumer that it is in their interests to adopt and promote a sustainable approach in their activities and purchasing decisions. Education programs and the development and widespread acceptance of codes of conduct are useful tools in achieving this step. Once this message has been conveyed, it is then important to back this up with the necessary information to enable consumers to make informed choices. It is here that "ecolabels" and award programs have value.

Solutions

Education Programs

The Foundation for Environmental Education in Europe (FEEE) seeks to promote environmental education by carrying out campaigns and improving awareness of the importance of environmental education. It is composed of a network of international organisations. The FEEE (headquarters in Denmark) runs three major campaigns in Europe for providing safe and clean beaches and marinas.

The award itself is given annually to beaches and marinas that satisfy a number of essential criteria in three separate areas: water quality; beach management and safety; and environmental information and education.

"Green Globe"'s Dodo Campaign, is based on a cartoon character, who features in 65 Travel & Tourism videos. Dodo explains and promotes the actions that visitors can take to reduce the impacts of their travels. The videos are aimed at children and are designed to be fun, whilst conveying important messages about sustainable Travel & Tourism. The aim is to have these videos shown on inflight and in-room television channels to raise awareness and influence consumer behaviour.

Codes of Conduct

Codes of conduct are also used to try and influence consumer behaviour. For example, "Guidelines for Responsible Environmental Tourism" are prepared and distributed by the American Society of Travel Agents to all customers who book holidays through their members' branches. The Guidelines aim to "encourage the growth of peaceful tourism and environmentally responsible travel" and include 10 recommendations to encourage tourists to act responsibly and show respect for their hosts and the environment of their destination(s).

The Pacific Asia Tourism Association (PATA) is an industrial association, which promotes the Pacific Asia area's Travel & Tourism destinations, products and services. PATA also serves as a central resource of information and research, travel industry education and training, as well as quality product development with sensitivity for culture, heritage and environment. In 1992, PATA introduced its "Code for Environmentally Responsible Tourism" to strengthen the principles of preservation in the region. Businesses, organisations and individuals wishing to affirm their support for the PATA Code are encouraged to participate in the PATA Green Leaf program.

The Africa Travel Association has produced "Responsible Traveller Guidelines"; the Japanese Association of Travel Agents has produced the "Declaration of Earth Friendly Travellers" and there are many more examples of industry codes aimed at educating and influencing their customers.

Eco Labelling

There are numerous examples of industry sponsored labelling schemes, whose aim is to recognise good industry practice and influence consumer behaviour into purchasing the labelled products. For example, the "Green Key, Denmark" certificate operated by the Hotel, Restaurant and Leisure Industry Association (HORESTA) has 56 criteria that includes environmental information, water & energy consumption and waste management. Special features also include ecological food products, outdoor areas, non-smoking rooms, and adaptations for access by disabled persons.

Awards

There are a number of industries that runs and sponsors award programs to highlight and promote examples of good practice. For example, British Airways has run the "Tourism for Tomorrow" awards since 1992 to encourage action to protect the environment. The awards are directed at tour operators, hotels, national parks and heritage sites, and other activities associated with tourism. By selecting projects showing best practice in their field as role models, others are encouraged to follow suit and consider the environment in the everyday running of their tourism business. The awards are run annually, with a winner selected from each of five regions and an overall winner. In addition, two special awards are made for mass tourism destinations. The awards are run in association with the British Tourist Authority, the Association of British Travel Agents, the Pacific Asia Travel Association and the American Society of Travel Agents. Entries to the awards have been increases every year.

American Express also sponsors a variety of environmental awards for international tourism organisations.

Agents and Partnerships for Change

A broad based approach is called for which requires Travel & Tourism to work with:

- national governments to raise the profile of environmental and social issues within the education system;
- NGOs to raise awareness of tourism issues in their work and activities and provide feedback to the Travel & Tourism industry;
- development organisations to communicate with host communities to understand their needs and requirements;
- local authorities to engage local people through the inclusion of tourism issues in Local Agenda 21 plans;
- national and international trade associations, labour representative organisations and training providers to increase awareness and training of staff in environmental and social issues;
- Travel & Tourism publications (such as travel guides);
- ravel & Tourism journalists to raise the profile of reporting environmental and social impacts of tourism among consumers and tourism businesses; and
- the Internet as a source of information for potential travellers.

Areas for Further Action

The WTTC/MORI data shows the scale of the task still remaining. The industry has developed a number of initiatives to influence consumer behaviour. However, if consumers do not understand or are not aware of the issues involved and do not demand more sustainable products then, in the long term, it will not be in the industry's interests to move in that direction. The priority for future action, therefore, should be to raise awareness among travellers of the issues associated with tourism and the impact their activities can have on local destinations and cultures.

Destinations

"Green Globe" has developed a specific "Destinations" program to recognise those tourist destinations where there is a concerted effort by all those involved in the local tourism industry to improve the quality of the environment. The Destinations process provides a framework to guide tourist locations towards achieving sustainable development based on the principles of Agenda 21. The Destinations programs are tailor made to reflect local circumstances, such as the level of environmental awareness, action taken to date and available resources.

Each program is based on achieving progressive environmental improvements. Targets are set within a realistic timetable and are developed by a steering group made up of key partners. The island of Jersey has become the first *"Green Globe"*. For example, in 1996 Lusotour SA, a tourism development company, enacted a management plan for Vilamoura whereby employees are given responsibility for individual environmental tasks.

The company has invested money into rehabilitating the surrounding natural environment, which includes pine forests and a lake that has significance to local wetland areas. Guests are provided with a copy of the environmental policy and are encouraged to participate in the scheme through specialized brochures.

The campaign includes recycling; treating diseased pine areas; regular cleaning of the beaches and marinas; development of a sewage treatment plant and new buildings in the resort are designed to minimise visual and environmental impacts. For its work in Vilamoura, Lusotour SA is also a winner of the British Airways Tourism for Tomorrow Awards.

The "Afrikatourism" brand has been developed by the Open Africa Foundation to encourage products, which embraces sustainable ecological, economic and social development based on Africa's unique cultural, natural and wildlife heritage. "Open Africa" is also developing a continuous network of "Afrikatourism" routes from the Cape to Cairo, known as the "African Dream". The Dream helps to create awareness of the many rural and environmental projects, which exist throughout Africa. "Team Africa", a transcontinental alliance of governments, corporations, institutions, professionals and individuals, provides leadership and motivation in the development of the "African Dream".

Host Communities

"Whale Watch Kaikoura" is an initiative of local Maori people from a small town on the East Coast of New Zealand's South Island. Within a kilometre of the Kaikoura shore is an area ideal for whales, where visitors are guaranteed to see them all year round. The Whale Watch began 11 years ago and is now a booming tourist destination, run by indigenous people with a strong sense of heritage and a view of the future based on strong principles of sustainability.

Jordan Tourism Investments, has revitalised the traditional village of Taybeh, in Jordan, into a cultural tourist resort, with the help and agreement of villagers. With many of the younger generation moving to the cities, the village was losing its character. By restoring its 19th century buildings and reviving old crafts, the village is now thriving again. The village lies 9km south east of the historic city of Petra. Opened in July 1994, the village now accommodates around 60,000 guests each year.

Uluru and Kakadu National Parks are both owned by indigenous Australians, the local Aboriginal communities, and jointly run with the National Parks and Wildlife Service. They are both major tourism destinations and involve indigenous participation in planning, management, and ownership of tourism infrastructure, as well as interpretation for visitors. They bring significant economic, social and cultural benefits to the local indigenous communities.

The Conservation Corporation in Africa has established a series of high quality game parks in which local communities are major stakeholders and beneficiaries of tourism. This initiative is also helping to re-invigorate local crafts.

Agents and Partnerships for Change and Areas for Further Action

The challenge facing the tourism industry in moving towards a more sustainable future is set out in "Agenda 21 for the Travel & Tourism Industry". To achieve the goals set out in this document will require a partnership between government departments, national tourism authorities, international and national trade organisations and Travel & Tourism companies. Working together in close co-operation such partnerships should aim to deliver the following:

- Close co-operation between the public and private sectors to deliver a regulatory regime, which encourages voluntary action but supplement, where necessary, with regulation in areas such as land-use and waste management.
- Agreed common standards and tools to enable the measurement of progress towards achieving sustainable development.
- Certification criteria developed and more widely applied to industry initiatives.
- A commitment to the controlled expansion, where appropriate, of infrastructure.
- Environmental taxes, where applied, should be fair and non-discriminatory. They should be carefully thought out to minimise their impact on economic development, and revenues should be allocated to Travel & Tourism associated environment improvement programs.
- International, national and local funding bodies should include sustainable development as a part of their criteria, so that in time, all funding would be dependent on sound environmental practice.
- Contemporary research into sustainable tourism needs to be funded and developed. Issues requiring attention include design, carrying capacity, tour operator activities, environmental reporting, auditing and environmental impact assessments.
- Environmental education and training should be increased, particularly in schools, for future hotel and tourism staff.
- Greater investment and commitment to the use of new technology.

Coastal Impact of Tourism

Problems

Tourism provides an essential lifeline for many coastal communities. Faced with the prospect of increasing financial hardship, more and more coastal communities have turned to tourism as a means of generating income and survival. Tourism's impact on the coastal zone has, therefore, been largely positive. Of course, as in any area, if Tourism is not properly managed and developed, it can be harmful.

Impacts arise from the construction of infrastructure (hotels, marinas, transport, waste treatment facilities, groynes etc.) and from recreation (golf courses, water sports, theme parks etc.). Coastal communities are now faced with tourism on a considerable scale, and the host to guest ratio can be very high in such areas. At the same time, coastal communities must try to maintain the resort's attraction as tourist demands change, sometimes quite rapidly. With coastal regions being primary tourist destinations, sensitive marine and coastal environments can suffer dramatically. For example, as a result of large-scale sea-front tourist development,considerable beach and dune erosion can occur. Tourism also impacts on environmental quality in the following ways:

- ribbon development, infrastructure requirements, particularly transport links;
- the treatment and disposal of solid and/or liquid wastes, particularly during peak tourist seasons, may be inadequate or at worst non-existent; and
- water is often consumed excessively, not only for drinking but for showers, laundry, swimming pools, maintenance of golf courses etc. This can affect the quantity and quality of fresh water available to indigenous coastal populations.

Recreational activities can also have a significant impact on the coastal zone:

- golf course's impact can be considerable, with those situated directly on coastal habitats (especially sand dunes) in particular;
- erosion of reefs and coral from divers and swimmers;
- pollution from boats and jets skis; and
- noise from motor boats and jet skis, cars and buses, nightlife and other activities.

Solutions

The development of a sustainable tourism industry in the coastal zone offers numerous opportunities. Opportunities includes, those for nature conservation – which, given the increasing interest in high quality natural and cultural experiences, can help to reverse the decline in market share of many coastal destinations. Tourism also provides important opportunities for strengthening local industries. Where industries are in decline, tourism ventures can help supplement declining income.

The following examples illustrate what can be done to make the most of the opportunities offered by tourism in the coastal zone:

Calvia is a Municipality on the Mediterranean coast that has undertaken an Agenda 21 project to assist the sustainable development of its tourism sector, in order to counter the negative impact of short-term tourism development since the 1960s. The local council has now implemented a transferable policy aimed at modernising, improving and diversifying the local tourist industry, involving all stakeholders, including the local population. A Project Plan was enacted, and achievements so far include:

- indigenous development, based on the sustainable use of available resources;
- high quality services and an appropriate bed night capacity;
- a ban on new development on 1,700 acres;
- active participation of the residents in community life; and
- environmental management of municipality buildings, waste recycling, reduction in spending on electricity, and use of environmentally friendly materials for office use.

Quicksilver Tours, Queensland, Australia, is owned by one of the largest tourism operators to the Great Barrier Reef. Quicksilver have five large catamarans, which take about 1,000 tourists a day to dive on the reef. They have their own reef site with fixed diving platforms. They employ a team of biologists, both for environmental management and assessment as well as widespread environmental interpretation. Recent assessment of the reef, in the vicinity of the operation, shows that it is being maintained in pristine condition.

Kingfisher Bay Resort is found at Fraser Island, Queensland. It is a large five star "ecotourism" resort built in a beautiful, but fragile environment off the Queensland coast. Its concept, design, construction and management were conceived using the latest ecologically sustainable principles. It is a state-of-the-art "ecotourism" resort, which has won Australia's top tourism awards, and its economic and environmental success has influenced new coastal tourism developments.

Maho Bay's camps and studios in the US Virgin Islands have based their product on a commitment to minimise impact on the environment, conserve natural resources, engage in active and passive environmental education of their guests, and contribute to the local economy. Specific initiatives introduced at Maho Bay include the following: use of new technology; purchasing policies; waste management; environmental education; energy and water conservation; and support for local communities and culture.

These initiatives show an appreciation of the need for alternative solutions to issues such as packaging and waste disposal through landfill. These are issues, which as the industry grows, will be increasingly important for the Travel & Tourism industry as a whole to address.

Agents and Partnerships for Change and Areas for Further Action

The agents, partnerships for change and areas for further action in relation to tourism in the coastal zone are similar to the development of broad based sustainable tourism in general as set out in Section D.

A number of issues do, of course, have particular importance for the coastal zone. Above all, the key to success is better participation at destination level among all the stakeholders concerned (such as at). In the case of the coastal zone, there are a number of additional organisations with an interest in coastal policy, marine conservation, shipping etc., which needs to be identified and included in partnerships for the coastal zone.

Successful planning for tourism is very important for the future of the industry in coastal regions, because a significant percentage of tourism occurs within the geographical parameters of the definition of a coastal zone. Concerted support from all countries involved (and the industries within them) is vital to protect the shared natural resources that coastal zones represent.

Historically, the influence most hoteliers have on the environmental impact of their business is limited to working within existing buildings, or after a new site has been completed. In April 1998, the IHEI convened a group of hoteliers, tour operators, architectural firms and sustainable development specialists with the goal of creating a partnership to be called the "Siting and Design Programme". The new initiative's mission will be to define responsible planning and design specifications that will cause minimal environmental damage at new sites. Particular attention will be paid to sites located within ecologically sensitive areas and upon waterfronts. The "Siting and Design Programme" will strive to reach hotel owners, investors and developers to bring these issues to the attention of the entire industry.

Conclusions

Travel & Tourism has a number of advantages over other industry sectors:

- it creates jobs and wealth whilst;
- at the same time, it can contribute to sustainable development;
- it tends to have low start-up costs;
- is a viable option in a wide range of areas and regions;
- is likely to continue to grow for the foreseeable future; and
- the industry is, in a large part, aware of the need to protect the resource on which it is based-local culture and built and natural environment-and it is committed to these resources' preservation and enhancement.

The industry is, therefore, making a concerted effort to build up programs for sustainable development. However, it cannot do this alone. If Travel & Tourism is to continue to flourish and to contribute to sustainable development, it needs help from national Governments. This assistance is needed in two forms:-both positive encouragement for sustainable tourism initiatives and an understanding that policy decisions in other areas can effect Travel & Tourism. In practical terms, what this means is the following:

The first point of action needed from Governments is to incorporate Agenda 21 principles into tourism policies at international and national level, and to promote their inclusion in regional and local tourism strategies. By providing such a lead and establishing a coherent global framework based on Agenda 21, national governments will make a vital contribution to developing a more sustainable tourism industry. Governments should also recognise that Travel & Tourism is a core service sector which should always be considered when looking at policies to expand trade, increase employment, modernize infrastructure and encourage investment-at both domestic and international level. It should also be included in national statistics with its economic impact calculated by means of a national tourism satellite account.

Governments should also consider helping Travel & Tourism by seeking to minimise regulatory impediments and by offering appropriate investment incentives. By supporting tourism and allowing it to compete in open and fair markets, tourism's benefits can be more easily secured.

Finally, governments can address some of the fundamental barriers to tourism growth by looking at how to expand and modernise infrastructure, to apply taxes fairly and to invest in human resource development.

If the program of action outlined above can be undertaken by national governments in co-operation with continued industry commitments and initiatives for sustainable tourism then we can look to a brighter future.

Tourism, Terrorism, and Tomorrow

As fewer overseas travellers pack their bags this holiday season, millions of tourism industry workers worldwide are losing their jobs. Before September 11th, travel and tourism was the world's largest industry, accounting for one in every 12 jobs. When the massive $3.6 trillion industry almost ground to a halt after the terrorist attacks, the ripple effects extended well beyond the United States, exposing the vulnerability of countries too dependent on international tourism, reports the Worldwatch Institute, a Washington, DC-based environmental research organization.

"The aftermath of September 11 has shown us how important travel and tourism are to the global economy, but also how over-dependence on tourism can devastate lives and derail economies,". "Now, more than ever, it is time to put issues of sustainability at the top of the global tourism agenda."

Revenues from tourism have been especially important in the developing world, which stands to suffer severe economic losses from the slowdown. "Tourism is the only economic sector where developing countries consistently run a trade surplus,". "It's especially significant in poorer countries that have few other options: for the world's 49 so-called least developed countries, tourism is the second largest source of foreign exchange after oil."

Businesses in the developing world are particularly worried about the sharp drop in bookings as the winter high season nears:

- India and Nepal, which are close to Afghanistan, are already feeling the effects of a drop in demand.
- In October, resort company Club Mediterrane was forced to close 15 of its holiday villages in the Caribbean, Central America, the Middle East, Europe, and Asia.
- Operators in Costa Rica report a 30 percent decline in bookings from last year.
- International tourism is now expected to grow by only 1.5 to 2 percent in 2001, compared with the robust 7.4 percent rise in 2000.
- The International Labour Organization estimates that as many as 9 million of the world's 200 million hotel and tourism workers could lose their jobs in the wake of the attacks. Nearly three quarters of these positions are outside the United States and Europe, many in countries with weak social safety nets.

Even in the best of times, the consequences of tourism's rapid growth have not always been positive. On average, as much as 50 percent of tourism earnings ultimately "leak" out of the developing world-in the form of profits earned by foreign-owned businesses, promotional spending abroad, or payments for imported goods and labour. And uncontrolled tourism development-on mountaintops, along coastlines, or in remote jungle areas-stresses many fragile ecosystems and cultures.

"Tourism does not have to have such negative impacts,". "Many governments and businesses, local communities, and tourists themselves are already paying more attention to the social, cultural, and environmental impacts of their activities."

Such changes can save money as well. Some hotels, tour operators, and other businesses are taking formal steps to restructure their management and operations along environmental lines-often at considerable cost savings. Between 1988 and 1995, for example, Inter-Continental Hotels reduced its overall energy costs by 27 percent, saving $3.7 million in 1995 alone. The Green

Hotels Association reports that hotels that have adopted such conservation measures and green practices have been better able to weather the revenue loss, falling occupancies, and higher energy costs in the aftermath of the September attacks.

Improving Sustainability

Regulation and Accreditation

Because the regulation of ecotourism is poorly implemented or nonexistent, ecologically destructive greenwashed operations like underwater hotels, helicopter tours, and wildlife theme parks are categorized as ecotourism along with canoeing, camping, photography, and wildlife observation. The failure to acknowledge responsible, low impact ecotourism puts these companies at a competitive disadvantage.

Many environmentalists have argued for a global standard of accreditation, differentiating ecotourism companies based on their level of environmental commitment. A national or international regulatory board would enforce accreditation procedures, with representation from various groups including governments, hotels, tour operators, travel agents, guides, airlines, local authorities, conservation organizations, and non-governmental organizations. The decisions of the board would be sanctioned by governments, so that non-compliant companies would be legally required to disassociate themselves from the use of the ecotourism brand.

Crinion suggests a Green Stars System, based on criteria including a management plan, benefit for the local community, small group interaction, education value and staff training. Ecotourists who consider their choices would be confident of a genuine ecotourism experience when they see the higher star rating.

In addition, environmental impact assessments could be used as a form of accreditation. Feasibility is evaluated from a scientific basis, and recommendations could be made to optimally plan infrastructure, set tourist capacity, and manage the ecology. This form of accreditation is more sensitive to site specific conditions.

Guidelines and Education

An environmental protection strategy must address the issue of ecotourists removed from the cause-and-effect of their actions on the environment. More initiatives should be carried out to improve their awareness, sensitize them to environmental issues, and care about the places they visit.

Tour guides are an obvious and direct medium to communicate awareness. With the confidence of ecotourists and intimate knowledge of the environment, they can actively discuss conservation issues. A tour guide training program in Costa Rica's Tortuguero National Park has helped mitigate negative environmental impacts by providing information and regulating tourists on the parks' beaches used by nesting endangered sea turtles.

Small Scale, Slow Growth and Local Control

The underdevelopment theory of tourism describes a new form of imperialism by multinational corporations that control ecotourism resources. These corporations finance and profit from the development of large scale ecotourism that causes excessive environmental degradation, loss of traditional culture and way of life, and exploitation of local labor. In Zimbabwe and Nepal's Annapurna region, where underdevelopment is taking place, more than 90 percent of ecotourism revenues are expatriated to the parent countries, and less than 5 percent go into local communities.

The lack of sustainability highlights the need for small scale, slow growth, and locally based ecotourism. Local peoples have a vested interest in the well being of their community, and are therefore more accountable to environmental protection than multinational corporations. The lack of control, westernization, adverse impacts to the environment, loss of culture and traditions outweigh the benefits of establishing large scale ecotourism.

The increased contributions of communities to locally managed ecotourism create viable economic opportunities, including high level management positions, and reduce environmental issues associated with poverty and unemployment. Because the ecotourism experience is marketed to a different lifestyle from large scale ecotourism, the development of facilities and infrastructure does not need to conform to corporate Western tourism standards, and can be much simpler and less expensive. There is a greater multiplier effect on the economy, because local products, materials, and labor are used. Profits accrue locally and import leakages are reduced. However, even this form of tourism may require foreign investment for promotion or start up. When such investments are required, it is crucial for communities for find a company or non-governmental organization that reflects the philosophy of ecotourism; sensitive to their concerns and willing to cooperate at the expense of profit.The basic assumption of the multiplier effect is that the economy starts off with unused resources, for example, that many workers are cyclically unemployed and much of industrial capacity is sitting idle or incompletely utilized. By increasing demand in the economy it is then possible to boost production. If the economy was already at full employment, with only structural, frictional, or other supply-side types of unemployment, any attempt to boost demand would only lead to inflation. For various laissez-faire schools of economics which embrace Say's Law and deny the possibility of Keynesian inefficiency and under-employment of resources, therefore, the multiplier concept is irrelevant or wrong-headed.

As an example, consider the government increasing its expenditure on roads by $one million, without a corresponding increase in taxation. This sum would go to the road builders, who would hire more workers and distribute the money as wages and profits. The households receiving these incomes will save part of the money and spend the rest on consumer goods. These expenditures in turn will generate more jobs, wages, and profits, and so on with the income and spending circulating around the economy.

The multiplier effect arises because of the induced increases in consumer spending which occur due to the increased incomes — and because of the feedback into increasing business revenues, jobs, and income again. This process does not lead to an economic explosion not only because of the supply-side barriers at potential output (full employment) but because at each "round", the increase in consumer spending is less than the increase in consumer incomes. That is, the marginal propensity to consume (mpc) is less than one, so that each round some extra income goes into saving, leaking out of the cumulative process. Each increase in spending is thus smaller than that of the previous round, preventing an explosion.Ecotourism has to be implemented with care.

Natural Resource Management

Natural resource management can be utilized as a specialized tool for the development of ecotourism. There are several places throughout the world where the amount of natural resources are abundant. But, with human encroachment and habitats these resources are depleting. Without knowing the proper utilization of certain resources they are destroyed and floral and faunal species are becoming extinct. Ecotourism programmes can be introduced for the conservation of these resources. Several plans and proper management programmes can be introduced so that these resources remain untouched. Several organizations, NGO's, scientists are working on this field.

Natural resources of hill areas like Kurseong in West Bengal are plenty in number with various flora and fauna, but tourism for business purpose poised the situation. Researcher from Jadavpur University presently working in this area for the develeopment of ecotourism which can be utilized as a tool for natural resource management.

In South-East Asia government and Non-Government Organisations are working together with academics and industry operators to spread the economic benefits of tourism into the kampungs and villages of the region. A recently formed alliance, the South-East Asian Tourism Organisation - SEATO is bringing together these diverse players to allay resource management concerns.

Tour Operators, Travel Agencies & Retailers

Some companies specialise in ecotourism, designing their trips to be environmentally, culturally and socially friendly. Companies such as Intrepid Travel, Adventure Life, Frontier, and Marine Conservation Society, Family Nature Summit, Peregrine Adventures, World Expeditions, greentraveller, Explore Worldwide and Exodus offer trips catering for the thoughtful traveller. Some tour operators are keenly aware of the impacts that they may have on specific areas and rotate clients around to different sites for snorkelling, bird watching, and other activities. Others are just beginning to see the advantage of "green" travel destinations.

Connecting the Sustainable Livelihoods Approach and Tourism

Tourism has been increasingly used for, and directly linked with, rural poverty reduction in developing countries. However, the application, and to an extent the principles, of the widely used organising framework for considering poverty reduction, the Sustainable Livelihoods Approach (SLA), may not fit fully the tourism situation, and vice versa. Based on a review of the literature we first suggest that sustainable livelihoods for tourism should be viewed in a broader tourism context, rather than merely taking tourism as a development tool. Second, the SLA seeks household livelihood sustainability at the individual or household level, while tourism sustainability is often applied to the industry and destinations at wider, more macro level scales. Thus, a reconciliation of the tensions and opportunities between the SLA and tourism needs to be found. Third, tourism research has demonstrated local residents" increasing concern about participation in political governance associated with tourism development, with less participation jeopardising local people's assets from a livelihood perspective. Therefore, an additional concept of institutional asset (mainly community participation) needs to be incorporated within the SLA. Given the above understandings, a sustainable tourism livelihood was defined and a Sustainable Tourism Livelihoods Approach (STLA) is proposed. The potential applications of the STLA are discussed and future research is recommended.

Although poverty is one of the most compelling challenges confronting humankind, there remains numerous issues when considering scale, form, and evaluation of response within the multiple poverty contexts. As the World Bank points out, 'policies targeted directly to the poor can hardly succeed unless governments know who the poor are and how they respond to policies and to their environment'. Based on this understanding, the World Bank adopted different approaches to rural and urban poverty, respectively, in implementing projects towards poverty reduction. This article focuses on the rural poverty context because up to 75% of the world's poor are in rural populations, and mostly in the 'third world' (World Bank, 2008).

Key economic activities aimed at rural poverty reduction continue to be primary industries including agriculture and fishing. While professionals tried to improve rural conditions through approaches to soil fertility improvement, land reform and advanced technology, these development approaches did little to alleviate rural poverty. In the 1980s, a new approach to poverty reduction, sustainable livelihoods (SL) and the Sustainable Livelihoods Approach (SLA) was proposed. It emphasised holistic and integrated thinking about poverty reduction and rural development, and soon gained popularity among researchers, practitioners and developers, while still typically being focused on agricultural practices.

Tourism is now the biggest and fastest growing industry in the world, having experienced enormous growth over recent decades (UNWTO, 2002). But only recently has tourism's potential of contributing to rural poverty reduction been widely recognised by policy-makers and others. Unlike agrarian change, the concept of tourism in rural areas originates from developed countries. Research regarding rural tourism has centred on aspects of tourism products, marketing, planning, and impacts. This trend has, however, recently been criticised for its reduced focus on rural livelihoods and poverty reduction, with some contending that this deficiency can be addressed by using the SLA. Thus, the question that arises is: will the SLA fit the case in which tourism is taken as a livelihood strategy for rural development? This paper addresses this question by reviewing the theoretical evolution of both the SLA and tourism. Possible gaps between their applications are explored and a sustainable livelihoods framework for tourism is proposed and discussed.

Rural Development

The SL approach arose from the broad context of rural development. In summary it can be seen that rural development has moved through three main bodies of thought since the mid 20th century, namely the population and technology model, political economy theories, and agricultural development.

In the 1950s the population and technology model was the main discourse. The model emphasises that rural population growth will increase agricultural productivity. Surplus agricultural output closely relates to the advancement of farming technologies, a major driver of agricultural productivity. In the 1960s, concerns with increasing income disparities in the rural economy led to the theory of political economy of agrarian change focusing on the equality of job opportunity and income, including appropriate social reform (Aziz, 1978). This theory, however, failed to stress livelihood diversification away from agriculture on which the rural poor have always survived (Ellis, 2000). The third stage of rural development, agricultural development theory, prevailed in the 1970s. Its emphasis on small-farm agriculture was very successful in raising agricultural productivity, so that for nearly 20 years it remained the dominant rural development philosophy (Ellis, 2000). In the 1980s, the notion of rural development in developing countries was critiqued and questions were asked about the overall success of 'small-farm enterprises'. While small-farm agriculture raised agrarian productivity it helped little to alleviate poverty, and worse, social inequality and unbalanced income distribution increased. More holistic, integrated, rural development thinking was called for. Thus, the sustainable livelihoods concept was proposed in the late 1980s, a concept that has subsequently undergone substantial theoretical and practical development.

Sustainable Livelihoods Approach

SL is a way of thinking about rural development. It calls for integrative thinking for poverty reduction rather than conventionally alleviating poverty through raising crop productivity and external aid (Cahn, 2002). Although the term Sustainable Livelihoods has been used widely in poverty and rural development research, there is no broadly accepted definition, and different governments, organisations and individuals have adopted their own understandings.

The notion of SL can be traced back to the first proposition of sustainable development in the Brundtland Commission Report of 1987 (Solesbury, 2003). In the same year the Advisory Panel on Food Security, Agriculture, Forestry and Environment produced a report to the World Commission on Environment and Development (WCED), in which the concept of SL was first, and officially, proposed (WCED, 1987). This report reversed the normal view that always starts with things rather than people, urban rather than rural, the rich rather than the poor (Conroy & Litvinoff, 1988).

Reviewing the WCED panel definition, Chambers and Conway put forth their understanding of SL:

A livelihood comprises the capabilities, assets (stores, resources, claims and access) and activities required for a means of living: a livelihood is sustainable which can cope with and recover from stress and shocks, maintain or enhance its capabilities and assets, and provide sustainable livelihood opportunities for the next generation; and which contributes net benefits to other livelihoods at the local and global levels and in the short and long term.

Chambers and Conway (1992), in their definition, accentuated the importance of capabilities, not only the ability of being and doing, but also the ability of recognising and recovering from the potential shocks and stresses which they consider are key features of sustainability. Ellis (2000) however, points out that the meaning of 'capabilities' in the above definition overlaps greatly with assets and activities, and use of the term 'capabilities' can bring confusion. Therefore, he argued that access to assets and activities mediated by institutions and social relations should be highlighted, rather than capabilities. When applied to Pacific cultures, Cahn (2002) notes that culture and tradition are prominent in a Pacific livelihood, and proposed a sustainable Pacific livelihoods model incorporating the integration of culture and tradition. Such deliberations indicate that a 'one size fits all' SL approach is neither possible nor appropriate—context is important.

World Travel and Tourism Council

The World Travel & Tourism Council (WTTC) was conceptualized in the early 1980s when a group of CEOs came to the realization that although Travel & Tourism was the largest service industry in the world and the biggest provider of jobs, nobody knew it. There was no consolidated data or voice for the industry to give the message to elected official and policy makers.

WTTC was established in 1990 and today the Council is positioned as the global business leaders' forum for Travel & Tourism, comprising the Chairmen and Chief Executives of 100 of the world's foremost organizations, representing all regions and sectors of the industry; a membership list is attached.

Mission

WTTC works to raise awareness of Travel & Tourism as one of the world's largest industries, employing approximately 220 million people and generating 9.4 per cent of world GDP, WTTC works together with governments to raise awareness of the economic and social importance of the industry across the world.

WTTC's mission focuses on three main areas:

Driving the Agenda: Raising awareness of the impact of Travel & Tourism and working with governments to make the industry an economic and job-creating priority. The Facilitator: Helping industry participants to understand, anticipate, interpret and act on global key regional development The Networking Forum: WTTC is the business leaders' forum to which Travel & Tourism players aspire

Blueprint for New Tourism

By 2003, events around the world such as the September 11th attacks, war in Iraq, the SARS crisis and increased terrorism meant that WTTC had to work to rebuild confidence among travellers. The Global Travel & Tourism Summit in 2003 was opened up to global press and media for the first time and the theme – Building New Tourism – came out of the atmosphere at the time. The outcome of the Summit shaped the Council's future vision and led to the launch of the Blueprint for New Tourism. The Blueprint for New Tourism provides a new strategic framework to ensure that Travel & Tourism works for everyone in the future. It promotes Travel & Tourism as a partnership between the private and public sectors, matching the needs of economies, local and regional authorities and local communities with those of business. The three main messages that form the framework for the Blueprint for New Tourism are: 1. Governments recognizing Travel & Tourism as a top priority 2. Business balancing economics with people, culture and environment.

Activities

WTTC Research

When the World Travel & Tourism Council (WTTC) was established in 1990, the founding Members decided that the quantification of Travel & Tourism's impact on world and national economies would be the most important contribution they could make to achieve their goal of raising awareness among policy leaders and decision-makers of Travel & Tourism's economic contribution and its potential for creating wealth and employment around the world. The subsequent 19 years of investment in research made a significant contribution to the development of the new international standard for Tourism Satellite Accounting (TSA) research, adopted in 2001 by the United Nations Statistical Commission. WTTC has also developed a Crisis Impact Forecasting Model to assess the potential impact of a crisis on the industry within 48 hours. It was put into place following the crises of the London and Egypt bombings in 2005.

TSA Commissioned Reports

Over the years, WTTC and its research partner, UK-based Oxford Economics (OE), have endeavoured to create a system of Tourism Satellite Accounting research, which now covers 181 economies around the world. Using a combination of macro-economic research and forecasts, national accounting data/information, Travel & Tourism variables and econometric modelling, WTTC/OE have produced a system of research covering many concepts of Travel & Tourism 'Demand', from personal consumption to business purchases, capital investment, government spending and exports. This information is then translated into economic concepts of production, such as gross domestic product (GDP) and employment, which can be compared with other industries and the economy as a whole to provide statistical information that can assist in policy- and business decision-making. Today, WTTC produces annual TSA forecasts for 181 countries and 13 regions and carries out commissioned TSA reports for a growing number of countries, regions, and cities each year..

Global Travel & Tourism Summit

The Global Travel & Tourism Summit is an annual WTTC gathering for both public and private sector leaders of travel and tourism. The Summit aims to facilitate meaningful dialogue among the world's Travel & Tourism industry and government leaders. Past locations of the Summit include Vilamoura, Doha, New Delhi, Washington D.C., Lisbon, and Dubai. The 9th Global Travel & Tourism Summit took place from 14-16 May 2009 in Florianópolis, Brazil.

Tourism for Tomorrow Awards

The Tourism for Tomorrow Awards were set up in 1989 by the Federation of Tour Operators to encourage action from all sectors of the industry to protect the environment. WTTC took over the Awards in 2004. Awarded annually, they recognise and promote the world's leading examples of best practice in responsible tourism development across four categories:

Destination Stewardship Award, Conservation Award, Community Benefit Award, Global Tourism Business Award

Winners and finalists are taking the stage in a Awards special session during WTTC's Global Travel & Tourism Summit.

Index

F

G

H

I

K

L

□□□